Four Years of Captivity in Cochons-sur-Marne

1900-1904

Léon Bloy is a cathedral gargoyle that vomits the waters of the sky onto the good and the wicked. – Jules Barbey d'Aurevilly.

I0542890

LÉON BLOY

Translated By Richard Robinson

Sunny Lou Publishing Company
Portland, Oregon, USA
http://www.sunnyloupublishing.com

1st Edition, Corrected: October 28, 2022
Original Publication Date: October 2, 2022

ISBN: 978-1-955392-34-1

* * *

This translation from French is based on
the Société du Mercure de France edition of
Quatre ans de Captivité à Cochons-sur-Marne,
Paris, 1905.

Contents

Preface

I ask the poor pigs' pardon, – those who go about on all fours, who are innocent, who are beautiful, who are beneficent, who are at the butcher's shop, and whom the human language dishonors unjustly.

I ask those humble brothers' pardon for having – by indigence of the imagination or penury of vocables – compared them irreverently to a category of stinking animals the least morsel of which the most knowledgeable industry of meat would not know how to employ.

Poor dear pigs! whose blood pudding and honest lard were the aliment of my youth, whose head appeared to me, at eighteen years old, the most desirable of cheeses, and who so often consoled me by the succulence of your feet grilled in breadcrumbs;

O pigs! so nice when smoked over wood; dear symbols of literary adolescence; you whom poets are duty-bound to sing under the laurels that they deprive you of;

I beg your pardon.

– Epilogue from *Léon Bloy Before the Swine*.

1900

*There was a virtuoso who played his soul like a
supernatural violin, and one had never heard so
dolorous a music...*

There is in our home a poor image that used to be precious to us, a sort of Calvary of the humble, borrowed
from I do not know what church in the countryside,
naïve work in colored pencils that one believed to be
the work of some admirable child. In the margins of it
one reads these words:

> *To Madame Jeanne Léon Bloy who
> honored me with the hospitality of her
> home, the charity of her best atten-
> tions, then when I was the poorest, the
> illest, and the most abandoned of
> men... Very humble and respectful
> homage of my most fervent and pro-
> found gratefulness.*

> – HENRY DE GROUX. July 1, 1893.

Now here is what I wrote on March 22, 1901, to my
friend Julien Leclercq, who passed away several
months later. – This letter has been published by the
bibliophile René Martineau in his booklet, *Un Vivant
et Deux Morts:*

> *... When we see each other again, we
> will need to speak about Henry de
> Groux; perhaps I could obtain from
> you finally an explanation of his mys-*

terious and monstruous behavior in my regards.

Here is what I know:

In return for an earlier hospitality of several months, in '91 and '92, during which that poor wretch, dying of misery and seriously ill, was taken care of by us like a brother and put back on his feet; in return for a second hospitality of only one month, but excessively demanding, in '97 (he was the father of a family then); in return for an absolute, celebrated, heroic friendship, which all my books, over the years, show the trace of, Henry de Groux, – when we came back to France from our exile in Denmark and when we were human wrecks – showed us the door of his home after four times 24 hours, in the middle of the night, – *having made to me, that very same morning, protestations of the most inalterable friendship – without knowing if we could pay for a hotel room, without known motive, without explanation of any kind. That at the risk of making our two little girls, who were asleep at the time, die for fright, our having no advance warning of that catastrophe. He wanted to be rid of us, simply...*

When I interrogate him, he responds

mysteriously that I know what I did to him and that he has nothing to say. Naturally, the listener is then placed in the position of conjecturing all sorts of turpitude. Having always had the valiance of my feelings or my thoughts, I esteem that such a friendship and after so many years must not be broken without a declared *motive and that one must neither condemn nor let someone go without saying* why, *– when one has testicles.*

I began bleeding painfully, then a healing contempt came. Today that man is like a dead man to me.

I think that it is totally appropriate to leave things where they are. Also, my courage fails me to add another extension leaf of anger or bitterness to the table of a feast of brotherly love which was devoured by filthy animals...

July

14. – After an immense fatigue, our move-in is finished. I can finally sit down and pick up my poor writing again. Five weeks have past since our return to France, and I have kept – as one has just seen – but one memory altogether. What difference does it make? At a distance of several years, certain facts that

one had believed important lose all their power over the soul, awaken nothing more than a vibration in the memory. I became aware of this when I wrote the two volumes that preceded this one. Writing every day what one observes in the visible and in the invisible, what poverty and how little to record among so many pages!

In sum, our prayers in Denmark were granted. I had asked God to deliver me from that kingdom, without suffering, without trouble, without sadness. If there hadn't been the great alarm that Henry de Groux had caused us, on the night of the 18th of June – the night of Waterloo! – and the excessive bitterness that followed, we would have thought we were feeling the gentleness of his Hand. Truth be told, our hearts had been prepared for a long time for that providential affliction that was admirable. What danger didn't we escape that night then, and how necessary was our flight! De Groux hasn't even responded to a merciful letter by my wife, whom he has so gravely and nastily offended. May Our Lord have pity on him!

But all the rest is marvelous. Our trip which was so easy, the help that we receive each day by that young woman come with us from Denmark, *to amuse herself*, and who has already shared one of our most unreal tribulations; the discovery of a pretty house in Ceux-d'En-Bas, a faubourg of Cochons-sur-Marne, at forty kilometers from Paris, and that even more surprising one of a publisher for the unpublishable pamphlet *Je M'Accuse...* What else do I know? And how many things that I cannot see! By excess of fortune, July 14th is, in this place, inoffensive.

15. – Received with calmness the news of the death of an old imbecile much admired in my childhood.

18. – Pilgrimage to the church of Ceux-d'En-Bas. One hour of walking. I am struck by learning that this parish possesses or has to possess, for centuries, the head of saint Veronica, unfortunately invisible or unverifiable at the back of an obstructed crypt. We want to believe it so that there might be, in our lives, a little more beauty. It is enough to make one think that we were expected here. The curate of this fold, which is our own, does not give the impression of doubting the existence of God. I learnt, later, that such a thing is remarkable in the diocese of Meaux.

22. – To a Naundorffist[1] who did not like my book on Louis XVII:

> *Dear friend,*
>
> *It is true, why would I not admit it? I thought that, unsatisfied with me for reasons I am unaware of, you had resolved to treat me, in the future, like a man of the world – which, for a Christian of my sort, is the supreme insult, humiliation beyond which there is no greater opprobrium. Pardon me if I*

---

[1]Naundorffist: a person who believes that Karl Wilhelm Naundorff (AD 1785-1845) was in fact the son of King Louis XVI. See Léon Bloy's *The Son of Louis XVI* (Sunny Lou Publishing, 2022).

am lacking in justice, but your silence, for several weeks now and under such circumstances, seems severe to me...

Of course, I had to explain my thought to please myself while pleasing God, without taking into account any "divergence" and you nobly understood. One can never ask a Léon Bloy, under any circumstances, *to appear to honor what he despises.*

However, I am not unreasonable and it is not right to say that, "even friends such as yourself and Friedrichs were unable to make me change a single *word." What inexactitude!*

Friedrichs had sent to me a rather long list of small corrections that he judged indispensible, historically, and docilely I did not hesitate to make them. If he had proposed philosophical or theological modifications, I very surely and very rapidly would have sent him on his way, make no doubt about it. But there, on the matter of Louis XVII, I saw in him my master and I would have been an idiot not to listen to him. For you, I did a bit more. I did what nobody obtains from me, litererary *concessions. Friedrichs had pointed out to me several things that annoyed you. I think that you were not wrong for the most part. In a society with neither grandeur not force, in other words profoundly hypocritical,* words *assume an excessive importance. It is the story of domestics having become masters. Now, I wanted my book to be able to be read by even the poor, that is to say,* men of the world, *and I made the changes you requested. I regret only one of them, that on page 137, line 8 – "bad place" for "brothel," – concession that I did not know how to refuse you, and which I confess I am inconsolable about.*

Another thing. You say that "this book has weighed on me," which is true, for very honorable reasons, I think, expressed in chapter XIII. But you add, while being absolutely mistaken, that I wrote it "in annoyance," in other words with the feelings of a slave, as if one were working on a chain gang. Now, it is just the opposite *that is true. I have a witness who will not recuse you. My wife can tell you that the greatest part of it was done in two months, in an access of* enthusiasm.

You said that "the first chapters are superior to the last." That is possible, but I don't believe it. They are different. *If I had kept the tone of the first four, my book would have been unreadable. I would never have em-*

barked on the subject even. I had
hoped that the "Duchess Cain" and
"The Last King's Hallali" would
please you, for I thought of myself as
an artist writing those pages and I felt
an extraordinary feeling in my soul.
But you are a man of the world, that's
invincible.

Enthusiasm for our curate. One has to come back from Kolding to appreciate a curate capable of saying that the presence of a Christian family is a benediction for his parish.

30. – Spoke about Saint Veronica with that pastor. He told me to see in her an example of heroism in opposition to human respect. Banal, seminarian, and sanctimonious point of view. I responded to him that the beauty of that Saint is incomparably higher and more profound. She appeared in the middle of the Passion in order to honor the Sacerdocy, the supreme Pontificate universally decried, and in order to venerate the Face that makes the human race both ashamed and fearful. In consequence of this idea, I think that it would be desirable for a very pious ecclesiastic to found an organization dedicated to Saint Veronica in view of assisting priests, both temporarily and supernaturally.

August

2. – Return of poverty. We had begun to forget that old companion for about two months while it seemed to distance itself from us.

3. – It was time also that a bit of bitterness should be offered to us by our curate. That threatened to be quite beautiful. Suddenly he begins to speak his mass with a rapidity, an inconceivable and unprecedented velocity. Impossible to follow him, no matter what one does. Profoundly sad and troubled, I wrote him a letter which he took very badly.

4. – Second letter to the same:

My dear curate,

My wife tells me that my letter offended you. Surprise and heartbreak for me. Supposing you on your way to becoming a saint and my being mistaken, alas! by several centuries, I believed that you would have come, simply, all in tears, and that you would have embraced me, telling me like the admirable Jean Tauler to a laic who accused him in an infinitely more severe and serious manner: – "It seems to me that what is happening to me, at this moment, is like what happened to the Samaritan near the well. You have pointed out my defects to me, my child, told me what I held hidden deep inside myself. Who could have told you? It is God, I am certain of it..." Why and how could you be vexed by so gentle a reprimand by the only one *of your parishioners who wants his pastor to be a* SAINT?... *You thought my letter insulting, alas! instead of seeing in it the sadness of a great love and the effort of a totally virile amity... You thought that I saw in you a bad priest. How little you know me! If I had thought that, I would have spoken to you in a different tone, and I would have spoken also to the Church, as it said in the Gospel. I thought merely that you had* a bad habit, *and I felt it was my duty to point it out to you...*

Recall what you had affirmed to me with such force, declaring to me that you were with me, resolutely, "eyes closed," and now see how strange it is that on the first word that touches you personally, *you distance yourself from me!...*

Why would you not want to listen to me and to believe me? I have few friends, having always spoken the truth to everyone who appeared insupportable and lacking in charity. Saint Philip de Neri, whose mass lasted an

> *entire morning, and the harsh Saint*
> *Ignatius who bathed his soul for three*
> *quarters of an hour in the prayers of*
> *the canon, were dragged to the feet of*
> *a vagabond who would have told*
> *them: "You scandalize me." Who in-*
> *forms you, my dear curate, that al-*
> *though greatly unworthy I was not*
> *sent to you?...*

Letter from Charles Morice[2] who declares his admiration for me, but who wants me to know that he is not fond of me. I will console myself as best I can. In the worst case scenario, I have the option of drunkenness.

5. – Reconciliation with the curate of Ceux-d'En-Bas, stormy the day before yesterday, but today resigned and who says his mass like a little saint.

11. – Every day practically, on our way to Church, we meet a married priest. It appears that that poor man is not an apostate, which is difficult to understand. Sacerdotal fornication, already monstrous given it implies theologically adultery, incest and sacrilege, does not necessarily imply apostasy. But a priest invoking civil code to sanction his turpitudes is forced to break everything, to destroy everything. The person I speak

---

[2]Charles Morice (AD 1860-1919): a French writer, poet and essayist. Born into a staunchly Catholic family, he later in life lost his faith and founded the anticlerical *La Nouvelle Rive Gauche*, a literary and political journal, which within a year changed its name to *Lutèce* and became the organ or mouthpiece of Symbolism. For more on *Lutèce*, see Chapter XII of Émile Goudeau's *Ten Years a Bohemian* (Sunny Lou Publishing, 2021).

about weeps, he says, over his cowardice. I know of nothing more tragic, or more mysterious than those tears that Anne-Catherine Emmerich saw fall, like drops of fire, into eternal wells.

Another priest who is not married, except to money, but in a manner that appears indissoluble, – the edifying curate of Ceux-d'En-Haut, adjacent parish, presents to me the scene of a pastor resolved not to turn away a single sheep, not the minutest trickle from the abundant source that he drinks from.

What is chance? It is the modern name for the Holy Ghost.

What is universal suffrage? It is the election of the father of the family by his children.

14. – Resumption of the *Eugene Grasset's Twelve Daughters*, that is, the twelve months, poems in prose inspired by his astonishing series of zodiacal signs and the three first of which were written in '96. I don't know if it is possible to understand them without having before one's eyes the admirable drawings in color that I have done my best to interpret. (Unable to find, thus far, a publisher who is rich enough or intelligent enough to attempt that double publication, I want to insert here, provisorily, my unfortunate poems, the last of which was completed on September 12 of the same year 1900. The *Mercure de France* published them, without pictures, in its November 1903 issue.)

Eugène Grasset's Twelve Daughters

For the great painter Eugene Grasset

To whom to dedicate these poems, if not to you who inspired them, my very dear friend? You will think what you will about them, of course. It sufficed for me to have held your interest for an hour.

You have admirably understood that your Zodiac could not be conceived of or interpreted by me except in the context of the Roman Catholic Apostolic Calendar of the Saints.

It would be unheard of for me to express, on any occasion, the base ideas of the world, and I entreat you to refuse any explanation to imbeciles.

Yours,

– LÉON BLOY.

October, 1900.

January

Is that my grave you are digging, charitable daughter? If it is, hurry up, for it seems to me that I am as dead as the year just past, that I stink already like Lazarus, and that my impatience is extreme to go and wait for the Resurrection in the bed of saints.

Do not worry about making it spacious. Do not forget that I must lie there with my poverty which is so great and which turns over and over without end.

The spot does not displease me at all, beautiful gardener. I like that holly which is not a bad symbol for me with its hard wood, its fierce leaves, and its fiery-red fruit. Its prickly leaves will discourage pilgriming sentimentalities, funereal loquacities, devotions after the fir, and its parsimonious shade will quite sufficiently protect The Ungrateful Beggar's sleep.

Doubtless, it is your ministry and your business to condition sepultures. Since your Mother who made, in an instant, from the tip of her finger of a Child of God, all the fruits of the trees of Paradise fall, it is almost unprecedented that a woman does not dig a small hole in her garden in order to bury some poor wretch. Isn't that right, my child, that you give me preference? Interrogate, if you will, all the polecats, they will tell you that there is no carrion equal to mine and that nothing is so pressing as burying me.

And then, there is your opaque crystal fountain, with its stalactites of ice that you must have frozen with your sighs. The fermentation of my entrails will unthaw it perhaps. Be at ease, my pretty redhead, I will not be a useless guest. Your round lawns will be greener and the sable edge of your mediocre paths will grow paler. The boxwood along your borders will no longer despair of being blessed, some Palm Sunday, in the parish church which your yellow scarf and brown skirt of a villager are assuredly unfamiliar with, accustomed as you are to working on the Day of Rest. The sad umbrella that I see behind the basin will finally know the glory of the cedars: your beeches with their pale trunks, your haggard fruit trees and the greenhouse where you hide your shivering flowers condemned to die for nostalgia on the impure bosom of our virgins – all those creatures afflicted with the feeling that you did not eat the Body of your Lord today will receive from my carcass an electuary that will prevent their melancholy.

You also, obstinate digger – and at this very phantomatic hour – of an illusory soil which the putrefaction of a hundred million living effigies of the Lord has transubstantiated, you will rise up with an attitude a little bit more than human, when, after having buried me in that fatherland, you divine that you have poverty beneath your feet of an animal, yes, truly,

Poverty itself, or, at least, its perfect image, which is totally divine, you may take my word for it.

Let's go! pleasant brute, hurry it up with your hole already. The time is right. I am full of consecrated hosts, full of psalms and penitence, full of joy and ignominy, and I will germinate for you.

February

I detest that rage of cutting down poor trees, melancholic trees that cannot defend themselves and that extend so voluntarily in all directions, whose branches would open the doors and windows of houses so well, and would tear down, as if with a very able-bodied hand, all the walls of gardens where the toad of the incontestable egoism of gardeners has become entrenched.

But who thinks of the captivity of those captives of human Gluttony? The executioners of Christ, who ought to have considered themselves happy squatting in vermin while singing very pure hymns and eating the bitterest roots of the flowers of tombs, have discovered how to mutilate those not ugly crea-

tures in order to constrain them to pour their essence into the fruit that are so sweet that one dies breathing them.

Surprising images of those Martyrs whose branches have been lopped off in the slaughterhouses of Christians so that they might engender, in their tortures, delectation for the Church. Also, doesn't anyone see how they twist and writhe, those miserable creatures, how they clench and sob under their bark which is bursting, how deformed and lamentable they are!

I think that formerly, before man's catastrophe – it has been centuries really – the trees did what they wanted, they moved about where they wanted in the Garden that one cannot speak of, under the eyes of the innocent Couple, in order to spare them the fatigue of walking under their foliage. Later, some sublime blind men, who had gouged out their own eyes and thrown them into the bottom of the gulfs of Paradise, saw very distinctly the trees of all species and all time running from the extremities of the earth – while passing by unintelligent men who thought they saw themselves passing – in the direction of a unique and prodigious Mountain: "Will that be me, Lord!" they said then, "will that be me?"

But behold a pretty person to prune that celibate whose dreadful, inconsolable carcass of a pear tree makes me bring to my lips a water that is more than bitter. That daughter of February does not look like she finds life too awful, and the reflection of the shears in her completely attentive eyes amply suffices, I suppose, for her contemplative instincts.

Would that she might be careful, however. It is terrible being in a perfectly closed garden where no poor person has the right to enter. I tremble really lest that pointed branch she is about to cut does not spring back into her face, blind an eye, and penetrate her brain, that little brain where the mendicant thoughts of heaven clearly have never been admitted.

For one does not recognize any tree, any more than any man. There is only one who is immortal and whose story is infinitely famous, but whom the formidable Cherub has so well hidden that God alone knows where he can be found. Now, it is always alarming to see a woman putting her hand on a tree, and what angel of darkness would dare say that that tree, precise-

ly because it looks so miserable, is not what was called the Tree of the Knowledge of Good and Evil which the ancient Serpent wound about?

March

On both knees! The soweress, on both knees! If only you are capable of understanding what you do. A single knee cannot suffice. For, I am telling you, in truth, that as soon as someone sows something, behold it is God passing through!... Something, you understand me, in other words anything.

Just supposing – I accord you this voluntarily – that your seeds had been bought in the shop of a demon and you were sowing Pestilence, Famine, Error, Destruction, Terror, it would turn out all the same, and you must kneel down even more. It is God passing through, I am telling you.

The Apostle who boasted knowing how to plant, and who is represented with a sword,[3] wrote one day to some Greek fornicators that there were only three ways to sow: in rottenness, in abjection, and in weakness; and now you know why that posture is the only one

---

[3]The Apostle... represented with a sword: St. Paul.

suitable. Because it belongs to the Lord alone to fecundate life or death, it is before Him that you act, and he watches you in a formidable silence.

It is possible, after all, that you think you are planting merely flowers. We will speak about that later, when the time for flowers comes. For the time being, we are only at March, anniversary of the Creation of the world. It happened then, in the time of times, a sowing of suns and reptiles, which you have no idea of. Your pretty head with its golden hair would appear to be nothing but a good story. Then, when the teeming was at the desired point, Man appeared who is, at one and the same time, a globe of light and a beast who crawls. He has to be the Sower par excellence, and I do not very clearly see why you have taken his place.

If however you were sowing during a night of new moon, as sorceresses do, it could happen that black flowers or the tenebrae's legumes, terrifyingly blessed by the incubi of chaos, continued in broad daylight the dream of injustice and prevarication that resides in your soul. But I see you in a clear and bright garden with deep, green paths, where the fresh air of Lætare

Sunday already stimulates the care of amorous birds. Ah! no, really, you have no idea what you are doing, that is quite evident.

You have never said to yourself, for example, that the merchants of grain are shopkeepers of Mystery and that one can never be sure of what they are selling. Eh well! listen. Little does it matter that you want to sow the wall-flower or the pumpkin, but there exists a prodigious Grain, only one, the smallest of all, says the Gospel, which is the impenetrable similitude of the Kingdom of Heaven and the infinitely exact measure of the Faith. *It is from this, doubtless, – I tell you in passing – that the celebrated pride of mustard merchants derives, for that seed is a vulgar mustard grain.*

Vulgar, but not just any *sort, given the Parable designates only the One that must become the excessively unique colossus where all the birds find shelter. What would you say if, in your box or in your little packets which make me tremble, was hidden the re-doubtable germ of that giant and that it might sprout any minute now – as is proper for miraculous vegetations – and that, devouring your flowers, your flower beds, your paths and your mounds, it plunged its longest root into your heart?*

April

It is the month of Easter, the month of trees in bloom, the month of ranunculus and adolescence's swoons. Formerly, thirty or forty years ago, I was rolling on the tender grass troating to the Infinite skies. Since then, I have found nothing in the flat external world to justify it. Mont Blanc seemed to me a hole, and I was disgusted by the oceans that any imbecile can cross.

Earthly Paradise, Eden Lost, whose recuperation is the effort of every human being, I can conceive of it in no other way than this: A prairie of the Annunciation filled with dandelions and buttercups, under some very humble apple trees that resemble Confessors and whose boughs, laden with chalices, look as though they are kissing the earth.

As for you, most savorous Redhead who arouse me, I admit, in this landscape of delights, allow me to tell you a story that you remind me of, a sweet story of days gone by. You will make of it, of course, what you may, like the first girl to come along, but that contingency is without interest. I seek above all to please my soul which is, in my eyes, the Beauty of the world.

A female saint got lost in the woods. Night was coming and everything was to be feared. So she prayed with great faith, as you yourself would pray perhaps if your father had taught you how to pray – imploring the assistance of fleet Angels. Suddenly a fountain appeared at her feet and became a stream the color of the sky which led her to her hermitage. And that is my story. It is not long, but it is immensely pleasing to my soul, once again, and it is that delightful river of yours that made me think of it.

Now, when I speak to you of my soul, o Redhead, are you able to understand me? Could you feel it trembling, that madness for the Passion of the Lord Jesus that does not stop bounding, crying, and sobbing in me, when it is not immobilized by a frightening dream?

Like you, it would have no idea how to dream standing up, under those trees and among those flowers. It is famished for Infinity, I tell you. It is enraged with a thirst for things that can-

not be seen and that exist in such a way that one dies for them.

If you were thrown alive to that monster, with all your paradise, you would not satisfy it for one hour even. Each morning, it needs God to eat and the crumbling of worlds.

Listen to me. That so pure water that flows through your beautiful prairie and which is, doubtless, an unknown affluent of Eve's immense River of Tears with its cataracts in the sky; – if you wanted to follow it, that lovely water, as the virgin of my story followed it; who knows, o Redhead, with your hands filled with flowers in the middle of flowers; – if you wanted to follow it just a little... who knows whether you would not arrive soon enough, all your trees having disappeared, at your true abode, your terrible house of a Godless young woman on the calcined bank of an Orinoco[4] of blood lit up by the furious stars?

May

Here is a fifth girl visibly resolved to be bothered as little as possible. She is

---

[4]Orinoco: one of the longest rivers in South America.

*neither standing nor on her knees, not
even on one knee. The attitude of contemplation and the attitude of prayer
are equally unknown to her. She is
seated quite simply on a garden
bench, like a girl of that majestic Juno
whose eyes of a cow impressed the
good Homer for the duration of centuries.*

*Perniciously inclined, she nonchalant-
ly culls big irises the color of the Passion that will die in her basket. Would
she not do better to leave them on
their stems, next to those bellflowers
and that viburnum* opulus, *not far
from that young chestnut tree that
pushes up its pyramidal flowers in the
glory of a Byzantine crepuscule?*

*It seems to me that you do not know
very well what you do, my sweet child.
You simply obey, I suppose, the instinct of destruction that is inside you.
I do not see you, with your red hair of
a magician, bringing those beautiful
plants to Mary in the church of your
parish. Do you know even who Mary
is, the very pure and very terrible Virgin, of whom it is written that "She
will laugh on the Last Day"? No, you
don't, do you? You think, like everyone else, if that is called thinking, that
the Queen's month of May is for your*

adornment, for the ornament of your altar, your altars, o wretch! And you would fall into a stupefaction never to be recovered from, if someone said to you that you will soon need to give an account of all that to the Holy Ghost, perhaps even before the first vespers of Pentecost ring out. Behold, the Holy Ghost has already turned into a ball of fire and descends on you...

Do you believe then that it will last forever, this impious farce of the glory of young ladies of high society who would make alligators recoil if their insides were exposed to those reptiles?

There is a voice that everyone will hear, when the other voices have gone silent. It is the Voice of the Consoler, of the Immaculate One's Spouse, of Love itself, and there will never be anything so frightening. I do not know what she will tell you. But by then the time of compassion will have passed, and you will feel it immediately, having made an attempt on the flowers. Your terror will devour you like a dragon, and the Morning Star will break out in laughter at the furthest reaches of heaven!

June

*There you are standing, you at least,
Antoinette-Baptistine, another killer of
flowers! If someone strikes you, you
will have something to fall over about.
But you are so young! Barely fifteen
years old, am I right? It is rather early
to be massacring the poor roses. Who
knows, after all? You do that perhaps
so as to strew their petals in the procession of the Holy Sacrament. I prefer to believe that...*

*Your hair is too poorly combed, more-
over, to have horrible thoughts, idolatrous thoughts, and your Eve-like gesture, I really hope, will not be the occasion of any catastrophe.*

*My benevolence is such, today, that
even the cherry tree that stands behind
you, o Pierette-Pauline, alarms me
very little, although I know that it was,
in times gone by, imported from the
Orient after the crusades, at the same
time as leprosy and ogival architecture.*

*However, the Mother of God is named
Rose mysteriously, one would need to
pay attention to that. It is so dangerous to touch things that are symbolic!*

The creation of flowers is as perfectly

incomprehensible as the creation of worlds. But after Adam had given names to all the beasts, as it is written in the Good Book, does no one see that he had to give flowers names too, by necessity? Who could relate the ecstatic trembling that the Father of all Prophets felt when he had to fix in that way and forever the essence of Her *among those admirable creatures who were bound for eternity to be the precise figure of the Chalice of Redemption!*

The most beautiful rosebush on earth is in Assisi. It is the one that Saint Francis rolls around in, totally naked, in order to discourage the devil. That miraculous rosebush is seven centuries old, and each year its petals grow back splattered with the blood of the Seraphic.[5] Your rosebush, poor little one, is of another sort. I presume, moreover, that anyone's blood on its petals would frighten you. Girls have little enthusiasm for heroes, much preferring boors to them. As for the Saints, they know nothing about them.

The roses that you pick are, despite everything, many visible examples of the Rose with the pistil of sorrow whence comes the Source of Blood

---

[5] The Seraphic: a nickname for St. Francis of Assisi.

that flows over you for nearly two thousand years now. Only, be careful not to prick your pretty fingers, for there is nothing so very like the Crown of Thorns as a bush of roses is.

It is in this way that I represent to myself the adorable Head of Jesus in Gabbatha, that is, at the culminating moment of the Passion, when one hundred thousand Jews in despair cried out to crucify him, and when his Mother exuded, through every pore, – a bush of roses!

July

Ah! yes, but what has become of the poor? Where are they then? Not only do I not see them, but I do not see any object that reminds me of them.

For some time now, I encounter only women, extraordinarily dressed, who walk or keep still in beautiful gardens. Not a single instance of those amiable people who are poorly dressed, of those dear persons dying of famine who put a bit of glory in the scenery and give some consolation after the appalling stink of proprietors.

Look at that tall lady who wears the sign of the lion on her blue dress, as if she wanted to devour everything. I have not the least desire to say the least word to her. For too long a time I have exhausted myself in harangues to these inferior creatures whom I would be tempted to find sometimes adorable if I saw them without a sou. This one has no need of me, that much is certain. She is, moreover, very busy and would not give me the time of day. She waters the lilies more splendid than Solomon, even though they do not work or spin.

It is for that reason that she cares for them, supposing them symbolic of herself, good-for-nothing and parricide, who causes to be crucified, at her expense, the good Savior, each morning, and who does not even have the energy to get out of bed to see him die!

She forgets or does not want to know that those same flowers express very particularly the purity *that can suit some bare-foot beggars, but that one must recognize as incompatible with the duties of the world.*

Has she already watered those magnificent poppies that I see behind her? Whether they be the poppies of sleep or those of death, they appear to me better paired with that spouse of a damned man. They bloom outside the garden, and they smell bad within. And I discover them as far as the eye can see in the neighboring gardens, in the gardens of other pashas who culti- vate them with no less love.

My God! It is to you, now, that I ask it. What have you done with your poor? Lord Jesus, where are they? I know by your veritable Gospel that there will always be the poor, because it is im- possible for you, being the Son of God, to do without them; because you can- not be a head without members and because all your suns would need to hurtle away on the day that there are no longer any poor.

I know also that it is a poor man who must fulfill everything, and I think that at this very moment he is making the world turn round on his finger, in some hovel.

Merciful Jesus! Do not allow the rich to inundate the earth. Behold how the day is ending and the night is falling. Send us the gentle lamps that are your poor, the calm lamps of sweet smell that illuminate your Paradise and that receive, by divine virtue, all the tor- rents, all the cataracts of light, all the conflagrations of brightnesses that the intelligence of a Seraph can glimpse!

August

Now here is a sky of a rather menacing color, so it seems to me. That young person whose blue ribbons make her resemble a child of Mary should not tarry in the middle of those suns and in the neighborhood of those somber trees. Then, there are those nenuphars emblematic of chastity which could very well attract lightning.

The month of August is, moreover, full of mysteries. To say nothing about Saint Peter-in-Chains nor about Saint Laurent, there is the Transfiguration, the Assumption... the Decapitation. It seems to me that those feast days are invocatory of cataclysms, the last more likely than the others.

But who thinks of that? When the Church has celebrated the œcumenical triumph of the Virgin, one would say that everything that follows succumbs, so great was the effort! It is only barely if one sees Saint Bartholomew passing in his beautiful purple robe and the sublime king of Mansourah and of Carthage on his bed of ashes. Nobody notices the Decapitation, the martyrdom of the Man, absolutely unique, the

*Man sent by God to be witness to the
Light and by whom all men receive the
Faith.*

*I tremble when I see a woman carry-
ing something. Even if it be a basket of
chestnuts in the month of December, it
is impossible for me not to think of the
Head of Saint John. I think that there
were two women to cause that Head,
inexpressibly blessed, to be separated
from its body and that subsequently
there were many others like them who
went to find it in a horrible sewer,
while weeping for love. I ask myself
then if all women are not made to carry, in one manner or another, the
Head of Saint John and if that is not
their profound law.*

*Go away then, young lady with the
blue ribbons. Hurry up and leave. I do
not know how I am aware of a violent
storm that is building. Go then with
your basket, with WHAT is in your basket, o pucelle who strikes fear in me!...
The Head of Saint John was cut off to
please a young lady who perhaps resembles you, and behold Saint Fiacre[6]
in person who carries lightning in his
chariot...*

Save yourself, I tell you, and if you be-

[6]Saint Fiacre: Irish saint who emigrated to France in AD 7th
century and is now considered the patron saint of gardeners.

lieve in God, go hide in the nearest church. Make yourself very small at the foot of the altar and pray as best you can for those who do not know the Precursor, while the winds and thunder are unleashed over the miserable world that cut off the Head of Saint John.

September

Yet another redhead who carries so-called flowers! She looks at me strangely as if she thought me her judge. Alas! how little she has to fear from me! Experience has killed any suspicion in me. Everything is so mediocre and so stupid! Where to find today a truly perverse woman, a heroine of Balzac or Barbey d'Aurevilly; a woman, more or less beautiful woman, but in cahoots with hell, capable of hiding, for the fright of souls, some terrifying relic under the flowers?

The scenery, I have to admit, suggests Romantic ecstasy. We are in a considerable garden, in an infanta's banal and grandiose promenade. But the vanity of all that! How many of these chatelaines who have spent thirty years behind a counter between the purchase order and the bill and whose lyricism is exhausted in phrases like this: "Anything else with that, Monsieur?" or "I did indeed receive your letter," or "I will send to your account an order for said sum with said due date," etc.! Can a Shakespearian peripeteia reasonably be expected from such hearts, from such brains?

May she put her mind at ease then, the dear soul, in the middle of the pale dahlias and under her service tree! I will not seek to understand curiously what she carries any more than what she thinks, only too certain that emptiness would be my discovery.

Then again, it is the hour when everything is about to die. Mary has just been born[7] and the Church is on the verge of exalting the Cross. After that, what are forms of Art and movements of Poetry? Here is autumn. Nature is profoundly, irremediably discouraged. With the exception of the Christian dead, if one puts something into the ground, it is without hope. It hurts to see the plants. Why would women, who are just above the flowers, want to keep, in the middle of universal agony, some mirage of victory?

Now, the tradition of poets which must

---

[7]Mary has just been born: The Feast of the Nativity of the Blessed Virgin Mary is September 8.

have its origin at the bottom of the Abyss, under magnificent lost Truths, absolutely wants that the triumph of woman be her mystery. *Mystery of her eyes, mystery of her mouth, mystery of her attitudes, etc. mystery also, I suppose, of her inexistent thoughts. What a pity for that guitar, when one knows that everything will die and that all is dead!*

But who then can have a need to live, when the Mother of God comes into the world, and what to say of a human triumph when the Cross of the Redeemer is exalted!

October

Let the leaves be, my child, I beg you. Don't you see that they make for a sublime scenery? Would you happen to be one of those sots who is always seen with a broom or a rake in hand and who have so low an idea of order that their diligence would efface divine Beauty even? Is it in order to sweep then and destroy those admirable leaves which two thirds of the palette, in October, is taken up by, that you have put on that magnificent saffron dress?

No one, it is clear to me, has ever taught you that the plane tree according to Holy Scripture, being one of the mysterious trees singled out to symbolize Mary, is of all trees the one whose leaves retain for the longest time and contemporaneously with the greatest display, the adorable colors of the setting sun.

Of course, I know precious little about a beauty as penetrating as any drift of its leaves on a lawn, and the nearness of the most beautiful chrysanthemums in the world would add nothing to the melancholic intensity of that vision.

Once again, then, let those poor leaves be.

Let them fall one after the other until they make a golden litter for Saint Luke's Ox. I would come and sit down with happiness beside that amiable beast, under Saint Francis and Saint Denys, the latter carrying his head the color of amethyst in his episcopal hands, the former completely beaming with the stigmata of Jesus Christ.

And if, after having put down your rake of a tidy little bourgeoise woman, you consent to stand back in the simplicity of your heart, you will see perhaps the Guardian Angels of October to whom was confided the sweet agony of nature.

Ah! how much need there is for those angels, when one is poor! It is the last month of the season before winter, the most frightening of the four. Seeing the forests and the more modest woods in their dazzling brocaded robes, the proprietors rub their hands together, thinking on the enormous tribulation of souls. They tell themselves that this here is their glory because, in order to pay them, by necessity the poor wretches need to work themselves to the bone, the mothers need to endure hunger, and the little children need to succumb.

The little children... the gold of heaven, the celestial Jerusalem, the eternal fatherland of the tortured members of the Redeemer... the proprietors! Ah! Jesus, Joy of Angels and Father of the poor, have mercy on us!

November

Finally! Here we are at the cemetery, the earthly Paradise according to Marchenoir. What peace! What sweetness! Who can express the refreshing feeling felt on seeing tombs? Those who inhabit them, grace be to God! they will not leave them voluntarily in order to torment, once again, those who still have to die.

It is true that if they could escape, the earth would not contain their supplications or their cries of despair... Long live silence!

There is no earthly consolation comparable to this, that all men must die and that while waiting for the miracle of the end of ends, there will always be, for each generation full of clamors, a corresponding generation of silence. One hundred thousand rise up, one hundred thousand lie down. Oh! What a beautiful law! The desire to inter someone in order to die a little while later oneself is so engrained in the nature of man that one can truly say that there is nothing but the Church to show compassion for the dead.

I want to believe that it is with the pious intention of adorning a grave that that young lady gathers those sad gillyflowers of autumn. She looks neither serious nor melancholic in her dress riddled with the arrows of Sagittarius. Why would she? At her age one does not believe in death or, if she believes, it is vaguely and with recourse to such sentimental effusions!

Her story, doubtless, is of an extreme platitude. She has been told, since a very tender age, that all roads lead to Rome, that when there's smoke there's fire, that great sorrows are silent, that business is business, and that God does not require much. Equipped with that viaticum, she has been taught, in addition, a little grammar, a little music, a little poetry and arithmetic, and she has read powerful books, such as those by Paul Bourget for example, between bicycle rides.

If she goes to the cemetery on the Day of the Dead, it is, above all, because of tradition, perhaps also because the carcass of her father or of her mother grows moldy in some hole and that it is more suitable and more touching for her to be moved over that carrion than to make merry in some brothel.

"My child!" hurls a desperate voice that she cannot hear, "my cruel child, why have you no pity for me? I suffer from infinite ills. If the smoke of my torment reached you, you would fall dead, and the hundredth part of a drop of my fearful sweat would set you on fire like a torch. Don't you have a prayer then to say for me, merely a prayer, on this day of the Commemo-

ration of all the dead?"

If the contemptible, pretty girl heard that she would think according to what her masters taught her that it was a hallucination, *and she would tell herself, while softly moved, that the dead are blest, as they have stopped suffering.*

Turn around then, wild animal, and look at that defoliated tree, that line of graves, that spent sun!... In several hours you will die.

December

God be blessed! it is the last. They will have finished passing before us, those beautiful strangers that the admirable Grasset has successively offered to us like representative species of the vanity of all that passes. My lassitude is excessive, and it is with a very gentle joy that I take leave of that druidess of Capricorn whom no one will follow.

My only interest is with the mistletoe that she has filled her apron with. Let her carry that parasite to those who suppose it to possess a mysterious virtue. I ask her only to take care of those beautiful roses of Noel that she seems not to see at her feet. And then, my God! that she might go, that she might disappear, into her large park filled with snow!

Frankly, I can no longer take all these godless creatures who would succeed in making me forget the Three Mysteries. Enough with your demoiselles, my good Grasset. They are pleasant to look at, I don't say that they're not, but they are so poorly bred. Not a single one who has let me see the least sign attesting to her being a Christian! And that is why I cannot contemplate them anymore without sadness nor, sometimes, without anger.

Recall what I said to the fourth, to that ravishing lady who wore the hieroglyph of Taurus on her Oriental-colored dress. To her who appeared to me to have more soul than the others, I spoke my soul, going so far as to say that it was a monster that nothing could assuage. She must not have understood much of that discourse. What to do about that? Your twelve ladies, Eugène, are impious simulacra, and I would not know how to speak to them in any other language than that of the ancient Witnesses whom one skinned and burnt alive and who were called Martyrs.

What would be the point of recalling

to this gatherer of mistletoe that Jesus will be born in Bethlehem where Angels, Shepherds, Kings will adore him, and where to welcome him with their breath, the Ox and the Ass, symbols of the New Testament, will gather, having hurried to the manger of the poor Infant, in execution of the instructions given to them by the prophet, twenty-six centuries earlier?

She would look at me with those big eyes, the color of snow, of eternally blinded idols.

Look at us then, far from the eyes streaming with tears that one would need to have to think only on adorable Poverty! And at what an infinite distance we are from eyes in the form of eternal wells that the Samaritan must have had when Emmanuel, having grown older, *asked her for something to drink!*

And even still, and finally, o dear great artist, what do you want me to say about the zodiacal women who do not know – among other things – that the Redemption of humankind was accomplished in the Sign of Pisces and that that is written in the Gospel. It is something of importance to them however.

The women of the zodiac, moreover, who are rich, – are they not frighten-ing? With the exception of the first who digs up her garden, all are mar-quesses including the last one with the look of a child who is a villager acting like a princess. None of them lack any-thing, the majority of them are evi-dently landladies. The Zodiac of land-ladies!... I give up.

17. – Encountered at the curate's a hypnotist, spiritist or occultist, – I don't rightly know how to call that animal, – who says he's a good Christian and on his own initiative pulls out his rosary beads. I learn with horror that ecclesiastical authority, far from violently rejecting such filth, claims that priests study it with the greatest attention under the pretext, a thousand times stupid, that they need to be armed against an er-ror *which could very well not be absolute*. That places us far from the Martyrs who would have preferred to sit down to a table of fire, a red-hot cooking pot on their head, rather than take half a step in the direction of demons. Terribly far, I dare say!

Occasion to cite a very fine page from the fa-mous seer of Dulmen (*Life of Anne-Catherine Em-merich* by Father Schmœger, tome I, page 485):

The practice of magnetism borders on magic; only, one does not invoke the devil, instead he comes on his own ini-tiative. Whoever should give into it

*takes from nature something that can-
not be acquired legitimately except in
the Church of Jesus-Christ, and which
cannot be preserved with the power of
healing and sanctifying except in
one's bosom. Now, nature, for all
those who are not in living union with
Jesus Christ by true faith and sanctifying grace, is full of Satan's influences.
Magnetic persons see nothing in its
essence and in its dependence on God;
they see everything isolated and separate, as if through a hole or fent. They
perceive a gleam of things through
magnetism, and God would want that
that light be pure, in other words
saintly. It is an act of God's kindness
to have separated us and shielded us
from one another, and to have raised
walls between us, since we are filled
with sins and dependent on each other; it is good that we are forced to act
in advance, before seducing one another reciprocally and communicating
amongst ourselves the contagious influence of a bad spirit. But, in Jesus
Christ, God himself made man is given
to us like our head in whom, purified
and sanctified, we can become one
thing only, a single body, without
bringing into that union our sins and
our bad penchants. Whoever wants, in
another manner, to stop that separa-*

tion established by God unites himself in a very dangerous fashion with fallen nature, in which reigns with his seductions he who brought him to his fall.

I see the particular essence of magnetism as real; but there is a thief who is unleashed in that veiled light. Every union between sinners is dangerous; mutual penetration is still worse. But when that happens for a completely open soul; when a state which does not become clairvoyant, except because it implies simplicity and the absence of scheming, becomes a prey to artifice and intrigue; then one of the faculties of man before the fall, the faculty which is not entirely dead, is resuscitated in a certain manner, leaving him more disarmed and in a more mysterious state, exposed internally to attacks by the demon. That state is real, it exists; but it is covered by a veil, because it is a poisoned source for us, but not for the saints. Etc.

20. – Trip to Paris. I'm told that de Groux, not satisfied with insinuating that I am a wicked man, now accuses my wife without providing details. My poor Jeanne who had previously saved his life! I return home flushed with disgust.

21. – Dedication of *The Son of Louis XVI* to Marguerite de la Tour du Pin Chambly: "Melancholic remembrance of a *fraternal* amity that she had promised me and that for unknown reasons she was unable to give to an unfortunate artist."

23. – I spoke today, with respect to *The Son of Louis XVI*, of the enormous injustice, nearly unprecedented, that weighs on me. It is impossible, I said, that God should tolerate it, that so undervalued an artist should live without recompense or, at least, without any compensation whatsoever. A poet, atheistic even, if men left him without any salary, is the creditor of God whom he has honored without knowing it, and he will be paid back very exactly.

27. – Testaments. When a man makes his testament, he undergoes a unique test. It is the last moment that he has to show his soul to men before showing it to God.

September

1st. – The curate of Ceux-d'En-Bas, informed as to the fix I'm in financially, speaks of introducing me to one of his other parishioners, the *Master of Forges*, that is to say the veritable protagonist of the author of the

Eaters of Filthy Things. That Vulcan, whose name is Trouduc, whom I saw from afar and who appeared to me not much inferior, insofar as distinction, to an overweight chamber valet on Kléber Avenue, is so rich, I am assured, that he spends 80,000 francs a year on ant eggs for the nourishment of his pheasants. It is enough to make a mist of blood rise up before the eyes of 80,000 poor people. The inhabitants of the countryside are admitted, on days of glory, to the honor of strolling in his park, the which, seen from the railroad, is quite certainly the most pompous thing one can imagine. I have never seen so abject a pleasure garden since the late Mme. Boucicaut, at Fontenay-aux-Roses, twenty years ago. I conceive the Hunchback Ohnet having been carried away for a such a strongbox, but I do not want to oppose the curate's plans. The result could be rather comical.

With the utmost attention, I continue not to visit the Exposition.

2. – *Animas pauperum tuorum ne derelinquas in finem...*[8] A small wine merchant from the neighborhood, who is also a mechanic, came to do a small job. I have him drink something, he stalls for a long time, talks a lot about his disinterestedness, the pleasure he takes in rendering a service, and finishes, in spite of a price agreed on in advance, by not returning to me the change for a piece of money that I slip into his hands. That brother goes by the name of *Dieuleveut!* So be

---

[8]*Animas*...: Latin for "Do not abandon in the end the souls of your poor." From the Gregorian Chant, the Introit *Respice Dominus,* part of the Proper of the Liturgy.

it.

4. – Annual pilgrimage to Saint Veronica in the church of Ceux-d'En-Bas. It is something of a feast day of the Holy Face of the Poor. In front of me, in the first row, the multimillionaires with the ant eggs, the male and female Trouduc, who have promised to enquire about me and to subsidize me in a princely manner by means of some *pieces*, in an indeterminate number of trimesters, if the information they receive is satisfactory. The commercial vulgarity of these "chatelains" is enough to make the Holy Sacrament recoil. I think of our curate counseling them, so he told me, to interrogate only *honest folk* about me. The comedy, on this score, is enormous. One can imagine a kind of central gulf of comicalness into which torrents drawn from everywhere rush headlong.

10. – There is talk of a band of inapprehensible robbers who let themselves into the most respectable houses, having sworn, I do know know on what relics, to "empty" all the habitations. (I learnt, later, that the gendarmerie itself had been broken into.)

11. – The hunchback Ohnet possesses, in the vicinity of Ferté-sous-Jouarre, a chateau des Abîmes. Yes, Ohnet and *the Abysses*! I had that stupefying affirmation repeated to me many times: "O Nothing," said Saint François de Sales, "thou art my fatherland; I am drawn by thy tenebrous abyss and by thy frightening

cavern."

13. – Banality. The rich are always absent.

14. – Continuation of silence on the part of the multi-millionaires with the ant eggs, good Christians who throw parties costing 10,000 francs and who can do nothing for a poor writer of God, who gives them the incredible honor of suffering that one might solicit them on his behalf.

17. – The appearance of *Je M'Accuse...* published by the Maison d'Art.

19. – Affliction of our curate who does not understand a thing in *Je M'Accuse...* and who believes me a Dreyfusard. His ill-humor and unintelligence getting to the point of deliriousness, he serves me with some clichéd phrases by Drumont, who poisoned them all, all these poor ecclesiastics. It is so stupid that I renounce defending myself.

21. – Letter by an unknown Joseph H***, calling himself my "brother and admirer" and offering me a mysterious, unintelligible communication.

To Eugène Gilbert, in Louvain:

Dear Sir,

When this letter arrives, you will have, doubtless, received my new book entitled Je M'Accuse... *which I requested be mailed to you yesterday evening by my publisher. The form is very rough, – your "good taste" will not fail to notice. However, if you consented for one moment to impose silence on that good taste that people do not cease proposing to a man who is alone against the world for twenty years now, riddled with wounds merely one of which would kill another man, and who is not rich save in his clamor; – yes, if that phantom of the Prince of the World whom you call Good Taste should permit you to hear me out for only a few seconds, I will tell you that this is a book in the service of God and, because of that, written* in the language that was necessary. *I think that this assertion is not temerarious nor needs any explaining. Through infidelity of the printer, an important line has vanished. The words* "Mercure de France, September 1894," *should be read below the last line of* "Cretin of the Pyrenees," *the two parts of my small book having been written five years apart. Certain readers won't understand a thing.*

And now, dear sir, permit me, even though it be a bit late, to congratulate you for the astonishing nobility of your conduct in my regards for so long a time. Despite certain repugnances that belong to your nature, the small equity of which will be revealed to you one day, you have invariably protested with a generous energy against the atrocious injustice that I suffer and die from.

Personally, I have no need of any man, and I do not implore any suffrage. I obey an order from on high, as did the man whom Josephus talks about the day before the destruction of Jerusalem. To the point that I am, like him, crushed. It is enough for me that a voice, infinitely sweet, should say to me from the bottom of my heart at every instant, "If only you knew how fine Jesus is!" What need have I for other salary? God will know how to nourish those of my children whom his terrible Hand has spared. But I rejoice, for the honor of Truth, with a little of human justice, and I entreat you to accept a vigorous handshake.

27. – Read almost in its entirety the book by Péladan, *Le Prochain Conclave*, which must have been published last year, without a date. It is impossible to be

more stupid, and it is certainly difficult to have as much talent. Who will explain that? Péladan is at one and the same time so stupid and so gifted that he writes remarkable things the which, *unbeknownst to himself*, are contradictory, restituted to nothingness, anterior and posterior heretical affirmations that he believes to be the foundation of his thought. That, almost on every page. What a prodigious and supernatural imbecile!

30. – Letter from a well-bred man reproaching me for the "unfortunate expressions" contained in *Je M'Accuse...* This socialite speaks to me about the World, monstruously supposing that I can have for an object of pleasure that mass of carrion.

October

1st. – Something horribly dark seems to be hovering over our house. We had to endure today excessive bitterness and transcendent churlishness. A person showered by us [with respect, goodwill, etc.], brusquely declares war on us. How many other troubles yet! We lie down with venomous serpents around our heart.

2. – Signing of a lease for the renting of a pavilion on a bank of the Marne.

A letter from Copenhagen informs me of the death of Prince Alexandre Ourousof. In 1891, this famous Russian lawyer came expressly from Moscow to Paris in order to defend me against Péladan who was demanding *ten thousand francs* in damages for my having made an attempt on his honor. The honor of Péladan! The case caused a great deal of noise for several days. He was the first Russian lawyer to plead in Paris, and it was the day after Kronstadt. And then it was a kind of great lord defending a kind of barefoot beggar. France and Russia acquitted me. I am perhaps the only Frenchman who has benefited from the Alliance. But who today remembers that extraordinary adventure that all the journals were talking about?

3. – Letter from Jehan Rictus, very enthusiastic for *Je M'Accuse...* (One knows, in the literary world, that I have become the admirer and friend of this poet. Some even believe that I wrote the *Last Columns of the Church* only to have an opportunity to assign to him his true place which appears to me to be the first. I thought that one might read with interest the response that follows. One will see the progress that I have made in three years and the extraordinary victory of him whom I have called *The Last Catholic Poet.* October 1904.)

To Jehan Rictus:

... Your Soliloquies *have given me the idea that one can have of a real poet, when one is the author of* The Desper-

ate Man, and the Doléances have added, I believe, something to that impression. I really do not know, you are perhaps the best contemporary poet, the greatest or the loftiest, that one could hope for. You appear to me like a prince who would have married for love a sexagenarian and misshapen slut, or like a painter of genius who would paint exclusively with shit. Ah! doubtless, you will respond that the poet alone is the judge of his procedure. Okay, I have often said it myself. However there is this. The French language must be respected... I am a true child of the people, me who writes to you these things, but I do not love slang. I have for ancestors, on both sides, very humble laborers. Since the age of fifteen, I blushed with despair over it. Since then I have made myself the marquis of the Marquisate of Myself, and I have built my heart like a tower. I shake your hand through one of my crenelations.

4. – The curate of Ceux-d'En-Bas dares to speak to the rich and condemn them. At least he boasts of it. That ought to be unheard of in the diocese.

The letter from a Belgian poet (who has never been wrong) and who claims to live in poverty. He came to my assistance, last year, when I was in Denmark, then left me, making me pay for his services. What can I do today and what must I do?

I write to Paul Adam, that he might create a little publicity for me at the *Journal*. I beg him to give me the alms of an article, me who never asks for anything from anyone. Last May 22, when I was in Denmark, several lines by him in a column were consoling and profitable to me.

5. – We decide, my wife particularly, to offer hospitality to the Belgian poet. Supposing him capable of interest, I encourage him with the following lines:

> ... *If you are a poet and a Christian, leave Belgium. That country is incontestably the headquarters of Catholic Hypocrisy, Avarice, and Imbecility. Nothing to be done with those ridiculous devils. The more genius you have the less you will penetrate the souls of that neighborhood of Sodom. They will not even read you. The bastards will arrange amongst themselves to suppress you categorically. Belgian baseness is* unique *and equaled only by the sottishness, assumed by it, of nations*

Extremely remarkable letter by Jehan Rictus. (Reproduced in its entirety in the *Last Columns of the Church*, published by the "Mercure de France," 1903.)

New response:

Thank you for your letter which I con-
sider myself very honored *by. You are*
certainly right, but not in the Absolute
which is my dwelling place. I will ex-
plain that to you.

(I never explained anything. One will see
why, if one takes the trouble to consult the work just
mentioned.)

6. – We discover that our curate is subject to crises of
extreme anger that make him sometimes unsupportable.

8. – To Paul Redonnel and Paul Ferniot, directors of
the *Maison d'Art*:

I have at your disposition the only one
of my books that has never been pub-
lished, Belluaires et Porchers, *a very*
personal view of the literary bustle of
twenty years ago, seen from today, a
copious series that I have had to cut
much out of. That book, offered for
many years, made many people trem-
ble. I have received letters that still
stink!... You seem particularly suited.
Could we come to an agreement
quickly? I have on my back a bitch of
a landlady, an overdue bill by a wine
merchant who is already getting the
bailiff involved, etc.

(Favorable response that the Maison d'Art's bankruptcy made ineffectual. *Belluaires et Porchers* continues to wait for a publisher, 1904.)

13. – Mailing of a copy of *The Son of Louis XVI* to Paul Adam who asks for it. Dedication: "Domestics becoming masters, and masters becoming domestics, such is the *secret* of the historic evolution in all the centuries. *Imperium œquiparat servitutem.*"[9]

15. – The curate tells us about his troubles with his ignoble chatelains who are indignant not to find in him a very obedient domestic, which country curates ordinarily are and nearly infallibly with respect to those accursed people. For him it is the opposite and, principally on account of that, he passes for an impossible priest. He wants to see the Master of Forges and obtain from him a definitive response. According to the woman who must know something about it, he would not dispute with me the art of writing, but he has something else doubtless to dispute with me. These bourgeois with their asses all in gold hardly ever quit the chateau of their admirable friend Georges Ohnet.

16. – To the curate:

> *I entreat you not to count on me tomorrow morning. I will return to your church which is dear to me when God grants me the grace to shake off the*

---

[9]*Imperium...*: Latin for "Mastery equals servitude."

horrible bitterness you gave me yes-
terday evening so unjustly. Without
even informing yourself of the purpose
of my visit, you had me sent away, al-
leging I don't know what fatigue. Now,
I had never had so great a need of my
pastor, and I left very miserable. You
have not understood that the alms of a
sacerdotal word is often needed by a
man whom God loves in so terrible a
manner, and that it is dangerous for
both our souls for you to refuse me
that word.

I have neither gold nor silver, but
what I do have, I give it, and when I
rise in the middle of the night in order
to pray for you, my arms outstretched,
as you have asked me to do, I am not
thinking of my own fatigue. Why are
you so stingy?

(I came, perhaps, to confess myself. The surprising pastor said that I had come to *hit him up*. I
learnt, a little later, about that seraphic interpretation.)

17. – It is monstrous – and banal – that yesterday's
letter was not sent in haste to our curate. (I never saw
him again. October 1904.)

Véronique becomes an extern pupil at the
boarding school of the women religious of
Saint-Joseph de Cluny who have at Cochons-sur-

Marne a considerable establishment. (I will have the occasion to speak about those servants of the Lord a little later.)

18. – The curate having decided to break off all relations with me, having sent back to me some of my books, I send to him the following texts: Matth. 25:43; Joann., 10:11 and 14; Ezech. 34:11; then, in enormous letters: *VISITABO*.

Wrote *The Fiasco of 1900*. (Article published, on November 5, in the first issue of *Partisans*, a periodical of ingenious stupidity which was able to remain alive for several months.)

The Fiasco of 1900

I am extremely displeased with the last year of the century.[10] It could have, and should have, been the year of Upheaval. It doesn't even leave any hope for the future year, which will obviously be the first of the Twentieth Century.

What happened to last year's promises? Where is the Affair? Where are

---

[10]Original footnote: many people have wanted, and continue to want, that 1900 be the first year of the XXth century. Incontestable proof on the universal enfeeblement of reason. It is as if someone were to say that the creditor of one hundred francs must consider himself paid in full as soon as his debtor has given him ninety-nine.

*Zola's filthy installments?[11] Where is
the slop of so many others and everyone's galloping infamy which appeared invocatory of the lushest of
catastrophes?...*

*Having assiduously and so reasonably
prophesied, for so many years, the discomfiture, I have the right to be revolted.*

*It is the effect of a bath attendant's
science or that of a traveling salesman
of knit jumpers, to believe that a
prophet is necessarily, exclusively, a
seer of future events.*

*The Prophet is primarily a Voice for
making Justice descend.*

*If people absolutely must, with or
without irony, give that magnificent title to a vociferator of my sort, one
consequence must immediately be accepted, drawn from the very nature of
things, that his cries will have the
power of accelerating devastations. It
is in this sense that he will be a
prophet, as much as one can be, without divine inspiration, exactly as a
man of prayer is a thaumaturge.*

---

[11]The Affair... Zola's filthy installments: in reference to the
Dreyfus Affair, and Zola's serialized novels. See *Je M'Accuse...*

*

* *

In brief, what were my predictions, that is to say what were my intimate and heartfelt wishes, my vehement and profound desires for an epilepsy of the earth, which made my teeth chatter and my body tremble from head to foot, like an excited adolescent?

Simply this. The Exposition, so greatly admired by the Hanotaux and so worthy to be so, not having taken place because Paris and peoples would have enough to do extending their arms against death.

Then the desolation of England, the squatting on her by all the demons, and that bitch among vilified nations letting out sobs and howlings enough to make the globe stop in its tracks.

Finally, and as much to say, the decisive and definitive disgust of a hypocritical Christian society, searching on all fours for its lost treasures in the popular excrement and even in dogs' vomit. There you have it.

Where is the multifarious cretin, exited from I do not know what putrid friction of two bourgeois pieces of meat, who will dare say that such postula-

tions were excessive?

Let him come to me, that sebaceous residue of the filthiest ejaculations of bureaucracy or group of notaries, that I might know finally from him what one must think of the inconceivable disobedience of Things!

But to what end? Is it not enough for me to imagine that puny runt who explains everything, in effect, in so frighteningly satisfying a manner!

*
* *

Contemporary flabbiness has gotten to the point of effecting miracles. Yes, miracles, I am afraid to proclaim it.

Then when the Exposition was being prepared, and all the vanities, all the stupidities, all the concupiscences of the universe were hurtling towards Paris, which had become more filthy, more stupid, more inane than ever, – if anything appears certain, it was the Collapse, the unprecedented Fall [from grace].

At the same time, the four or five parts of the world bellowed against England whose ignominy astonishes the oceans and discourages all hyperbole. How not to be twenty times sure of the cataracts of filth that seem no longer to await a sigh, an imperceptible nod, by a Captain of the Angels before submerging that shameful part of the earth?

After that, I ask, what could have been the destiny – each person receiving his due recompense – of so-called Christian society, nearly infinitely wicked, which bears down on human consciousness with its turpitude and casts doubt on the Redeemer?

Assuredly, and a thousand times assuredly, o invisible Lords, angels, and ministers of Grace, but listen to this:

There are no more men, and bankruptcy is at such a point that there are no more rabble even, something never before seen.

The human species is so prodigiously degenerate that it can no longer produce honest men, but soft and clingy monsters instead, equally incapable of the abominations of vice and the abominations of virtue!

In this terrible mess what to expect from a poor prophet?

*
* *

> *Nothing at all, am I right? Unless it is to escape and hide among the humble animals, imploring God, with a shower of tears, for the smooth and mellow cataclysm out of which his Magnificence will appear.*

19. – Dedication of a copy of *The Desperate Man*: "I am Job on his dungheap and I hand to you one of my shards. Scrape yourself."

Another dedication for *The Son of Louis XVI*: "Ah! It is all the same a funny sensation to be the son of the king, unbeknownst to his concierge, and primarily the son of an imbecilic king. I felt it myself several times, by identification, while writing this joyous book."

25. – Paul Adam delivers on *The Son of Louis XVI*, with benevolence. It is the story of the executioner by Villiers de l'Isle-Adam. – "I spoil you," he said to one of his victims whom he had just favored by a small kindness, moments before the chopper. If that attracts a single reader to me, it is because God will not have stopped making miracles. My response:

> *I am too much of the profession not to see what this article must have cost you, having been targeted at so great a distance, so prodigiously distant! I wonder even, with a bit of anxiety, if there was not, on the side of your*

gazette, with the Journal's beating of the drum, some nastiness already. You have given, o Paul Adam, or you have tried to give some free publicity. You sully the Eucharist of Pimps! It is frightening.

26. – I undertake, as I did for Zola, to make daily notes on the novel by Bourget, *Un homme d'affaires*, published by the *Journal*. Read the first three issues. For starters, Balzacian intentions, as always. There is even something clearer in that little ploy by Paul. At all costs, he must be Balzac. Ah! for example, what the great man becomes after having been passed through the sieve of that brain, it is not easy to say. Fundamentally, all that the miserable son of a peon got out of *The Human Comedy* was the golden lantern of shady dealers and the backdrop of aristocratic elegances. And my faith! given it is not precisely Race that is his gig, he takes aristocracy where he can. "In that avatar of a stockbroker in the process of playing a gentleman, Nortier appears to have merited quite a few reproaches: that of the most ferocious egoism towards his poor family or his ruined colleagues, that of the most immoral absence of scruple in his choice of the means of fortune, that of the most brutal utilitarianism in the matter of relationships. *He has never been ridiculous.*" Then all is well. Supreme aristocracy for our eunuch means having lots of money and knowing how to wear a habit. Let us remark in passing that, without even realizing it, he has already disclosed his cancer to us: the fear of being ridiculous.

Naturally, adultery cannot wait. Gentlemen, such as Paul's little cerebral mechanism conceives of it, cannot dispense with "sleeping" with others' wives. It is a manner he has of collecting and smoking cigarette butts. In general, inform yourself as to what MM. the Flunkies think about it, and you will have the thoughts and sentiments of that academician.

Citation to complete the precedent: "When the enormous fortunes of the stock market have only this advantage of saving the several master works of our national architecture from definitive ruin, having escaped the imbecilic vandalism of the 'giants of 89,' all the misdeeds of the worst lynxes of speculation would need pardoning." Always the domestic.

27. – A gem found in Paul's feuilleton: "It is not very common in France: *a house that has never* LEFT *the hands of the family that built it.*"

Visit by a friend come to try to make me understand that he is no longer eighteen years old and that, by consequence, I must no longer count on his enthusiasm.

28. – Dedication of *Je M'Accuse...* to my very faithful Auguste Marguillier, secretary of the *Gazette des Beaux-Arts*: "Here is Zola's hide, while waiting for those of a batch of sad priests and some other servants of the Devil."

Installation of the daughter of our old maid,

engaged for the service of the Belgian poet who will arrive in several days. What a strange life is ours! The less we possess, the more numerous we become.

November

1st. – My satiety of men seems to grow each day. Grief and horror martyr me. On Sundays and feast days, that already almost unsupportable problem augments. I feel it today, with what force! The hideousness of those *Christians* involved in commerce or employments who come to edify their parish become completely intolerable to me. Their nearness literally suffocates me.

The young Danish woman who came with us from Kolding asks our old maid whether her daughter, a child, *has a fiancé*. That's Denmark in a nutshell.

3. – The ancient and redoubtable tribulation of errands through Paris recommences, with the ball of images and onerous thoughts I drag along with, like a galley slave, for so many years! In the omnibus, a young bourgeois who is reading the last novel by the hunchback, the *Ténébreuse*, I believe, is determined to step on my feet. A kind of irony that makes the anger brew inside me for one instant. I was reading the cover of the book of I don't know what enormous number of print runs. But I was praying like so many times before, being perhaps, of all moderns, the per-

son who prayed the most in the streets of Paris, *tristis incedens* and on the point of sobbing with each step. I endured my sorrow then. It is a great deal, doubtless, that God does not let my heart fall down the shaft. After such a terrible day, I end up by finding myself on the street, with sore feet, at the door of a mont-de-piété, the last resource.

Protestants always give the advice of walking. Always walking, but not going anywhere, such is Protestantism, in effect. – JEANNE.

4. – It is a quite certain thing that the Words of the Holy Book nourish the soul and even the intelligence, in the manner of the Eucharist, *without the need of understanding them.*

5. – Paris streets again!... I think, like people who grow bored in a solitary place, on my destitution of friends and on this, that at the age of fifty-four and being the author of such and such books, I do not know what door to knock on in a moment of distress. Then I remember, with what horrible bitterness, Henry de Groux.

"Troubled spirits walk without repose, from one extremity to the other, in the field of their thoughts," said my friend Ernest Hello.

Bourget continues his serialized novel. I have had to renounce the daily analysis of it. How to follow an *icoglan* whose only ambition consists in de-

scending each day into the heart of young women of
high society, like the foreman of cesspool emptiers
who descends into the hole at the decisive hour of
gratin?

The *History of the Late Empire* by Lebeau
continued by Ameilhon, a dispassionate prig, which
the academies themselves have forgotten, does not
cease, for fifteen years now, to bring me delight. Here
is what the continuer offers to me today, book CVIII:

> *The young Andronikos congratulated*
> *himself for the success of his last expe-*
> *dition against the Tartars, when a*
> *piece of upsetting news came and*
> *clouded his joy. He learnt that the em-*
> *press, his wife, had died. He felt that*
> *loss acutely...*

6. – To Rachilde, who wrote an amical article on *Je
M'Accuse...*

> *Dear friend,*
>
> *I read your article from Friday, The*
> *Day of the Dead, and we have not had,*
> humanly, *any other consolation for*
> *many days now... You are right,*
> *Rachilde, "the truth does not* get off
> *easy" and I am poor, even more than*
> *you think. One can come to terms with*
> *poverty which is a malady like so*
> *many others, the most dolorous, if one*
> *wishes. But* the impossibility of living,

were it in torment, and each day, for quarters of centuries, with the people one loves!...

Do not think that I am too naïve, however. I knew what I was doing by dedicating Je M'Accuse... *to Mirbeau who, to this day, has shown no sign of gratitude. I had read, in Denmark, in* l'Aurore *of November 29, 1899, a long article by him, entitled, "Fecundity," wherein the son of a bitch was declared, in no uncertain terms, an "evangelist... prophet..." and finally "*GOD.*" Yes, Rachilde, God, no less, I kid you not, with a paradise and a hell – which gave me incontestably a view onto the future. It was said, without shilly-shallying – and I assure you that that had a very strange effect on me in Denmark – that the aforementioned son of a bitch "had spread over all the cogs of contemporary society the* inexhaustible oil of his genius."!!!!!!! *I kept that article which could well have paid two or three thousand pretty sous, isn't that right? Then, having been decorated gratis, two years earlier, with another impassioned article by the same on the* Femme pauvre, *could I do better than to dedicate my new book to that "contemnor of false great men"? There are malicious people who would call that viciousness.*

One does what one can. I console my-
self in that way, feebly, for the disdain
of "chamber maids" and for the suf-
fering of my poor ones, — suffering
that could turn into agony, whenever
God wishes.

The Belgian poet says he will arrive on Friday. Should we be rejoicing or afflicted?

7. – Read in the *Journal* an imitated tale and even a bit copied from my *Histoires désobligeantes*. Œuvre of a young careerist known formerly.

9. Arrival of the Belgian poet, along with his wife and a little fella clinging to the breast, and an orange tabby, enormous and devouring like a jaguar. Sinister impression the lot of them. *In manus tuas, Domine.*[12]

10. – Letter from a Mme. Tuparle, proprietress of the pavilion leased on October 2. That old woman informs me that having received some very bad information about me, she desires to rescind our lease. Keeping in mind that she is a Christian and even a devout one, at the same time a proprietress, she adds this noble phrase that makes one think of the detachment of Saints: "I would prefer to keep the pavilion without renters than to have any that would not pay

---

[12]*In manus tuas, Domine*: Latin for "Into your hands, Lord"[, I confide my spirit]. From Psalms, 31:5.

me exactly." *Beatius est magis perdere quam dare,*[13] rumbles quietly the choir of demons.

After several minutes consecrated to admiration, I respond to her that the desire to break the lease, thirty-nine days after her signature, is a bit late and that I will take it up with the justice of the peace.

Besides, my present landlord, M. Le Bison, has communicated to me a message of dense churlishness, claiming an October move out date.

What a beautiful day! It would be sublime if the old Harpagonne[14] who insults me, without motive, were designated to pay my rent to the ridiculous and atrocious bourgeois just mentioned. It is time that renters began finally to touch some rent, to receive, in turn, money from landlords.

13. – Response to the sending of an invoice:

> *Monsieur, I really want to pay all that I owe, but I still need to know what it is and above all to understand it. Now, your statement of account is absolutely unintelligible to me. In my quality as an artist, I understand nothing about commercial usages whose formularies make me nauseous. When 100 francs is owed to me and someone*

---

[13]Beatius... dare: Latin for "Much more blessed is it to lose than to give."

[14]Harpagonne: female miser.

pays me 100 francs, I consider myself paid, and I would not for one minute think to collect. Eh! well, I owed you 100 francs, which had been established by you yourself. You accept a note for 100 francs to be due on January 31. Naturally, I think that that is that. Not at all. You demand, in addition, 9 fr. 75 centimes, which is the purchase price of a very fine book. Why? I would be much obliged to you if you could explain it to me in an intelligible language.

(I soon found out that those 9 fr. 75 cent. were the price for a written protest. Swine! swine! swine!)

23. – Appeal in Conciliation Court. Bloy vs. Tuparle. Just as I hoped, I won. The hypocrite came in person, little anticipated. I plead my case and my demand for two terms, to which she responds with the exhibition of a copy of her stinking letter and my response, having counted on, doubtless, the judge getting the impression of a blackmail attempt. At first, I believed that that effect was obtained, the judge exclaiming the high virtue of the late Tuparle, "benefactor of the commune of Ceux-d'En-Bas." He did not say benefactor of the poor. I was about, at that moment, to lose it. I saw myself on the verge of speaking violently to that imbecilic magistrate. My good angel happily made me keep my mouth shut. I limited myself then to observing that Tuparle's glory did not authorize his widow to injure me and that, having the long-standing

habit of honorable visits [to the Church], it was difficult for me to accept the insolences of a cook. With
an incredible dignity, she responded that she was
Mme. Tuparle and that that ought to suffice. The
judge estimating, happily, that that did not completely
suffice, offered me one lease term, according to the
custom of those counselors who have retained since
Solomon not much else than the precept of *compro-
mise*. I wanted nothing better. The widow of the
beneficent Tuparle could have spared herself that
snub by settling it herself, several days earlier, with a
globule of rudimentary equity. But the pious old
bourgeoise lady, deep down, had hoped for a break by
the magistrate who would have saved her very dear
money, her sweet, beloved dough, which she would
certainly not have failed to use in an manner agreeable to God.

24. – Visit by a young man who was not long ago my
effervescent admirer and who now, the possessor of a
pretty fortune and judging me in the light of a full silver moon, has gone so far as to   contest my literary
form, preferring to me... Fénelon! From now on, for
him, there is no more truth, and Buddhism is as plausible as the Christian faith. That miserable fellow's
inferiority shines as if it were made of light. Sadness
replants its old claws into my heart.

29. – Touching letter from a poor Czech inhabitant,
not far from Austerlitz, a small town in Moravia
where he reads me compassionately. His name is

Josef Florian, calls himself "son of the victorious Virgin" and propagates me as much as he can.

December

1st. – Apropos of the secret of confession, a very nice word by Jeanne: When God finally speaks his secret, *secretum meum mihi*, the priests will be cleared of theirs.

4. – Painful trip to Paris, after plenty of others the enumeration of which would be fastidious. Office of Deposits and Consignments. I discover that a pension-fund booklet, buried deep in a drawer, from twenty-three years ago when disgust forced me to quit a miserable employment with the Northern Railway Company, gives me the right to *fifteen francs* of annual rent, starting in October 1901, and that after my death my heirs only will be able to withdraw the original capital, that is to say the 48 francs invested *obligatorily* in 1878. The State which has need of the bread of the poor in order to force feed its Hanotaux or its Trouillots, usuriously keeps the sum of 700 francs formed by the accumulation of composed interest for a quarter of a century. Splendid. I am finally a rentier then!

8. – Huge grace. I lose a nasty friend.

My dear Georges,

This morning, on returning home from mass where I had tearfully asked for pity and assistance, one hands me your letter, so similar to so many others from you these last twenty years now.

Reply: it is of no importance that a poor painter, deprived of reason, should have said this or that to you.

It is of no importance that the things said should be true or false, exact or inexact.

It is of no importance that you decide or do not decide to see me again.

It is of no importance that you have done this or that on rue Lafayette or on boulevard de la Tour-Maubourg.

It is of no importance that you "regret" or that you do not regret such and such a thing.

We are, the two of us, approaching death, and all that is of no importance.

Except this:

1ˢᵗ. Two years before at least, knowing that you could one day assist him with some money which you had neither earned nor saved and which, by con-

sequence, not having cost you a thing, absolutely did not belong to you; two years before, I say, you received from the mendicant Léon Bloy, a continual and more than once heroic hospitality, which a son, even degenerate, of a gentleman would perhaps have wanted to protect, at least, the memory of.

2. For a long time now, we have gotten our two little daughters into the habit of including you in their daily prayers.

This morning after the mass of the Immaculate Conception, after your letter, hearing that prayer for the thousandth time in those voices, both innocent and terrible, – I asked myself what it was bound to accomplish. Do you want them to stop?

10. – Fifth anniversary of the death of little Pierre, our second son, very probably murdered, at two and a half months, by a wet nurse with the Office of Public Assistance. What does God want from us, in the end? I am agitated with anguish and love. Will we be protected by that child who has grown, for five years now, in Paradise? The world is horrible, inexpressibly.

11. – A sum [of money] was necessary for us to ward

off a certain calamity, and the only possible remedy had just failed. Suddenly the individual who was solicited, while showing me the door, changed his mind: "You have children?" he asked me. On my affirmative response, he came through. It was then two thirty in the afternoon. *At that precise moment*, my little Madeline was praying for me, her arms extended, imitating her mother.

12. – Departure of our young Danish friend called back to Denmark by her father. She was very sweet and consoling to us more than once, and her departure is a blow. Here we are alone now, face to face with our two execrable maids and our two guests, male and female, whose mediocrity of mind and heart, a little more visible with each passing day, frightens us.

14. – To Otto Friedrichs:

> *... F. has grown completely distant from me. It is too easy to understand why. Mme. B., furious for having spent money on an artist, when she had believed she was paying for a flunkey, will have filled his ears with bitter complaints. That poor F. reproaches me above all for not writing* like everyone else!!! *It is frightening, it is enough to make one want to cry. The miserable man is a* MAN OF THE WORLD, *in perpetuity. Nothing to do about it. I*

could have written masterpieces to make the stars quake, but I would always be, for those minds, a hooligan. It may very well be that F. was a hero, a sublime reckless fellow in speaking up for me, – I say that very seriously. But he has had entirely enough of it now. Must it be that what one calls, by antiphrasis, the spirit of the world has had a debilitating effect, so that the Catholic and very noble man who wrote the book that you know has come to espouse in opposition to me *the indignations of a cook and a Calvinist cook at that! When, three years ago, he spoke to me – not without admiration – about that lady's immense fortune, I did not ask him what the* origin *of it was. I knew all too well. It is as if one were to ask for a baptismal certificate from a Scandinavian cathedral transmuted in the XVIth century into a pigpen for Lutheran swine, or the instruments of transfer for such and such a seignorial property in the epoch when children dripping with the bran of the sodomite Calvin turned Catholicism upside down. F., who believes himself to be a Catholic, will never understand that Mme. B., had she given me millions, would still be in debt to me.*

Is it not surprising, all the same,

Friedrichs, that, for more than six months now, after a separation of two years, that man whom I loved, whom I continue to love, and who has shown to me, formerly, demonstrations of the most lively affection, has not felt the need to come and see me again?

As for Mme. B.'s judgment,... *about my book, apropos of the very mediocre article by Paul Adam, what do you want me to say? If people and things were in their proper place, which could happen, the epoch being highly unusual, I would not refuse taking that person into my service, to assist with the washing...*

18. – Nastiness and disgusting behavior by our two maids. Nothing comes in, and the danger starts all over again. What an end to the month! What an end to the year! What an end to the century!

19. – Reread *Ursule Mirouet*. Unbelievable stupidity by Balzac. That book is the story of feelings or evolutions and peripeteia of religious feelings among people ignorant of any religion, told by the most complete ignoramus of all, by an ignorant person of genius.

21. – My Belgian poet, not content with being onerous and even overwhelming, is trying hard to become
totally unbearable. Jeanne tells me with ennui about
the extreme liberty with which this so-called Catholic
judges the priests, *in front of our children.* She informs me that this type of discourse greatly scandalized our young Danish Lutheran who told her, a short
while before departing, her astonishment on hearing
priests judged so strongly by a Catholic, as if there
were not a one who merited esteem and respect. Immediately I express to our guest my desire for a little
restraint on his part, especially in the presence of the
children. That without vehemence, but very firmly.
Then, all of a sudden appears the monster of a all-en-
compassing, frightening, absolutely invincible pride.
He does not admit for one second that it is possible he
was mistaken, and my strongest objections mean
nothing. Jeanne's objections are less than nothing and
irritate him all the more given he has no response. But
it is the practice of pride to retire while grumbling. I
told him quite frankly: You have scandalized a young
girl raised in the misery of Protestantism by exposing
her to the appalling danger of rejecting the Grace that
is offered to her. He "couldn't give a damn," repeating with an idiotic, exasperating obstinancy that the
truth must come out, basing himself on texts that he
does not understand and which he abuses. He is ready
to begin again and goes so far as to say that he will
raise his son in contempt of the clergy, alleging with
inconceivable stupidity that it is the only way to pre-
serve that child from probable undertakings that despicable ecclesiastics could, one day, try on him. He
wishes, – such are his words, – that a child might

make, like a man, the distinction between generality and universality.

In vain, I object to him the law that a child be nourished on milk and not raw meat: that does not take. He grows irritated and becomes insolent. So it is over. I see that I was mistaken, once again, and that I find myself in the presence of a vicious cretin whom I cannot immediately unburden myself of. Enormous suffering for which my awful life has prepared me.

22. – Long letter by Johannes Joergensen, the great Catholic poet of Denmark, in response to one that I didn't keep a copy of. It appears that I said brazen things about Leon XIII. He declares to me his absolute respect for the Sovereign Pontiff, unfortunately trying to explain to me the NECESSARY *dispensation* for "*Nolite conformari huic sæculo.*" All that permeated by a filial simplicity and gentleness. What a difference from that which is at the current moment right before our eyes! And how admirable it is that such a letter should arrive at a such a moment!

To Joergensen:

... Desolate because of that cruel imbecile whose presence has afflicted us, never has anything human seemed to us so sweet as the apparition, under such circumstances, of your honest face of a pious Kalmouk. You respond to things that I have only a vague memory of. I do not keep a copy of all

my letters. It would seem that I spoke rudely about Leon XIII, whom I do not like at all, it is true. I would have ref-erenced Nolite *with respect to that pontiff's undertakings in favor of the atheistic, renegade, apostate, sacrilegious, parricidal, infanticidal and concordatory French Republic, and apropos of the democratization of the clergy, things that cannot be justified by any Text. I add this: A disciple of Our Lord, the least of all, a witness to the Denials of Saint Peter, would have been in the right to reproach with a most extreme indignation the Prince of Apostles for his cowardice, and he would even have had the obligation to do so, on the condition that immediately after that act he openly declared his formal will to obey the Head of the Church. Such is my case. You know, dear friend, that I would consent to the most complicated of tortures,* Deo adjuvante, *before refusing obedience in matters of faith and discipline to the infallible Successor. But all the rest is my own stuff, and every Christian ought to be afflicted by a human weakness in the Pope. There you have it, and I think it is extremely simple. I am with you in* obedience, *I was established thereon before you were a Catholic, before you even came into*

*the world, and I have suffered a lot
from it. How could we be separated,
as you seem to fear?...*

23. – What is particularly, strangely disconcerting is
that God seems to do what bad rich people do (In fact,
why say *bad rich people* as if there were any *good*
ones?), the which rich people make [others] pay horribly dear for what they give and do not give except
in the last extremity, when there is no more means for
refusal. There is an infinitely mysterious and melancholic answer. It is that God is poor and, until a certain hour, powerless. *What he gives, he must obtain it
himself at first,* with unknown sufferings which our
finest sufferings are merely a reflection of. *Elijah
must come.* What a book to write on Money, considered in my own way, in other words as a symbol of
God! There is but one man in the world capable of
writing it, and I do not know that man. His name is
Léon Bloy.

25. – Terrible Noel. Enormous sadness, and a moral
and intellectual stagnation of black sadness in the
company of our poet and his wife. Terrible sensation
of solitude, of dereliction.

31. – We learn that, according to Leon XIII's wishes,
a mass will be celebrated at midnight in all the parish
churches of the world to bring in the twentieth century. I renounce attending, being forced to go there

alone. At midnight, however, we are anxious to join in this great act by asking for as much as we can, eternal life for ourselves and for our poor children.

Thus ends, in sadness, in love, in prayer, the grievous and very base XIXth century. Thus begins for us the XXth century.

1901

There is room to presume, – in view of the duration of Prussian occupation in Cochons-sur-Marne in 1870-71, and considering the practical sense that the bourgeois class rightly prides itself on – that the majority of citizens today in this canton seat were fabricated with German semen.

January

1st. – Demand for payment by the baker who has chosen today of all days, with a great deal of tact. Such are our New Year's gifts. God has sat down to the table of my suffering as to a great feast, and he demands again without cease.

2. – Steps taken for the exhumation of my son André, whose five years of lying in a common grave are about to expire. If I do not find the money before the 19th, appointed day, I will need to kill someone.

6. – Unbearable cold. We have no coal, money is not to be hoped for from any quarter, our two maids have become enraged and the appetite of our guests seems to grow... I would really like to be beside my innocent children in the cemetery of the poor!

(October 1904. Rereading today these old

pages, my heart fails me and I am forced, quite often, to renounce transcribing them. The uninterruption and the paradoxical intensity of the torment, and the uniformity of the clamor, are enough to upset one's reason. That reading is dangerous. One comes away from it no longer understanding anything at all, by no longer knowing where to find God, and if one comes to consider that the same man is on that anvil for more than twenty years, it is enough to slam shut the notebook with terror and ask for grace for oneself, shuddering.)

9. – My Belgian poet does not appear to notice that his situation here is that of a heavy pachyderm on the shoulders of a poor wretch who is drowning. On the contrary, he [thinks he] protects me, being one of those whom I ought to rejoice over for having the occasion to regale, for omnipotence will be theirs tomorrow morning. (See, in my *Exegesis of Commonplaces*, pages 128 to 132, a rather faithful portrait of that funny man and his partner.)

Read in *Le Siècle*, posthumous book by Hello, a chapter on M. Dupont, the "Holy man of Tours" who recommends, lest he should suffer from a *lack of faith*, prayer in the form of a commandment or a summons from God. That holy man never lit a fire under me. He came up terribly short. That, however, is not too stupid. If one tried!...

10. – A friend gives me 100 francs for the exhuma-

tion of my child.

11. – Obsession by a grocer with the face of a stuffed tomato who firmly demands that I must go rinse out his chamber pot, every morning, because I owe him several pieces of one hundred sous.

17. – Paul Adam is an ultra-modern myope who gropes about in a dark and filthy place, hoping to find the electric light switch.

19. – Saint Canut, the great Danish saint. Exhumation. Having spent the night in a miserable hotel on avenue d'Orleans, I hear the first mass at Saint-Pierre where I am very fortified for the redoubtable thing. I arrive at the cemetery in very humid and cold weather, the morning just breaking. I find the open grave, I see the little casket. The employees come. One of them opens it and, *with his hands*, piece by piece, transfers the poor little corpse into the new bier. The horror would be enormous if God was not assisting and if the shapes had not become more or less indistinct. Noticed only the head which was divided, it seems to me, and the ribcage... Some instructions to the monument mason, and I take my leave.

20. – The awful insolence of our maids, and the complicity of the poet and his family who seem to be greatly amusing themselves while the others are

yelling. For we have gotten to that point. And no money to throw the lot of scoundrels out the door.

21. – Certain healings at Lourdes resemble diabolical maneuverings. The pilgrims are Christians (!) preoccupied principally with their flesh, who are not healed except to be put into a state of damning themselves even more. In the fire at the Charity Bazaar there had to have been some miraculously cured people. In reality what burned there was the triple extract, the quintessence of the superfine rabble of the World.

23. – Demise of the old cow Victoria. Leon XIII said that the Church has suffered a great loss. Hanotaux has given, this morning, at the *Journal*, a column whose abjection astonishes, even for him.

Harassed by demands for payment, assaulted by threats, idiotified by bawlings out, sullied by the filth of souls, I wrote to Edmond Picard, the wealthy lawyer of Brussels, a rather crazy letter asking him for *end-of-the-century New Year's gifts*.

26. – Letter to Demolins, editor of *Pays de France*, a Provençal review, and one of the most remarkable men of our time. (See my book, *The Last Columns of the Church*, pages 168 and following.)

> ... *Men tall enough and firm enough to see, – in spite of the unqualified exhortations of a strange Pontiff – the* abso-

lute *incompatibility of the Gallic Coq and Democracy, have become so rare that one should see in them historic monuments. The terrible political or philosophical bullshit that we are in the process of dying for have always given me the horror that you know. We are entirely in this together then, I congratulate you and I congratulate myself, being a little surprised, all the same, that a writer of your clairvoyance and virility should mention capons like Barrès or Paul Bourget, appearing to mistake them for something.*

As for the reestablishment of Sovereignty, I believe it not only probable but as incoercible as the translation of globes. But this time it will be the sovereignty of true *Lilies, the others, the lilies of the earth which represented the celestial Flower, having grown out of the dungheap and dust. There would need to be a few more than the fourteen hundred thousand Dominations guarding over, for three hundred years, the Cross of Jesus in the tenebræ in order to say what the twentieth century will* discover. "Tunc manifesta erunt abscondita cordis nostri." – Brev.

rom. in Inventione S. Crucis.[15]

Insofar as what concerns me personally, you have seen quite clearly all that I wanted to show, and the noble pages that speak of my "phantom King" have made me happy, have consoled me...

Your letter to me arrived unexpectedly, at the moment that I was expecting something else... Today is the fifth anniversary of the tragic end of the eldest of my two murdered sons. I have recounted that more-than-dark drama in the Femme pauvre, *for my books in general are composed of my sorrowful memories. The coincidence made me think. It is pointless to tell you that I believe in the very sure protection of those of our defunct who died sinless and who speak for us in the light. I was immediately preoccupied with you then, and I asked myself, as always in like cases, why you appeared thus in my life,* why you were sent...

Atrocious scene with our two foul guests who were supposed to depart this evening. We needed to wait until night and to endure their continual insults, for want of the last one hundred sous of their pledge which did not arrive until very late. What an agony to

---

[15]*Tunc...*: Latin for "Then what is hidden in our hearts will be made manifest." – *Roman Breviary on the Discovery of the Holy Cross.*

be unable corporally to punish such miserable people!

29. – Total destitution. One suffers for the cold and one begins to feel hungry. The Belgian poet, fortunately, continues his protection of us and is surprised not to be better fed by indigents whom his gratitude will enrich.

31. – To the curate of Ceux-d'En-Haut, a prodigious abbot Vignoble, protector of commerce and industry, refusing the sacraments of the Church to Christians who have debts among the shopkeepers of his parish, and thus leading one to suppose a sort of canonical prebend, a certain percent over payments:

> *Monsieur the Curate,*
>
> *You have shamefully abused my presence this morning at the confessional, not far from the Holy Sacrament, in order to offend me in the most serious manner – without the shadow of a licit motive, no Christian being expected to give an account of his affairs at the tribunal of penance and the presentation of any* settled invoice, *never having been required by the Church for the absolution of a penitent whom one does not even know. In consequence, I demand an explanation* at my place, *if not I will address myself to your superiors to begin with, and then the Press.*

(He came the following day. For the recounting of that interview and the portrait of that worthy priest, I ask the reader to read page 166 and following, from my *Exegesis of Commonplaces,* wherein I think I have exhausted the matter.)

Apropos of that curate (transplanted since, I do not know whereto), excellent response to an ecclesiastic of the same ilk, objecting that when one makes war on the priests it is ill-advised to cast filth on the soutanes. – It is better, someone retorted, than that the filth should be on the inside of the soutane.

"Every Christian lacking in heroism is a pig," an envoy of the Holy Ghost will pronounce, one day. "That expression is hard, and who can understand it?" the scandalized Pharisees will say, as in St. John.

February

2. – General rule without exception. When there is conflict between a priest and a laic, the fault must always be presumed to lie with the laic.

That is what I am made to understand by the deacon of Cochons to whom I had been stupid enough to go and complain about his subordinate colleague in Ceux-d'En-Haut. – "You are hot blooded!" he told me with the surprise of a poor man used to whispering among the dead.

3. – Excessively painful day. For the thousandth time, I endure that redoubtable melancholy which I cannot give a proper idea of except to say that whatever there is of the most cruel in the sensation of *fear* is one of its ingredients. Active torment because of the cold that freezes the bones for the entire day. Read Well's *The Island of Dr. Moreau*, in the *Mercure*. I do not believe that hell has ever proffered eternal abomination by means of so panic a voice. If one is compelled to avow that Poe drew his inspiration from subterranean Places, what to say about that frightening Englishman?

5. – Prayer of Our Lord in the Garden. Read the last volume of the *Life of Our Lord Jesus Christ* by Anne-Catherine Emmerich. What the admirable saint recounts, on almost every page, about the Pharisees, accords so well, so naturally well, with the contemporary clergy that that gives to her book the frothing sensation of a prophecy. Ah! if a saint showed up in the diocese of Meaux, the diocese of Bossuet! what a welcome [he or she would receive]! And if God showed up!!! I would like to find in that subject something that might console me.

8. – I am inundated with bitterness thinking about this abomination of the world and about the Church's appalling ignominy. More and more, the curate of Ceux-d'En-Haut appears to me a perfect example of sacerdotal mediocrity. Even at my communion I am pursued by his repugnant image. The cold increases and

the coal diminishes.

11. – *Die Apparitionis B.-M.-V. Immaculatæ.* At the same time as the Immaculate Conception is made manifest at Lourdes, Jeanne is miraculously insulted by a friend of the grocer from January 11. The impossibility of living in a more swinish countryside is made evident.

13. – *Nix abundat, tribulatio redundat, constantia mox deficit.*[16]

14. – We have an ataxic maniac for a neighbor, a barker during the day and an artilleryman at night. He rises at the hour of the stars in order to discharge his revolver on passersby. Our poet returning from Paris by the last train thought he would die, which would have been a mourning for Belgium. The artilleryman being a millionaire continues his firing.

Excessive cold, immense distress. It becomes almost impossible to keep our little girls warm. We were sold coal, at the most elevated price, coal of an inferior quality that does not burn. The merchant is one of the fine riffraff of this countryside.

15. – Our poet and his family moves out. Separation

---

[16]*Nix... deficit*: Latin for "Snow abounds, tribulation overwhelms, constancy soon ebbs."

without sorrow. *Someone* knew that we were at the end of our strength and courage. Ourselves, hoping to escape this loathsome countryside and speaking of our eventual move to Paris: We will probably be forced, we tell ourselves, to spend the first night in a hotel. Of course, exclaimed the strummer of the lyre, we could not lodge you. We lodged them and fed them for three months, and they cannot give us one single night of hospitality. The Belgian poet smashes through the ceiling of chaste stars.

17. – I do not recall any time in my life when I felt so demoralized. Jeanne has the same sensation. We find ourselves without resources, and defenseless, in an execrable neighborhood where everyone, curates in the lead, seem to hate us instinctively, and we haven't any means of escaping...

Fundamentally, pride, at all levels, consists in believing that one is God and that one created the world.

18. – A friend (who died today) had come up with a plan to assist me by subscriptions. It has to do with finding one hundred people who would commit to putting 25 francs per year into my small fund. I would thus have a princely revenue of 200 francs per month if each one came through, under the moon. Paul Adam, made aware of the schema, sent this to me:

My dear Master (sic),

I am in the process at this moment of realizing your modest wish, in an efficacious manner, and I hope soon to arrive at a result that will satisfy you in a certain measure. Please believe me a devoted friend. – PAUL ADAM.

19. – Mardi gras. Abstinence and fasting.

21. – An ignoble cafe-owner lets me carry away a bottle! Credit in the blink of an eye. Ten minutes later, he visits us under a makeshift pretext. I give him back the bottle intact, not without expressing my disgust in terms rather difficult to support. But what to do with these rascals who would happily swallow vomit in order to gain or save 50 centimes? I think of the novel of opprobrium that this countryside could be the theater of. But I have already done that for the Grand Montrouge, and the suburbs of Paris resemble it.

The saints have said that one of the most horrible sufferings of hell was not to feel anything around oneself but hate...

The cold augments.

I imagine, as if in a dream, that there are days when God is wringing his hands with despair at the back of heaven.

22. – "Entrust your soul unto God and die." Surprising dispatch by my friend in Moravia (see November 29), despairing that he cannot interest certain millionaires in me. The day's large breaking wheel turns heavily on our heart.

23. – We thought, in fact, that we were going to die of hunger when ten francs arrived from a poor priest whom I have never asked anything from. – When a friend is dying of hunger, he writes me, it is bread that one must send to him, not phrases.

To Gabriel Randon (Jehan Rictus):

The individual who was my guest for more than three months and who has just established himself in Paris, told me that he met you, several days ago. He spoke about me in his conversation with you and I'm led to understand that that Belgian, whose discernment and precision do not appear indisputable to me, supposes between himself and me a solidarity of judgment that I had not authorized. You would have offered this lament then: "Everyone is against me for some time now." Insofar as it concerns me, I wish to efface from your mind such an impression. I am not against you, Randon, I am with you, even against Jehan Rictus. I hope, my friend, – I know you will understand me. I said that I didn't like your language, in other words the slang, several vocables of which can be beautiful, but whose allure is not noble. I said also that your manner of speaking through several Individuals seemed profane to me, revolted me. And that is all. Miracle, if you wish, but your person remains very sympathetic to me. I want you to be persuaded of it. I want it all the more given Laurent Tailhade honors you with his insults – to the point of seeming like a sycophant. It appears that I enjoy the same privilege and that I caught it at the same time as Barbey d'Aurevilly, qualified [by Tailhade] as a sot *in an edition from Sunday or Shrove Monday! I believe that I wrote to you that Laurent-le-Borgne always has an ax to grind with me. The mortal wound for that failed writer would be to demonstrate to him his literary impotence, which is easy enough to do at any rate.*

Read together several pages by Anne-Catherine Emmerich. Ah! how beautiful and holy our life would be, if God wanted!

25. – (This day was so painful that I renounce transcribing anything from the alarming *memorandum* that I have before my eyes. My daughters alone will read it much later in life, when I am groping my way

"on the stairway to heaven's palace," as my little Véronique sings, and they will help me then by their prayers. "But how Jesus treats his friends!" said to me, one day, an admirable priest, now dead for more than twenty-five years. November 1904.)

26. – To Randon:

Dear friend,

I received with emotion your ten francs. The suffering had been almost intolerable. Certain signs seem to authorize a bit of hope. Who knows? Do not put yourself out. I am not unaware of how much some people detest me and how much the majority of those who abhor me would be embarrassed, if one asked them to specify their grievances. That there is a very curious case, a sort of little miracle insufficiently observed. It is as if I was for that multitude a completely mysterious individual; a disquieting individual because one believes to understand that he is not what he appears to be... *You seem to put great stock in my esteem. I will have expressed myself very awkwardly then given you were able to fear the opposite. I deplored slang, perhaps wrongly, precisely because it seemed to me that that language harmed the superior poet that I dis-*

cerned in you. I could be wrong on that point. I am not a critic. To be perfectly forthcoming, I am barely literate. My very exceptional case is exactly expressed, I believe, in the Femme pauvre, *which you have read perhaps: "Pilgrim of the Holy Sepulcher." That and nothing more, in all honesty. There are people, and you are not one of them, who are rather shallow, believing that my Catholicism is an attitude. The truth of the matter is that I am a devotee, absolutely, a man of continual religious practice, of confessions, daily communions, rosary beads, scapulars, etc. So, you see, we are on opposite banks of the torrent. But you are too deserving of the insults by a Tailhade not to feel how extraordinary it is that you are admired, – for better or worse, – by a man such as myself.*

You call yourself a Christian. So be it. Perhaps even you are more Christian than you think. But you seem to see only a Christianity deprived of the supernatural, *which is unintelligible and a contradiction in terms.*

Jesus came for the poor, you say. Well! of course he did, but he came for the rich too, so that they might end up poor because of love, and you must know that hundreds of thousands of saints obeyed. Jesus came for souls, that is what a person must say. Slang would not bother me if it served to express the Love of God. But see what you make your poor wretches say. Was there ever a sadness more base, more carnal, more desperate, more demoniacal? For such beings, there is evidently no Redeemer, nor Consoler. It is the most hideous form, the most terrifying form of an anticipated hell. Of course, nobody has more right to speak to Jesus than the poor, as Jesus is the true Poor man. I have written several volumes to say only that, but one must speak to him in hope, in obedience, and in humility. Otherwise, why speak to him at all? Finally, when you introduce the holy Mary Magdalene, for example, whose name makes me tremble, as if you were introducing a girl from boulevard Ornano, and when you suppose a love of the flesh between the Second Person incarnate and that Penitent, come on, frankly, what do you expect me to feel? etc., etc. I have told you, I love you nevertheless because I hope that one day we will meet...

28. – Letter from a famous Belgian lawyer who made

himself formerly a literary reputation on two or three streets in Brussels, by articles composed of phrases or scraps of phrases *borrowed* from one of my books (*The Desperate Man*), with no attribution. I had informed that great man who is, at the same time, a millionaire, of the subscription project mentioned earlier. He does not refuse to subscribe for three annuities of 25 francs, but, – being drunk at the moment that he wrote to me, I want to suppose it charitably – he wants to make me understand that Belgians "couldn't give a damn" about me. His expression.

My wife and children are in Paris. I am alone and I wait for a bill that I cannot pay. Enormous anguish. The Tormenter of souls inflicts on mine the illusion of an inexpressible danger. I have never felt so miserable. The rain taps on my window panes and the least sound sets me on edge. Only a poor orange tabby that sleeps at my feet, before a desperate man's fire, consoles me...

March

1ˢᵗ. – To the Belgian lawyer:

Dear Monsieur P.,

It goes without saying, doesn't it? that I do not believe a single word of your alleged efforts. You will have spoken about me, with much finesse, at the hotel Ravenstein where very noble minds will have rejoiced believing *that*

Léon Bloy is finally down for the count. That's all. Your memories of the Congo make you hallucinate. Even when I was a "vulture," I never fled before any "band of parrots." Why would I begin today? How little gener-ous your friends are to "not give a damn about me," as you say, in the middle *of your letter, with a Brabant's tact! I don't give a damn about them, myself, as you might well imagine. I refuse your twenty-five pieces. I would think it would offend you if I accepted twenty-five louis from your hands. Oh! it is incontestable that five one-hun-dred-sous pieces are completely what is needed to offer "the illustrious mas-ter" that I was for you for so long, but at what point would I not dishonor a disciple of your importance by accept-ing them? Poorly informed about all things Belgian, I was uninformed of your efforts in that neighborhood. I supposed you to be a capital fellow and lawyer, completely inoffensive. Brusquely, I'm overwhelmed by reve-lations. What am I supposed to think?*

3. – To Demolins:

I told you in writing, it is a marvel to-day to encounter a man who thinks deeply. But precisely because you are that man, I wish to be treated justly by you.

*One has wanted, and one wants abso-
lutely, that the author of* Salvation
Through the Jews *be nothing but a
pamphleteer, a "critic" at best. I accept that from many people, but from
you it is too bitter. Another error. Barbey d'Aurevilly was exclusively an
artist and even an immature one, in
the same way that my poor Hello, despite his craving for art, was exclusively a thinker, when his wife didn't
get in his way. It would have been necessary to delimit...*

5. – Visited apartments in the new quarter of Lion de
Belfort. Nothing more hateful than the avidity of the
landlords asking, for example, for 800 francs for three
sad, small rooms. It is a universal conspiracy against
the poor who have never been so hated. Doubtless
one wants Paris to be inhabited exclusively by rich
people and domestics. But is it possible, and how
would that end? The devil of centuriate beginnings
must know what he is doing.

6. – To the organizer of my subscriptions:

*One person whom it would be com-
pletely fitting to reapproach is Ed. P.,
the Belgian lawyer. I had counted on*

him to secure for me many subscribers in Brussels. Inexplicably, he wrote to me an insolent and churlish letter wherein he said: "the Belgians don't give a damn about you." I responded immediately as expected, and he retaliated by pouring Belgium on my head. Nevertheless, because he is an extreme imbecile, he got it into this head, after the insults, to want to crush me with an alms fixed bizarrely at 75 francs. Take him at his word and ask for it immediately. It will suffice to say that I informed you of his intention and that you are impatient to begin saving a writer whose character *is no less admirable than genial... For it is that Belgian's will that my soul be as fetid as my eloquence is aromatic. Why that new opinion by a lawyer who fawned on me for ten years? There were rumors, someone told me... Ah! life is too short!*

10. – *Scrutiny* Sunday.[17] We are looking for a new place to live. *Passer invenit sibi domum...*[18] Those words of the day, are they for us? Nothing is found, and here we are once again not knowing where we

---

[17]Scrutiny Sunday: the third Sunday in Lent.

[18]*Passer... domum*: Psalms 83:3 (Vulgate). Latin for "The sparrow found its home."

stand in the Hand of God.

11. – Huysmans having learnt of the subscription, and immediately solicited by a friend, has sent 50 francs. Afraid to refuse, he sterilized the promoter's effort as much as he could by giving very little. He gave *pro respectu*, like the Pharisees. May God judge him and not me. Formerly, I greatly sought after his soul, I accomplished acts of love, I accepted to suffer and to pay, and I am deeply certain that that miserable man received something very precious in vain. Every appeal to his conscience since then seems pointless. Encouraged by wretched priests who did not warn him of the danger, he chose, in his sad books and in his life, to consider nothing but himself.

12. – I remember having *seen* very clearly, in my sleep, what it means to help one's neighbor. In a very intimate way, I felt – and I'm sorry not to be able to express it – that there is but one help. It is the absolute gift of oneself, such as Jesus practiced. One must be slapped, shouted down, flagellated, crucified. The commonplace: *throw oneself into someone else's arms*, says it all. All the rest is vanity.

13. – Forced to spend a night in Paris, I think of my poor family in our isolated house, and I feel a great pity. This is really the most painful point to be at, powerless pity. This enormous torment was bound to be, like all others, contained in the Passion, in an un-

known fashion.

Saw Le Bison, our landlord, one of the most hideous old men in the countryside. He has an atelier where he paints the paintings of a landlord. As for intelligence, that is his level. Around the end of October, I gifted him *The Son of Louis XVI* and *Je M'Accuse...* naïvely hoping to disarm him, to dehorn him. He sent the two volumes back to me, almost immediately, with a worthy letter informing me of his disdain for politics, the which "has no meaning," he said. That delicious "proprio," old dignitary of the postal administration, where he left the memory of a very old swine, mistook me for a political fomenter.

The gaga, after a moment of hesitation, decides to consent not to prevent me from renting, declaring that after all it is not in his best interest. Being an artist, he does not fail to point out to me that "business is business." (See *Exegesis of Commonplaces*, p. 33)

14. – Visit by Le Bison's cook, a septuagenarian woman laden with jewels, invested with a portfolio of rents and payments. The gaga received a letter from a female colleague of the place Denfert-Rochereau, where I had thought I found a place. It appears what was said yesterday does not suffice. Le Bison makes me wonder imbecilely what I need to respond. I say that it must be affirmed that I am a very honorable man, which annoys him. His conscience of a post office worker and painter-landlord permit him only disdain for a writer of my level. Fundamentally, the fun-

ny man has decided to submit a bad report. May God have pity on us! I fear I'm about to lose all courage. The absence of compassion and the hatred for the poor surpass the imagination today.

Saw other stinking animals who claim that I owe them more or less. I have never been able to express in a satisfactory manner the throes of melancholy that contact with, or the mere approach of, these cursed people causes in me. To have a sinking heart is a rather exact commonplace. But it does not say everything. There is something there of the movement of a slow claw that would crush, while shredding that organ of sorrow and joy. Ah! I know it, the helpless feeling of tearing one's own heart out!

15. – To the landlady-colleague of rue Denfert-Rochereau, one Mme. D.:

Madame,

Being a Christian and the father of a family, I had the duty to gather some information about you and I received such bad stories that I am forced to renounce my plan of renting an apartment in your building whose appearance is, moreover, sinister. I am told, among other things, that you do not allow your renters to have poor friends!!! It is diabolical, it is shameful, and it is ridiculous.

Accept, Madame, the consideration

that you deserve.

16. – Tearing down and sawing up a poor structure made of wood that Véronique used to swing on and which had cost me a great deal of effort to erect. It has to do with building a small fire for my little Madeleine who is suffering. But whatever I do, I feel such a need for God! Ah! if only he wanted to treat me with great compassion, to give me peace, security, finally! certainly, I would work to become a saint and sanctify my family. Literature, then, would have to take a back seat!

17. – *Lætare* Sunday.[19] Bad night for Madeleine... I go then to request that Dr. N. come. He is the great savant of the countryside and even a rich doctor who will fleece us, of course, I like to believe. (He never fleeced us. He is a real doctor, I believe, a good man and very gentle. He will die without having known me.)

At mass, I am extraordinarily touched by the *Nobis peccatoribus*, read so many times before without love. Repeating that prayer in the street, I am on the verge of weeping in the middle of the vermin dressed in their Sunday best. To become a saint! To obtain *aliquam partem et societatem...* The hope to suffer, the joy of suffering! I had asked Mary to have a share in the joy of the Church, in *Lætare*.[20] And here

---

[19]*Lætare* Sunday: the fourth Sunday in Lent.

[20]*Lætare*: Latin for "to rejoice." Here, substantively, "rejoicing."

I am, my wish granted.

Brutal letter by my organizer of subscriptions, reproaching me for a lack of "that practical sense that literary genius does not give." Response:

> ... *"Practical sense," you say! My God! as far as concerns me, I am forced to admit, all the same, that I utterly lack it... You are greatly afraid lest I might ask you for a personal assistance which you ask for from others [on my behalf]. I am not however so audacious a mendicant, you may have noticed. You go so far as to want me to pledge "my faith as an honest man," as if I was one. I should think that my word as a* Christian *ought to suffice...*

Strange consequence of my strange destiny! Would it not be correct to say that heroism is absolutely indispensable, as soon as one has decided not to be hostile to me?...

18. – Those who love me the most find it very simple that others insult me. Excellent reception of that nearly. Certain friendship and even devotion.

Simple remark. Nobody, even among the best of Christians, seems to seek out God or even to think about Him. People sit down to table like dogs, and they go to bed like swine. Impossible to obtain the least attention when one speaks about God.

19. – Endured, this morning, one of my most terrible crises of melancholy. Bodily torture can be imagined voluptuous in comparison.

20. – The poor never have a choice. Forced to move out in April, one must be content, at 40 kilometers from Paris, with any sort of apartment on a street in the countryside, with a view onto a little shambles and without the appearance, even telescopic, of any garden. The truth is that the mayor of Cochons-sur-Marne is our landlord.

21. – Found – at what a price! – enough money to stop, by means of a downpayment to the bailiff of the justice of the peace, the enterprises of an effervescent grocer who is after my hide. That payment, accompanied by the most ample maledictions, constitutes what the bourgeois call "a proof of good intent."

22. – A letter to me by Charles Morice announcing the next issue of the *Plume* dedicated to the glory of Tolstoy, who is about to die, one hopes, and asking me for "a page of prose" to contribute to the apotheosis of the celebrated Muscovite cretin.

25. – I rise full of sadness, having had my sleep disturbed by horrible images of our misery. I tell myself

that it is really hateful to submit to such violence and that a man such as myself, forced to consume every hour of his life in abject preoccupations with money, instead of employing them solely to eating and drinking the Word of God, is a spectacle of compassion for the Angels.

To Paul Adam:

I send you a card that I received, yesterday, Sunday, from my friend J., the organizer of the subscription that you know of. He is one of those men – improbable and incomprehensible in ten or twenty years – who love and sacrifice themselves without empty words. J., who does not think of himself as a hero, is persuaded that I ought to be saved at all cost and that it would be unconscionable of him not to try everything in his power to obtain the desired result. Naturally, I had him read the generous lines that you addressed to me on February 18.

26. – Gloomy, silent, desolate day. Behold winter starting all over again, and the wind from the north and snow. Reread the admirable sermon by Bossuet on the rich who "die in beauty" entitled *De l'impénitence finale*.[21] It is true then that at a distance of only two centuries there was still enough of Christianity for one to speak in this way to the sons of Cain: *Quia*

---

[21]*De l'impénitence finale*: French for "*The Final Impenitence.*"

non pavisti, occidisti...[22] That reading places me furiously far from the curate of Ceux-d'En-Haut and the sacrilegious multitude of ecclesiastical flunkies, chamber-pot cleaners on both knees before the bourgeoisie, who constitute, today, monstruously, the greater part of the Sacerdocy of Jesus Christ.

28. – To George Dupuis, illustrator known by the pseudonym of Géo:

> *My dear Dupuis,*
>
> *You have acted, I believe, very badly in our regards. To begin with, you have set us at odds with Rémond, by giving him an inexact report; then you have completely abandoned us, afraid of being compromised by me, you confessed it yourself. Finally, you were not afraid of depriving your children of their godfather and godmother, which you could, one day, be terribly reproached for by them. All that lacks splendor.*
>
> *However, as I cannot nor do not want to forget the bond of spiritual affinity that is between us, I do not believe I have the right to hide from you that we are in grave danger. In spite of your*

---

[22]*Quia non pavisti, occidisti*: Latin for "Because you have not fed him, you have slain him." Possibly a reference to St. Thomas Aquinas, in his chapter on "Alms Giving," in the *Summa Theologica* (II, 32:5): "Si non paveris, occidisti."

cruel and horrible negligence, I do not want you to be exposed to the calamity of letting poor people, who have only done good to you, perish, without seeking to see them again, without making an effort to assist them.

Of course, that is everyone's usual practice, more or less without exception, to leave me, with or without pretext. It seems even that that might be part of the duties of a citizen. But you do not have to be like everyone else.

Recall your abjuration, your baptism, the hospitality that you found with us so long ago, the bread we shared, even in a time of terrible distress, finally the assistance that I was able to give you under various forms, even under the form of 20-franc pieces, sometimes.

If your furniture has not changed, it is difficult for you to look around you and not see memories of Montrouge. If nothing else, that is something.

Now, enough talk. If you absolutely want to be a lout, be a lout at your leisure. But if you are still, despite everything, the good, very soft fellow I knew and loved, prove it. It is time.

(No response. For more on this person, see

Mon Journal, pages 83, 86, 139, and 319.)

29. – Particularly devoted to the Mother of God, I have asked her forcefully to rouse a Christian who might deliver us. Then I ask this unknown person, by the faith that God gives me and on the promises of the Gospel, to make himself known and to act.

30. – New visit by Le Bison's old housekeeper, mentioned earlier. They wish to know whether we will be moving out the day after tomorrow. I respond that I will pay the funny man in three days and that I cannot do any better than that; moreover, that the flu that our children have contracted will force us, in any case, to defer the move-out to Thursday, possibly, which is accepted grudgingly by the ambassadress. Le Bison is very afraid of not being paid, of being deprived of the flesh and blood of the poor. No pity to be expected from that direction.

31. Palm Sunday. Letter from a Tourangeau by the name of René Martineau.[23] Would this happen to be the *unknown person* that I was invoking the day before yesterday? That thought strikes me. My correspondent speaks of a small collection of select morsels, with a view to making me known to not-so-well-read bibliophiles, and he offers to submit his

---

[23]René Martineau: author of *The Biography of Léon Bloy* published in 1921 (in English translation by Sunny Lou Publishing, 2022).

manuscript to me for my review. Immediate response:

Under other circumstances, your letter would have been well received, perhaps. At this moment, it resembles irony. It arrives just at the moment when, on the verge of being thrown out into the street by a landlord whom I cannot pay, I am also as near as possible to despair while considering the terrible fate of my wife and the more than somber future of my poor little girls. You must have penetrated my character, having read much by me. Judge then the effect that your letter could have produced on "a writer of genius" – as you say – exasperated and disgusted beyond words by the atrocious injustice that he dies of. And how might you expect that that miserable man could be in a proper state of mind to examine your manuscript as long as that terrible anguish lasts? In the midst of such torment, how could the admiration or execration of contemporaries or posterity hold his attention, and how is it possible that he would not be disinterested in his own works?

It is well understood, of course, that writers of genius are everyone's servants, but, all the same, it is too much to ask, and when one does not wish or when one is unable to do anything for them, it would be at least equitable to let them die in peace. Note, monsieur, that I absolutely do not ask for anything from you, my being persuaded, for about ten or fifteen years now, that that would be absolutely pointless and that I would find myself as always in the presence of an admirer sorry for his powerlessness. These lines are a simple response to your letter.

The old woman of yesterday again, bearing a comminatory letter from Le Bison, an ultimatum by the landlord. If kicks in the ass were hanging from trees, what a zoological garden one could offer that ruminant! We launch desperate letters on Paris. It will take more than genius to describe the anguish of this procession in our house of the Palms of Sorrow.

April

2. – Holy Tuesday. The necessary sum of money arrives finally through the most unexpected of means...

25. – A gap of twenty-three days. We have moved out, we have paid, we continue to live. From the moment of the first Sin, in the declining splendor of Eden, it had been decided that we would move out on Good Friday, seven thousand seven hundred seventy-third anniversary of the Expulsion from Paradise,

according to the probable calculation of the Septu-
agint. Good Friday cold and dark. Rain without inter-
ruption. For us, no ceremonies, no adoration of the
Cross, impossible meditation. We have with joy however quit that house so little conformant to a paradise,
where we just finished one of the most terrible win-
ters of our lives. A letter from the Belgian poet was
waiting for us in our new abode. Base and venomous
letter. He sensed or thought he sensed that we had
crawled out of our hole, and that displeased him. Correspondence with Martineau who appears without
question to be the *Unknown person* and whose opus-
cule: *Un Vivant et deux Morts*, examined carefully, is
very publishable. I give him some unpublished material to spice up his brochure, wherein I occupy, in the
quality of the one and only *living person*, a large
place. The two dead are Ernest Hello and Villiers de
l'Isle-Adam. Surprising particularity which has something of the supernatural to it, Mme. Martineau has an
uncle by the name of Hercule Joly – like the fictional
Tourangeau in the *Femme pauvre* – and the physical
shape of my individual is exactly that of that authentic child of Touraine. I have known and detested oc-
cultists who would have found that very simple and
who would have been right perhaps. As for myself, I
remain confused, and my surprise grows every time I
think about it.

26. – Mass at the chapel of the Friars of Cochons. Almoner, an abbot Galette. I have never seen a mass
sandblasted like that. It is unprecedented. Yet another
man of the cloth who is going to make himself loved

by me, and whom I will have perhaps the occasion to offer a bit of agreeableness to.

28. – Delicious and recomforting reading in *Voyage en Tartarie et au Thibet* by M. Huc. I imagine that there is no moral penalty associated with the presence of that extraordinary book.

30. – Deprived of mass for an unknown reason, I put in a request to the deacon for communion. Response brought by the sacristan: *He does not have time*. Always the same. These priests make themselves judges of their own duties in order to dispense with what riles them, even if it means souls perish. What is the point of complaining? Is there one single example of a priest who was wrong?

To Paul Adam:

My admirable friend J. who has taken on himself for me an infinite difficulty and who has succeeded in procuring for me several unfortunately insufficient resources, writes to me, about two weeks ago, that he had seen you and found you in the most generous of dispositions towards me. He terminated his letter by affirming that, according to what was said, you would not fail, immediately after certain steps were taken, to have passed on to me "the first ten louis" of your collection.

I ask your pardon for that importunity.
I launched that friend on you because
the promise of your letter of February
authorized me to. However, despite my
horrible reputation, it would displease
me to be onerous on my confreres and
particularly on you who have spoken
nobly of me. I give you back your
word then and your liberty, asking
only that you pardon me.

Here included is your letter from Feb-
ruary 18.

(Paul Adam received the slap in silence. He
believed, perhaps, to have received only a kick in the
derriere, a sort of occultism accepted by contemporary careerists.)

May

5. – Saint Pius V. Mass *Statuit*. Gospel of the talents.
The first servant who receives the five talents, would
that not be the Hebrew people receiving the Law, in
other words the Pentateuch? The second who receives
two talents, would that not be the Christian people receiving the two Testaments? Finally the third who receives but one talent, would that not be the mysterious people of the Holy Ghost, the reformed Church,
regenerated by Love?

What will he receive, the one prefigured by
the servant called "bad and lazy", who buried his tal-

ent? *Unum est necessarium...*

13. – Celebration of the Mother Superior at the boarding school of Saint-Joseph de Cluny. Each pupil must
give five francs. Such is the usage. Those religious
put into their hands, on that occasion, a thousand
francs gleaned from two hundred pupils.

15. – Visit by our new friend Martineau, come for
twenty-four hours. He has all my books written in his
face and seems to have really given us his heart. I
give him what I can in return, among other things, a
posthumous photograph of our son André with this:
"Souvenir of our blessed son André, taken in the
bloom of his innocence and who is, since six years of
age, at the right hand of Jesus Christ."

17. – Since having moved into our new place, we frequent a fat grocer, the accredited supplier of priests
and women religious, probity guaranteed by the finest
chaplets in the parish. He's a Lorrainian through and
through in joy and stoutness, assisted by a crumpled
flatterer like those September chestnuts that the grocers of Paris and its suburbs fight over with the swine
of Périgord and Brittany each year. That symbolic pa-
troness has one eye made of glass and the other of
faience in order to keep an eye on the cod or the
gruyère at the same time as a silly goose exited from
her flanks – and devoted, like the authors of her days,
to the merchandise, – which she sprinkles with the

verjuice of her experience. They go to mass, Sundays and holidays, attending even the ceremonies and sermons, but never closing their shop. Interrogated, they respond: "Our clients would go elsewhere." Translation into the vernacular: The commandments of the Church and even the commandments of God are not made for merchants. When one risks losing several ecus by observing the commandments, one is dispensed with, *ipso facto*. There you have them, edifying Christians such as they are, and entirely beyond reproach, whom no priest warns of the frightening state of their soul as profaners and renegades. *On the contrary.*

20. – Trip to Meaux. A benevolent canon gives us a tour inside the cathedral which is extremely beautiful. It appears that the remains of Bossuet are still in the choir on the right under the tile where his epitaph is engraved. Our guide saw them with his own eyes, without having been able, he admits, to identify them. Poor great man who did not know how to become a Saint and who has a need, enough to make one's hair stand on end, of the compassion of poor wretches!

23. – Visit by our poet. He is clean shaven, hideous, and humble. He bores us hideously and humbly for three hours, and finishes by leaving with provisions that one stuffed his pockets with. It is astonishing how closely a freshly-shaven Belgian poet resembles an imbecile!

25. – New experience of mass at the chapel of Friars. It is more exceptional than the first time. It is evident that the celebrant who, moreover, passes for an ecclesiastic of prey, absolutely mocks Jesus Christ.

To Gustave Schlumberger, a member of the Institute:

Monsieur,

I received successively, from the publisher Hachette, The Killer of the Bulgars *and, from the publisher Didot,* Nicephorus Phocas, *this last one comfortably bound. I have but one means to recognize this very gracious present, and that is publicly by saying what I think of your immense work on points of history that have remained so obscure, despite their interest that nothing surpasses.*

For three years now, I am familiar only with the colossal drama of Tzimiskes and the Two Bardas, surprising reconstruction of an epoch almost as scantily documented as that of Ninus or Hycsos. I have always devoured with an unusual cupidity all the books, superior or mediocre, that treat of Byzantium or the Late Roman Empire. My passionate taste for that period in history is quasi famous. I do

*not at all despair writing then, after
you and according to you, some pages
that might satisfy you. My enemies
themselves whom I have given up trying to count, have sometimes the kindness of conceding that I am capable of
something. I ask only that you grant
me all the time I need, having to read
altogether and very attentively the two
thousand copious pages that make up
your three volumes and also charged
with the care of providing subsistence
to my family. You will excuse me for
having sent to you, at the same time as
this letter, the* Femme pauvre, *a kind
of very sad, personal novel that has
generated some attention. There is
mention of Byzantium in it in two
places.*

(The promised work is yet to be written. M.
Schlumberger having announced a fourth volume before completing his *Epic*, I had conceived of a furious
need for the entire collection, completed today. Here
is the letter that I just addressed to the illustrious historian of Byzantium:

November 24, 1904

Dear monsieur,

*I have just seen arrive, with an ex-
treme joy, the magnificent book so
long awaited. Here it is then, your
completed work, given you do not*

want the Komnenos, who do not begin in reality but with Alexios and not with Isaac, who was content "showing his family the way to the throne," as the excellent Lebeau said.

Would to God that, going back to the IXth century, as far back as the alarming death of the Drunk, you had told the story of the first Basil. One would then have all that beautiful Macedonian series. But it would have required a bit more, doubtless, than the strength of one man. Your four volumes already represent an immense labor. I have before my eyes finally the entirety that you had wanted and announced. Rest assured that you will not regret having placed your confidence in me.

I have no more valid excuse then not to act. I have already read the first three volumes two times. I have even read Tzimiskes *and the* Two Bardas *three times, and I am perhaps the only contemporary who has done that. The new and latest tome will be the voluptuous occasion of a new feast.)*

29. – Mass, once again, at the Friars, by necessity. I leave full of indignation, decided never to return. If an angel told me that that abbot Galette does not omit

any of the liturgical prayers, I will respond to that angel as Angela da Foligno: "I do not know you, it is
you who have fallen from heaven!" I will need however to say something about these abominable priests.

June

5. – Resumed the *Exegesis of Commonplaces*, begun
September 30, '97 and interrupted the following October 30.

10. – To a madame Frusquin née Visible, landlady in
Cochons:

> *Madame,*
>
> *Yesterday evening, my wife, strolling
> with our two children on route Saint-
> Laurent, met a group of people among
> whom Mlle. your daughter and a
> young man. Those individuals got it
> into their heads to want to mock her
> very ostensibly, with so much boldness
> that she was without defense. That has
> happened* multiple times *already.*
>
> *Of course, madame, you are free to
> raise your daughter as you see fit and
> to give her the companion that suits
> her. But as for me, I inform you that I
> do not like churlishness and on occa-*

*sion I know how to make my family be
respected.*

*So I alert you to the fact that I am an
old soldier and an artist, that is to say
a man possessing a ready slap for im-
pertinent young people and absolutely
not giving a damn for the bourgeois.
Expect a pretty little scandal at the
next instance of insolence.*

Two hours later, visit by that lady. Physiognomy of a
potato with red kidney beans. It would be difficult,
even with a harp, to sing appropriately that interview
which surpassed the heights of comicalness. Seeing
her out of breath, I naturally suppose that she dropped
everything in order to come and make excuses. What
naïvety! She expected the same from me, her having
four sous honorably acquired, I wish to believe, and
possessing a ridiculous apartment building where tor-
mented souls groan. In the lower-intestinal brain of
that bourgeoise woman who watched over cows in
her youth, I'm told, that must suffice to give her the
right to the most deprecatory and most wallowed-in
consideration. I forced on her the counsel of keeping
quiet and framing my handwritten letter luxuriously,
like the most precious of family documents. Then, I
invited her to rid me of her carcass, having better to
do than to engage in sophisticated banter with chamber women of a certain age. Rarely have I contem-
plated a more repugnant gob. The ugliness and vulgarity of that duenna are barely credible. I was struck
stupid, as the great Corneille said. Suffocating with
rage and having become completely doddering, she

took off, feet on the ground, like Ajax's cattle, repeating multiple times that things would go much further than I think... That evening, the Holy Sacrament being exposed in the parish church, I saw her again, kneeling, worshipping, not far from me. Ah! the piety of landladies in the countryside!

15. – What hampers love is the senses.

19. – A man, rich or poor, takes a trip. Before leaving, he gives instruction not to have any letter follow him, not to send to him any object capable of reminding him of God or men, and he calls that a "sage precaution." By which gesture, you may recognize a servant of the devil.

26. – Received a fragment of a journal wherein is found an insulting and horribly written comment by Tailhade about *Blood of the Poor*, apropos of I do not know what. At the time of *The Ungrateful Beggar*, when he wore out – literarily – my old pants, I thought the old devil was menaced by senility, which could have been a future for him. A senile old man is a ruin, and ruins can be interesting. I was wrong. Tailhade is only an imbecile, and nothing menaces him.

29. – Letter by the Belgian poet enjoining me, *on God's behalf*, to send him 200 francs *which I do not owe him*. Immediate response which puts an end, I

want to think, to so dear a friendship.

July

1st. – New letter by the same poet and same Belgian who unmasks himself finally. It is impossible to be viler, more churlish, more foreign to all nobility, to all generosity, to all equity. Letter evidently inspired by his woman, wherein Jeanne above all – who nourished and took care of that man, as she did before for Henry de Groux – is insulted in the filthiest manner. I will hold on to this monument of turpitude. He goes even so far as to wish evil on our poor little girls, calling maledictions down on their head, because I was unable to give him an alms of 200 francs... Among other things, he menaces me with his "quill," poor hussy of an old quill gathered from among my sweepings, saying that he will not *leave me be* from now on.

Short response: "You are right to not *leave me be*. It is your only literary resource."

7. – It is a national holiday, the holiday of firemen. Great agitation outside, and sweet to stay at home. Nothing more idiotic and miserable than that gala of firemen. Exited for a necessary errand with the children, and towards the end of our maneuvers we were just lucky enough to escape the spraying of the square in front of the town hall by those enraged people who launch torrents of water on the spectators.

10. – First idea of a small book on contemporary apostles: Coppée, Huysmans, etc.

(Realized in 1903 under the title of *Les Dernières Colonnes de l'Eglise*.)

I learn that Georges Dupuis, called Géo, appointed draftsman for the publisher-bookseller Ollendorf, is committed never to seeing me again. I asked for it and he consented. Not to mention the surprising ignominy of that flake, what to think of that publisher-bookseller who cannot even hear my name spoken without immediately feeling the *need* to give to the best books in his shop their veritable destination?

28. – Jubilee, plenary indulgence. Last year, only the rich, that is only those who could spend three weeks in Rome, were admitted. This year, by a sort of modesty, that privilege is extended to the poor and is translated into a *triduum*[24] in the parishes. Ah! One must have one's faith sealed with bronze crampons!

August

2. – New insolences written by our poet. How much we have suffered for that dirty bastard!

---

[24]*triduum*: Latin for "a period of three days."

12. – We are, for three days now, in Pouliguen, with the Martineaus who give us the hospitality of Ker Saint-Roch, rented in order to spend, altogether, two weeks there. It is the first time that I have seen the Ocean. The last perhaps, the poor not having the right to contemplate God's works. In the neighborhood of an ancient chapel of mariners and of one very old calvary, which was visible, two or three hundred years ago, from the high sea, before the rock had been covered with habitations. Dedicated to Saint Anne and Saint René, the chapel, as poor as it is old, is served four or five months out of the year by thirty or so priests, ever-renewed boarders of a nearby ecclesiastical hostelry. All that is very nice. Our hosts go out of their way to show us testimonies of their affection.

13. – Read *Quo Vadis* the immense success of which appears inexplicable to me. It is mediocre, however, as much as the riffraff can desire, and so boring!... Torment over one of our lost parcels. It contains our dear little ones' dresses. In vain, complaints lodged with the railroad company. This dollop of bitterness in our poor joy was necessary, doubtless.

18. – To a Jesuit:

> *... I have received no letter from Father G., which does not surprise me in the least. If that religious promised you that he would write me, he must have, after reflection, considered that*

promise with surprise and wrote to someone else. The contrary would be unprecedented... I am persuaded that there is, here and there, in communities or outside communities, excellent and cherished souls of God, full of desire for his glory. But those souls are too small in number to save Sodom, and I think, after the admirable Anne-Catherine, who was appalled by it, that there are no more Christians in the true sense of the word.

The proof is too facile. If a persecution occurred, you understand what I'm saying, a real *persecution, do you want to tell me how many of our Catholics would choose black misery, ignominy, and tortures? One out of one hundred thousand, maybe. There would be an immediate, universal defection, a terrifying apostasy. To hope for better, one would need to be blind or a sot.*

Ah! well do I know that you are going to speak to me about Grace, but I will stop you immediately with an extreme indignation. The Grace of God is not for dogs, no more than his Word or his adorable Body is, and I call them dogs those who want to receive without any preparation. Jesus said Væ vobis divitibus, *and modern Christians say:*

*"Happy are the rich." He said also
that one needed to leave everything
behind in order to follow him, and that
that was needed in order to inherit his
kingdom, and never has cupidity, even
in religious houses, been more violent,
more unbridled. They say: "The Order
is rich perhaps, but each religious, individually, is poor." What miserable
sophism and fundamentally what infernal derision!...*

*Since the beginning of your letter, you
lead me toward the edge of a gulf,
inviting me to leap. You speak to me
about the* elections!!! *of 1902 which
you and your colleagues expect something from! Another denial, rather un-
conscious on your part no doubt, but
all the more deplorable. You implicitly
affirm that a bad tree can produce
good fruit, for finally you are forced,
under pain of condemning yourself to
the worst mediocrity, to recognize that
universal suffrage is an absolute evil,
an execrable disguise of hell's anarchy.*

*God has the power to draw good from
evil, I know, but he alone has that
power, because he alone can draw a
being from nothingness – which,
moreover, is totally incomprehensible.
What a surprising presumption for you*

*to present to him the matter of that in-
conceivable prodigy, to tell him in
summary: Here is that invention of
Disobedience, Wickedness the daughter of Envy, Pride and the Stupidity of
men in this last century. Issue the com-
mand, not that it be destroyed or confused, but that the triumph of your
Church be the consequence of it; and
that this inventiveness, which is a per-
manence of the spittings on your Face,
continue to remain with us and be
more and more honored, even in your
sanctuaries, even on the chair of truth,
right in front of the Holy Sacrament of
your altars!*

Nolite conformari huic sæculo, *said
the Receptacle of election. "To be one
with one's century" the Imposter had
responded for an extremely long time
already, but is it not something to
weep over, to tell oneself that it is
Leon XIII himself who inaugurated the
so-called Christian politics of attribut-
ing such denial to the affirmation of
the Holy Ghost! Well-known example
and forever lamentable!*

*Since then, the ambition of the majori-
ty of Catholics is to appear as democratic as the most criminal or most insane Jacobins, and that, o indescribable misery! is believed by them to be*

the culmination of hability. To that de-gree of blindness, how to express the distress and horror of the Christian soul?

However Deus non irridetur... *you know how dangerous it is to touch the divine Third Person, who does not for-give. The Charity Bazaars and other attempts to serve two masters are scant profitable. It can happen that the Fire leaps up and swallows the beauti-ful ladies who mock the Gospel. I have written pages about it, which none of your fathers would support and which would have had me skinned alive if they could have been published at the right moment.*

What do you want me to say, my dear Paul, to such a world? You are often indignant of the horrible treatment I have suffered because of it. But my friend, I am merely a unity. It has al-ways been so and will always be so. There is no hatred that surpasses in intensity the hatred of modern Cath-olics for what is or appears to be su-perior, especially in Art; Beauty be-ing, in their eyes, an indecency. These are not new ideas to you. You know also about the ignoble history of the Assumptionists... I do not recriminate, dear friend, persuaded that suffering has been good for me, whatever the judgment of Our Lord might be on those who inflict it on me... "You would be assured the wherewithal to live," you say, if I consented to make a certain journalism which I do not like at all. I know too well what monsters mean by those words, the "wherewithal to live," when it is not them we are talking about. You know what I need. If one really wants to give me the wherewithal to live, I will recognize in that sign that the sacrifice of one of my most vivid repugnances is called for. I will then say yes *immediately, and I will act in consequence. Ah! for example, I would not need to be asked to cook up an election, nor to admire Coppée or Jules Lemaître or the author of* Quo Vadis, *nor to find out that Huysmans is an apostle or that the imbecile de Mun is a great man. To hide in the secret of my heart that the Orléans are rotten and that the cowardice of modern Christians is enough to disgust demons, there you have all that I can promise. You see to what generalities I would find myself reduced, but you know what I can do, even in that genre.*

19. – Excursion to bourg de Batz and to Croisic. Saw

in Batz two churches, one of which is in ruins, like the ancient abbey of Cochons-sur-Marne, with this difference that the ruin of Cochons is polluted, horribly pissed on by an entire people who received its baptism there, one thousand years ago; while that of Batz is a closed ruin, inaccessible, and falls to pieces under the sky for over a century, without profanations. In Croisic, nothing but the Ocean, the road of the world.

There are also automobiles. A kind of homicidal and demoniacal delirium. No security. This morning the driver of our car showed me one of those machines that killed an old woman recently and which seems ready to begin all over again. No punishment. The crusher gave a little money, and all is said and done.

22. – Excursion to Guérande. For the first time, I see an entirely fortified city, as in the XVth century. The famous novel by Balzac appears largely in my mind, while contemplating that adorable vestige, "that magnificent jewel of feudalism." I see the du Guénic again, Mlle. des Touches, and Claude Vignon; I see the detestable Béatrix again especially, and I have, once again, that grandiose sensation of the Emptiness of all the Visible world that the immense *Human Comedy* continually unleashes.

23. – Refound finally, after ten days, our lost trunk. If the railroad company administration consents to com-

pensate us, that vexation will be fortunate. Providence is an abundant Source of tears.

24. – A little boy, the son of our host, was stung by an animal, and his hand swells up before our very eyes. On my counsel, we have him blessed at the altar of Sainte-Anne by a priest whose reverence at mass touched us. This evening, the swelling went away.

25. – Hopeless letter to the director of the Eastern Railway Company, in view of obtaining a compensation.

30. – Sad return home. We return like poor people. First stop, the Mont-de-Piété. Such is the end to our holiday.

High mass in honor of Saint Fiacre, patron saint of gardeners. Does anyone know in all of Brie, where he is particularly honored, whether this saint, otherwise authentic, didn't replace very probably in the VIIth century, in these still idolatrous lands, old Priapus, the God of gardens? The transference must have happened in the simplest, most *spiritual* way in the world, BY ASSONANCE, as with all savages. Whatever the case, it is a custom in Cochons to solemnize this day religiously. The deacon, very unfamiliar with Priapus, gives an important discourse. Noted this: "It is not asked of everyone, as [it is] of Saint Fiacre, to leave everything behind. One can gain heaven while living in the midst of riches." Calling to mind *Væ div-itibus*[25] and several other formal Texts on *indispens-able* despoilment, I am ashamed and disgusted to be a parishioner of that old blasphemer.

31. – Saint Raymond Nonnat, that is to say *non natus*, one who was not born. They had to cut open the belly of his dead mother to extract him. That happened in Catalonia in the XIIIth century. He became a shep-herd, whose angel guarded his flock; he became reli-gious, he became a priest and missionary among pi-rates who pierced his two lips with a hot iron poker and locked his mouth to prevent him from pronounc-ing the name of Jesus Christ. He was ransomed in the end, and the pope made him a cardinal, a dignity that he profited by in order to give his red cape to a poor person. Then Jesus Christ placed on his head the Crown of Thorns and, soon thereafter, he died, having received communion by His Hand. One would like to be slapped with the entrails of a rotten fish when one thinks on such men.

September

5. – Against all hope, the administration of the East-ern Railway Company compensates us.

---

[25]*Væ divitibus*: from Luke 6:24-26. "But woe unto you that are rich! for ye have received your consolation" (KJV).

10. – Beginning of the expulsions of men and women religious. Soon there will no longer be any in France. What will become of the religious and, a little later, secular priests? Later still, what will they do with Christian laics? For ultimately, it is the abolition of Christianity that they wish for and hardly anyone tries to hide it. It will go, if needed, as far as a massacre. The Catholics have earned it all. Perhaps God will want to give back again thus a little beauty to that flock which has become so repugnant, so abominable.

11. – Read in *Raison*, a paper by the ignoble Charbonnel, an article by my old plagiarist Laurent Tailhade. That one-eyed character suffering from a democratic softening, not content with serving mass each morning to his spiritual father, seems to have promised, furthermore, my demolition to the abbot Victor. It is disarming. Read this, in the same asswipe: "'Let's let the dead,' *said a poet*, 'bury their dead.'" Unprecedented.

12. – Visit by an expelled religious, in route to Holland. Several hours of visiting with him greatly encourages my disdain for the present Catholic world. The infamy of the secular clergy, seen in its entirety, is perfect and also a bit apocalyptic. That clergy rubs its hands, joyous of being rid of the *competition* of regulars and persuaded that one will spare them. Stupidity and ignominy. Dark, appalling future.

13. – Motto on an old sun dial: "It is later than you think."

18. – Lamentable trip to the Mont-de-Piété for a derisible result. The Republic spends tens of millions to welcome the Tsar and his wife and to expulse religious. *Usquequo?*

19. – No mass at the parochial church. Trip to the Friars where I barely arrive on time to receive communion from the hand of the horrible bodger almoner. I wonder whether such a bad priest takes the time to consecrate and whether he does not give me poison with the assumed Body of Christ.

Lord, deliver us from our misery and from our anguish!

Continuation of the Franco-Russian farces. Dreadful domesticity of everyone. History, one day, will tell in what unprecedented proportions human servility was aggravated by our fourth republic.

21. – After some awful errands in Paris, while forced to wait for a track to clear, I am witness to the deboarding of guests from the train returned from the tsar's spectacle in Reims. Ah! my friends, what a spectacle, what an explosion of caparisoned, damascened, plumed flunkeys! Ah! the gobs of those proud Republicans all still vibrating with their enthusiasm for the Autokrator! The train station is teeming with

deputies, senators, important functionaries with their women in gala toilette. I looked in vain for Hanotaux whom I had a thirst for admiring. A sad and fatigued disgust "mounts in me like the sea."[26] At my arrival this morning I had seen in the same location and here and there still, in the omnibus offices, frightened religious leaving for exile, a traveling bag in hand, and I had read in an obedient sheet, a beautiful piece by Rostand, who has become the national poet, wherein it was said that the Tsarina is *our* empress. Retained a copy of the Compiègne lunch menu, this Ember Friday of *quatuor tempora*, feast offered by atheists to schismatics.

27. – We had learnt yesterday by public crier that soldiers were going to arrive today and that our street would have to lodge them, each inhabitant supposed to expect the visit of two men. In our situation, that announcement sounded terrible to us. It was to put an enormous surcharge on a poor boat already about to sink.

Today then, those soldiers arrived in town and invaded all the houses on our street, on every floor. Our neighbor, a greedy old woman who lodges above us, saw *four* come her way! of which two for us, very probably. We had prepared ourselves to receive them, having put wine on the table and sacrificed two francs to send them to the inn. Now we had nobody. The old

---

[26]"Mounts in me like the sea": from a poem, "Causerie," in the *Fleurs du mal*, by Charles Baudelaire: "Vous êtes un beau ciel d'automne, clair et rose!/Mais la tristesse en moi monte comme la mer..."

woman, furious because of her squad, cried injustice, filling the street with her clamor. Several other wandering soldiers complained of not having found a place anywhere; neighbors spread lots of stories; the mayor came in person to perorate under our windows, preoccupied, I imagine, to ensure that the most strict justice be enforced. All that in vain. Nobody thought of us and *could not*, it seems, think of us. We had been forgotten by everyone, an absolute forgetfulness, invincible, supernatural.

October

1st. – Apropos of Saint Remy. In *The Son of Louis XVI*, I spoke of my conviction of the irremediable fall of the Bourbons. I forgot a fact of capital importance however, which proves that God had had enough of that race and that he has truly rejected it. It is the profanation and irreparable destruction of the Saint Ampoule by the French National Conventionalist Rhul, in 1793. That would have been a beautiful chapter to write.

To a Belgian priest:

Your letter which I just received fills me with a profound indignation. I understand too well that you were unable to enter into the project I was proposing, but to divulge my distress which you had received in confidence, *going so far as to mention it to redoubtable gossips, to undertake or only dream about a* collection *that could not have been for the honest people of Brussels anything but an occasion to rejoice like devils, – what a lack of tact! not to mention, moreover, an absence of delicateness and of veritable love! If you were so powerless, you should have simply declared as much to me and stopped there, without compromising me by steps that I had not allowed. This is rudimentary behavior what I am telling you here, monsieur the abbot.*

As for your counsels, the practice of which would dishonor me in the eyes of men and angels, how to qualify them? They were often given to me by my worst enemies. Ah! to be sure, if I wanted to act like everyone else, to write platitudes, as you invite me to, to betray my faculties, my vocation, my pressing call by Him whom I appear to be presently the one and only *witness to; if, writing from now on for the multitude, I sought the suffrage of Judases, imbeciles, or cowards who do not want the kingdom of God; yes, of course, my editors would easily sell my books. In summary, you advise me to vilify myself in order to earn some money. Long live misery!*

*A question. Why did you write to me in
the first place? For, finally, I did not
seek you out, I had even a great dis-
trust of you and I told you why. What
do those reiterated, continual protestations of your admiration, of your desire to be useful to me mean, if all you
have to offer me in reality are Belgian
refusals, lessons!!! or horrible advice?
Once again, I did not seek you out.
Would you happen to be a practical
jokester?*

2. – At Véronique's school, among the women religious of Saint-Joseph de Cluny, one requires that
each pupil come *in gloves*, so that – as the mother
charged with that important communication said – the
pupils of said school, in the exclusive practice of
well-todo families, cannot be confused with the poor
children from the school of the sisters of Saint Vin-
cent de Paul. That abominable prudence explains better, and in an otherwise profound way, the explosion
of impiety, the present discomfiture of religious Orders. They perish by worldliness. They despise the
Poor, and Jesus Christ abandons them.

4. – Learnt of the death of Marius Tournadre, one of
the most impoverished beings I have ever known.
How did he die, and what has become of his poor
soul? He was an unimaginative man without culture
and an unwavering *fumiste*, as a result of an obscure

need for justice. He mystified landlords or shopkeepers as one might accomplish a religious act, and I saw
him giving money to the poor which he had appropri-
ated at the risk of going to jail.

5. – To a benefactor:

Monsieur,

*I hasten to acknowledge reception of
the money order for 50 francs that you
wanted to send to me. Having read
me, you cannot not know that I am a
devout Christian for whom all events
of this world are sufficiently explained
by the certain dogma of an infallible
Providence. Before this morning, I believed myself in need of an abundant
alms. I see now that 50 francs was just
the amount I needed, as it is precisely
the assistance that God wanted and allowed. From this point of view, it is
clear that the numbers no longer mean
anything, and I consider you a benefactor in the same way as if you had
given me 50,000 francs.*

*What a shame that you were unable to
avoid speaking to me about the* future
*so frightfully! My letter, I believe, was
not without nobility. Why so prudent a
response? Why mix some bitterness in
with the morsel of bread that one gives*

to an indigent? Do not fret, I entreat
you, and remember me only as you
might remember Sesostris. It is point-
less to revive what I said. I would like
to deliver to the public very beautiful
and, above all, very noble *pages on*
that monarch, on the occasion of your
books. If I fail, you will not be as af-
flicted as me...

(I am not concerned about this letter being
published, after and before so many others, *because* I
am a man preoccupied with Death. I think on it continually and, many times, amorously. So, what should
the world's opinion matter to me?)

8. – A journal, very little read fortunately, and edited
by imponderables, publishes a sort of appeal to the
generosity or rather to the compassion of its readers.
Title: *Léon Bloy's Distress*. Very painful impression
for starters. But what does it matter? Am I not a
stranger to that reasoning? Let's let God act as he
wishes. After all, I am a beggar. (Pointless to add that
this appeal had no effect.)

10. – We voluntarily took part in the recitation of the
rosary at our church, and this practice was very beneficial to us. The deacon deprived us of [the opportunity for] participating going forward, deciding to move
the time to eight o'clock in the evening, instead of
six, which diminishes at least by half the number of

attendees. The earlier hour doubtless annoyed someone, a beautiful lady with a golden belly button, silver
pants, let's suppose. I often think of the affirmation
by Anne-Catherine Emmerich: "There are no longer
any Christians *in the true sense of the word.*" This
morning, after mass, Jeanne having run into one of
the rare and truly pious people of the parish, said
apropos of the present persecution, which is not yet
bloody, the intensity of which however, it seems, augments with each passing day, that perhaps one should
get ready for a martyrdom.

"Ah! no, my word!" responded that Christian
lady with extreme vivacity, unmasking thus naïvely
the frightening poverty of heart that is the reality of
all modern Catholics. What will happen when the
Judgment Day arrives?

16. – Prayer to the Holy Virgin:

> *Immaculate Mary, my Sovereign and
> Mistress, here is the very humble
> prayer of your slave. I possess nothing
> but my sufferings, and you know that
> they have been serious. I offer to you
> this unique treasure like a spray of
> sorrowful flowers. Being already old
> and perhaps near to dying, I present it
> to you on my knees, my eyes and heart
> in tears, in my excessive distress, so
> that you might have pity on me and
> mine, and I beg you, o Mother of Jesus
> in agony, by the Seven Swords of your*

*Compassion, to obtain for us the grace
of becoming Saints.* Maria, Immaculata
Conceptio, per Septem Dolores tuos,
adjuva nos.[27]

1 9 . – Reread together the *History of Christopher
Columbus* by Roselly de Lorgues, a much studied
book formerly. Disheartened, disgusted at first by the
writer's odious commonplaces, the beauty of that exceptional Life soon seized us, and immediately we
can believe that an angel visited us, so marvelous was
our emotion! That reminds me of the extraordinary
impressions of my first reading, 27 years ago. A miracle of a book, absolutely mediocre in its form, nevertheless all-powerful on the soul.

20. – Read, for several hours, *Du Pape* by Joseph de
Maistre. I was passionate about the author at the time
of my adolescence. Today, I enjoyed it even more,
within certain limits. Incontestable genius, but limited. Exclusively traditional genius. One would think
that his "Providence" is a mechanism. He did not understand that in 1789 God had changed the face of the
world.

21. – "I heard Mary saying a *Pater*, kneeling before
God. The Holy Trinity responded to her by an *Ave
Maria* and all the creatures added: *Sancta Maria,*

[27]*Maria... nos*: Latin for "Mary, Immaculate Conception, through
your Seven Sorrows, help us."

Mater Dei, etc." It is my dear wife who speaks thus.

22. – Deliverance is so near that I believe I see it and hear it, so thin is the wall that separates me from it. But, after twenty-five years, it is impossible for me to reach it.

23. – A preacher makes an effort to put on guard against the world the young girls who have finished their classes this year and who will begin their very low existences as shopkeepers or bourgeoise women without a profession. Infinite inutility of that effort.

28. – Read the old booklet by Michelet: *Poland and Russia*, published in 1852. Despite his unbearable Jacobin sentimentality, this little work interests me because of Russia. I have the deep certitude that nothing good can come to France from that monstrous and fierce empire. But who wants to listen to that? The delirium of a Franco-Russian alliance, the which will end by a horrible deception, is, in my eyes, a diabolical prestige of the most dangerous kind.

Found this, on page 16, against lying publicists: "... If they have extinguished the daylight, may they be lit up by lightning!"

29. – To René Martineau:

This morning I received, with emotion,

the portrait of my poor Villiers on his deathbed. Thanks to you, I have finally the consolation of seeing that deplorable visage that I was unable to kiss a last time, in '89. Huysmans' orders were opposed to it, and I was admitted only to kneel before the nailed bier.

I have recounted that dreadful story, more or less. Huysmans is today "in piety." I think that he would like to do, and believed he did, for Saint Lydwine what he did for poor Villiers. There are wolf traps on the PROPERTY. *Those farces, of course, succeed and appear to succeed when God permits them, and in the measure that he permits them. We will see in the end. I have interred others.*

I have just prepared for an excellent man, who had asked me for it, a key to The Desperate Man.[28] *There were twenty-four in all, those who 'got it' in that book, much more moderate than one generally believes. Eh! well, since '87, the date of publication, there are already twelve who have died and of the twelve who remain alive still, there are certainly six or eight who hold on by a hair...*

---

[28] A key to *The Desperate Man*: the book was a roman à clef.

November

1st – In a state of decline, Beauty is a monster.

2. – Day of the Dead. I learn of the death of Julien Leclercq. Extremely sad news which devastates me. He was one of my rare friends. Where is he now, that poor wretch? What a frightening thought! But he was not a bad person, and I hope that he found mercy. Who will pray for him, other than me only perhaps?

Civil burial. I do not even have the right to attend his funeral. What assassins of journalism would I not encounter?

(I knew, or learnt, a little later that I had not been informed of anything, out of *prudence*. Some feared lest I might run and exhort the moribund, which might have prevented the renegade's death by starvation, which was the hope.)

4. – Saw Mme. Leclercq who appears to me less saddened than unshakeable in her will not to pray for her husband or have him prayed for. She admires him for dying Godless and does not believe for an instant that he could have need of any assistance. What to say to that? Her Scandinavian and Lutheran ignorance or obduration are invincible. The moment, moreover, is hardly favorable. At three paces away, on a settee, the poor little orphan girl of two years of age sleeps. The sight of that little innocent, doomed to a homicidal education, tightens my heart and I exit overwhelmed

with sadness, with the sensation of [wearing] a coat of ice.

5. – Last night, extraordinary dream. It seems to me that I am king and that it is the time of my coronation. Then I am conflicted, telling myself that it would be better if someone helped me to pay our grocer. That is ridiculous or appears to be. However, my feelings were strong and profound, and those things must have a meaning. But how to make sense of what happens in dreams?

6. – Gloomy and cold day. Renewed sensation of our interminable misery. How greatly this sorrowful life resembles what is said of Purgatory! Privation of the sight of God. Desire, never satisfied and more and more vehement, for infinite Beauty. But who suffers with us not to see God?

Finished the new novel by Wells, *The First Men on the Moon*. He is a Jules Verne *writer*, that is to say a monster. Anglo-Saxon atheism. That man gives the impression of someone writing from the bottom of a well. All the same, that book, very inferior in terms of inventiveness compared to *The War of the Worlds*, has nothing of the capital, primatial, and transcendental abomination of *The Island of Dr. Moreau*, one of the darkest of atrocious books, wherein the Demon himself seems defamed.

9. – Véronique returns from school so suffering that she must go to bed immediately. The woman religious who teaches her class is an idiot, incapable of seeing what all her little comrades saw. She is contented with telling her to go take some air for a moment, that is to say *fog*. We were told that in the case of emergency we would have the resource of entrusting our children to that house. Poor Véronique would not come out alive.

10. – While Véronique has a fever and delirium, and while we are on the verge of being short of everything at home, I read, as best I can, the *Histoire de Bossuet*, by the cardinal de Bausset. Mediocre book that rejuvenated me by two hundred fifty years.

14. – The women religious of Saint-Joseph, informed, after four days, of Véronique's illness, have not made one move to visit. If we were rich they would have come every day, and if they thought us to be millionaires, the mother superior would come in person.

17. – Apropos of automobiles and electric trains, Jeanne points out to me that modern inventions tend more and more to give men the means to *run away*.

19. – Saint Élisabeth. God have pity on the poor little Élisabeth de Groux, if she is still alive! Will we never see that poor child, our goddaughter, again, whom her

horrible parents have so harshly separated from us? Exceptionally painful day. That torment of black poverty which lasts since the Second Empire begins to be stronger than me.

21. – The greater part of the bourgeoisie die without confessing because they would need to *restitute*, a necessary consequence that terrifies decent folk primarily. Such is the profound reason. The curates know it well. In this case, one can strictly apply the evangelical story of the young rich man to the moribund. *Abiit tristis.* There is a detestable article by Paul Adam that reminds me of it. (See my *Exegesis of Commonplaces*, page 226. *One must not see things too negatively.*)

24. *Histoire de Bossuet*, 2nd vol. Assembly of 1682. Frightening mediocrity of the great man.

25. – Feast Day of Saint Catherine at the convent of Saint-Joseph. The pupils have fun, but it is not for free. The good mothers are very attentive to collecting the money.

27. – Here is, I believe, an absolute law: Inferiors always *protect* their superiors.

To a person who is indignant to learn that we have rented a small garden for the spring:

Know that I am the holder of a life annuity of 15 francs per year with a pension fund, having been in '77 and '78 a commissioned employee of the Northern Railway Company. The compounded interest of deductions over the course of several months having finished by forming at the end of twenty-three years a small capital, the State takes its share and I ought to consider myself happy for not having lost everything.

So those 15 francs will be employed to pay two-thirds of the annual rent of a small piece of uncultivated land, but in the shade of half a dozen large trees. We suffered so much, last summer, to see our little girls deprived of a garden. At all times, even in Denmark, even in periods of our worst poverty, we have always had a garden, not for cultivating legumes, but for sowing some flowers. We need it. That is necessary to us, you have to understand me, not only for the health of our children, but for the health of our souls which would perish for disgust and horror if they were to be deprived of it. Sometimes we have paid too dearly for it. Today, it pleases God to give it to us for nearly free. Why would we not take advantage of it?

December

1ˢᵗ. – 1ˢᵗ Sunday of Advent. *Hora est jam nos de som-no surgere*,[29] says the epistle of the day. It is exactly the opposite for me. I sleep in poverty.

6. – Saint Nicolas and the little dead children, and my immutable distress, and my captivity which has no end, and all the tortures of my life! I weep and I hope.

10. – To Rachilde informed by Martineau's booklet, *Un Vivant et deux Morts*, of Henry de Groux' terrible act, over eighteen months ago, and who is surprised by it:

> *You cannot be more "flabbergasted" than I was by the story of Henry de Groux. I thought at first that he had gone mad, and I am still of a mind to believe it. When you think that three or four hours earlier he had spoken to me with* the most tender affection *and in complete confidence...*
>
> *Mysteriously, that poor wretch has become my enemy* instantaneously *and my enraged enemy, to the point of threatening to* kill *me by signed letter. His rage, nonetheless, is not exempt of villainy, given, as I wrote to Julien*

---

[29]*Hora... surgere*: Latin for "It is time for us to rise from our sleep."

Leclercq in the letter that you read, he refuses to offer any explanation, insinuating thus whatever one wants. With the atrocious reputation that I benefit from, you can see where that leads. If though there is some madness in his case, it is certainly not a very innocent nor very sympathetic madness. As I know that there is wrapped up in it, moreover, much of Dreyfus, much of Zola, much sex, much absinthe, you will not find it surprising that I found refuge in contempt, after having greatly suffered. Would you believe, Rachilde, that he had gotten to the point of suspecting that I was dedicating myself to religious practices in order to keep Dreyfus on Devil's Island!

... It is clear that you almost never see him. Otherwise, you would have doubtless noticed the rapid and lamentable instability that the Dreyfus affair has caused in him. To think that he has painted a Zola aux outrages!!![30] *Yes, Rachilde, he did that!*

16. – Threat of expulsion of our women religious of Saint-Joseph. It all depends on a municipal vote that

---

[30]*Zola aux outrages*: Henry de Groux' most famous painting was, perhaps, from when he was in his early 20s: *Le Christ aux outrages*. More on it and de Groux' relationship with the Bloys can be found in Bloy's first journal.

will soon be known. It appears that the municipal council, which could be nothing but imbeciles, is here mixed with a lot of scoundrels and that anything is to be feared. In the case of expulsion, what will become of us! It is for Véronique alone that we have remained here. That threat, added to all the rest, succeeds in overwhelming me.

18. – Nobel Prize (200,000 francs) is awarded to Sully-Prudhomme, who is envisaged by the academicians of Stockholm, desalinated Lutherans and perspicacious moralists, as a worker of the "most beautiful idealistic work." Patriotism in person is forced to agree, even in Paris, one cannot be any stupider than that. The happy victor has declared his intention of employing that sum to come to the aid of poor poets, without keeping a cent of it. (*Idealistic* joke, the derision of which did not take long to break out.)

23. – The reading that is done at home, for a month now, of the history of Christopher Columbus, compels me to modify some of my old ideas. Isabelle, whom I praised in *The Revealer of the Globe*, disgusts me today, and the abject praises by Roselly, when he speaks about that princess, make me want to vomit.

What a misfortune to write *definitive* books, when one does not have experience!

24. – Despite Noel, I have an ankylosed, rusted, un-

moving soul. I am like an old clock full of dust.

25. – Darkness of Night, darkness of Dawn, darkness of Day. Infinite desolation.

26. – Letter from Joergensen who hardly ever writes to me anymore. This time, apropos of the *Mercure de France*: "... And then the intellectualism of Remy de Gourmont. It is completely atrocious. He says things that make me tremble, as if at the edge of an abyss of malice!"

Henri Fouquier, one of those lambasted in *The Desperate Man* (Nestor de Tinville), has just given up his good ghost: "He is dead," said the *Figaro*, "with a faint smile." – This is so ignoble that it must be true, said Barbey d'Aurevilly to me one day, apropos of another bit of muck.

30. – A more-than-painful day.... Has it ever happened to me that I was so miserable and in a way that appeared so dangerous? There is a tightening of the brain, a suffocation of the soul! Frightening state. That, without any new cause of affliction and even, one might think, with consoling news. I should consider myself *delivered* and yet I ask myself if it is not too late, if an irreparable blow has not been made. What is certain is that everything I could say of my suffering is miserably short of the truth.

1902

> *The damned have no other refreshment, in their pit of*
> *tortures, than the vision of the terrifying faces of*
> *demons. The friends of Jesus see modern Christians*
> *around them, and it is thus that they can conceive of*
> *hell.*

January

2. – Finished reading *Histoire de Bossuet.* Complete disgust. What to think of that "Church father," as the historian qualifies him, who dies without repentance after having troubled the Church for a century, having by his own authority condemned, like a criminal error, pontifical Infallibility which was bound to become Dogma one day?

5. – When any event happens, if one could contain in a single look the infinite multitude of the concomitant gestures of Providence, and if one saw, as if in a ray of lightning, with what intelligence and marvelous docility all facts correspond and rush forward, tripping over themselves, *one would understand everything*, and the dazzlement of the mind would be little different from beatific ecstasy.

6. – Epiphany. When we have so great a joy in the discovery of, or rather in the meeting up with, a di-

vine verity, what exactly is the cause of that joy? – It is that we feel, on that occasion, that *three make one* and that the basis of all natural and supernatural joy is contained therein. All truth is this: *three in one*, and there is no other truth. This is what Jeanne received this morning from the holy *kings* of Kings.

In the same way, with respect to one of our friends who believes himself a Christian: "It is nothing to die with Jesus, it is following him that is difficult."

7. – Woke up at midnight by a bell tower that seemed to be sounding the Angelus, I get up very tired and full of sleep, understanding that one must obey. The prayer of a sleeper for "sleepers."

8. Better spiritual state. My extreme difficulty of speaking to God, these last few days, diminishes. My soul paralyzed by grief and retired into its darkest cave begins to exit.

14. – *Exegesis of Commonplaces*. For the nearly eight months that I have been working on it, and it is time that I wrap up the book. It has been the most difficult of all, and the one that cost me the most. But I am far from having finished, and my fatigue is great.

17. – Dangerous overworking of Véronique at school.

I am forced to complain energetically.

I learn with stupefaction that Leon XIII has just instituted a commission charged with studying the *Question of divine inspiration* in the Holy Books. Why not the QUESTION of Christianity's Divinity?

Peter's three denials prior to the crowing of the Coq, in other words prior to the Redemption, must have prefigured the three denials of the Papacy which are the undivulged story of the Church Militant until the final advent of the Holy Ghost. I have often wondered whether we had not come to the Third Denial and whether the Coq of France was not going to crow!...

19. – Feast day of Saint Furcy, the inconsolable apostle of Cochons-sur-Marne. Translation of relics from an old reliquary into a new one. Act which will be done publicly this afternoon. But the deacon cannot do without ridicule, even in circumstances where ridicule could not be produced except by a miracle. So, this morning, announcing the ceremony, he said this: "After vespers, *opening of the reliquary...*" then he hesitated an instant.[31]

20. – To a faithful admirer:

My dear friend,

I am ill and extremely sad. Fearing to

---

[31]Opening of the reliquary: the phrase in French could also mean "opening of hunting season."

see a last illusion disappear, I didn't dare ask myself about the result of your endeavors. There is no getting around it however and the illness has gotten to the point that anything is preferable to incertitude. My illusion or, if you will, my hope is moreover a very weak plant sprouted in the cave of anguish. Since the first day, it appeared to me unheard-of that a man like him whom you know could be interested in me. But I was thinking at the same time that your efforts could be blessed. Tell me plainly, brutally. I have endured so many cruel operations in my life!...

22. – The *Times* publishes a letter by Sully-Prud-homme, the recent Nobel Prize winner, informing people that he reserves for himself the right to employ the prize money that he obtained "according to his conscience. " No doubt. When a Protestant or a philosopher speaks about his conscience, one can be sure that he will not do anything.

A young Champion sends me a copy of *Le Tombeau de Louis Ménard*. I knew, thirty years ago or so, a Louis Menard, prolific and virtuous physician, protected by the good fathers of the Assumption, who distanced himself from me splendidly as soon as he had discovered that I didn't earn any money, but this is not him. Response to the sender of the *Tombeau*:

When you wrote to me a year ago to ask my opinion on the works of your Louis Ménard, I could not make any other remark than that of Royer Collard to de Vigny. I knew absolutely nothing about him. Even today, I know merely several verses by that poet which I have just read in your little book, and that is certainly not anything that would whet my appetite. Olympus, Stoicism, and filth, thanks! "He was sordid and rich," wrote my old comrade Haraucourt. Figuratively as well as literally, that suffices for me. Ah, yes, and how!

Moreover, he looked the part. Impossible to find a more antipathetic physiognomy. Look at your heliogravure. He is a pawnbroker with the symbolic frog leg in the corner of his eye. That man there has never known any pity. Then the "dear master" Barrès pushes me away, I dare say, as if with his hand.

Let's leave him there then, your poet, who must know at the present hour and at the time of his death whether it is true "... that a God can neither suffer nor die."

23. – Sufferance for not seeing my deliverance com-

ing, for my prayers not being granted. Strange sorrow for finding God very little faithful in his promises, or rather not giving any visible fulfillment to certain signs come from him and which seemed like true promises to us. I recall strange deceptions. I have the honor of being treated like Saint Bernard to whom God inflicted the humanly insupportable test of the fiasco of the Second Crusade, after having certified success to him. It is true that Saint Bernard had committed a big mistake (See *The Ungrateful Beggar*, p. 400.)

25. – Our housemaid on learning that Véronique has chicken pox immediately beats it with an impetuosity of churlishness that discourages our admiration. To be honest, she takes our last sous with her. We are ill, without resources, and perfectly alone... God loves me more than another, of course, as, for so many years now, he treats me thus, with extreme rigor. Tonight will be the seventh anniversary of the blessed death of our André.

26. – Sully-Prudhomme again. Three or four friends having written to that winner to know whether that [prize money] would induce him to prevent me of dying of hunger, he responded to one of them through a secretary by the name of *Bourgeois*. The Bellerophon of the Ideal has a secretary by that name. The response expresses the indignation of that recompensed academician upon seeing that the city and department I inhabit "don't do anything for me." The excellent

idealist would have me in the bureau of charity.

27. – To one of the imploring friends just mentioned:

> *… You do know, my dear Alexandre, that I would not wish, for fifty million [francs], to be in Sully-Prudhomme's shoes. That miserable poet loved by lukewarm and detested souls has been put by incommensurable goodness into a situation of redeeming his vain existence by applying a mass of gold,* which he did not earn, *to the noble works of mercy. Eh! well, that is something he absolutely does not want…*

We are acquainted with a sentimental and unappeasable oaf, one of those certain men who send a friend to the guillotine while saying to him, with tears in his eyes: "I did it for the best!"

February

1st – Insolence and villainy of our grocers, male and female. My word does not suffice those vermin, they need "guarantees." – It's a great misfortune, Barbey d'Aurevilly used to say to me, to live in an epoch in which one can no longer strike with a stick those who are beneath one.

3. – Thinking on the insufficiency of Balzac's study on the *Grocer* of his time, I search for a short-story idea that would allow me to paint ours, whose grotesqueness superabounds. Can I not, in addition, celebrate the serene leaden and ballasted hypocrisy with which they sacrilegiously rig out the Son of God and the Son of Man, sweating blood in Gethsemane?

4. – Very late mass because of a ridiculous patronage. There are some ladies, so-called of Providence, the high society of Cochons. Those individuals get together "to do good," as Coppée used to say. But unable to raise their carcasses early, everything runs late on days of reunion. The Deacon, naturally, is at their beck and call. They must not be fat, the poor assisted by those Christians!

5. – According to the *Journal*, Sully-Prudhomme simply founds an annual prize of 1,500 francs for young poets, to be awarded by the literary Society. And that is where the immense publicity of his immolation for the poor leads to. 1,500 francs is a quarter of the revenue of 200,000 at 3 percent, that is to say 4,500 francs of bene and capital, without prejudice to the reputation of a holocaust. Idealism is rather good business.

8. – Atrocious poverty. To a friend, speaking to him about our terrible life:

> *It is as if I was going in discovery of a*
> *new world, with a leak, a fire, illness,*
> *and famine on board. Happily, my*
> *poor crew does not revolt.*

9. – Quinquagesima Sunday. "*Manducaverunt et sat-*
urati sunt nimis..."[32] Letter from a very poor person
whom I did not ask anything from, and who sends me
ten francs.

12. – Ash Wednesday. Madeleine's great joy when
we told her that the priest will call her: *man*.

25. The convent of Saint-Joseph, Véronique's school,
appears more and more to us to be a factory, a manu-
factory, a refinery of virgins where the stupid women
religious create shop girls or future cashiers, exclusively. There is the pretty woman religious for the
battue[33] of pupils. They know us, or think they know
us, to be poor and they disdain us, as is right. I begin
to be unable to think of that house without feelings of
disgust and horror.

One is so prudent, so adjusted to the world,
among these female sellers of arithmetic and soup,
that Véronique will leave them without having re-

---

[32]*Manducaverunt...*: Latin for "They ate and were extremely
satisfied..." Psalms 77:29.

[33]*battue*: a hunting term; literally a "beating" of quarry [from
around the bush].

ceived a single one of those religious impressions that one can receive even in the most lay of households, when war is not openly declared on God. The poor child who prepares for her first communion has not even learnt a single canticle.

26. – Here I am finally seriously ill. My number one head cold, which does not go away and turns me into an idiot, announces itself. Pointless to add that we are sou-less.

Today is the hundredth anniversary of the birth of [Victor] Hugo. Great patriotic and literary parade. Hanotaux *gives* a discourse at the Pantheon!

27. – O the filth of the newspapers this morning! The story of yesterday's celebrations, the discourse by Gabriel at the Pantheon! What ridiculousness, and what a shame to think that there was not a *single* listener of that imbecile's speech doubtless who believed in Victor Hugo's "civic virtues" and that it would not have been possible to find among them twelve capable of citing one line of verse from the *Legend of the Centuries!* Hanotaux, roundly applauded, had the goodness to remark that in '85, Victor Hugo had been the occasion for closing down the Pantheon. "He had the doors opened again before him, in order to restore its glory." One way of expressing that that bastard had replaced the Holy Sacrament.

March

1st. – Serious letter to a Jesuit. I speak to him about his Company which is perhaps the religious society where a saint today would find the least number of hangmen. But on the subject of the depressing and mediocre distinction between the evangelical precept and counsel, I add this: "The Precept is given by the Second Person and the Counsel by the Third, the which are *One* with the First, in such a way that there is no means of escaping. *Estote perfecti.*"

4. – Visited a moribund in the neighborhood, a destitute worker who appeared to wish to see me, even though he did not know me. He has already refused one of the parish priests. I find him so exhausted, comatose, near death, that I cannot get through to him in any manner. His family, moreover, is atrocious. His wife to start with, later his daughter, said to me very firmly that, above all, I should not mention the word priest to him; that they knew and were respecting his opinions. The *opinions* of that dying man! That appeared to me the strangest of horrors. Jeanne told me that an important neighbor woman, learning that I had been to see that dying man, expressed the most naïve stupefaction, which really opens our eyes on the depths of soul of these bourgeois.

5. – End of *Exegesis of Commonplaces*. That work which cost me more than I could say, is completed amidst exceptional tribulation. Never have I seen my-

self more completely abandoned by men. *Never*, and yet...

6. With respect to the moribund who continues to agonize and refuses to see the priest, our housemaid, out of nowhere shows herself to be thoughtful. She said to us, with a satisfied look on her face, that there is not one dying person out of thirty who feels the need to call for a priest. This idiot expresses what everyone thinks. There are no more Christians.

7. – Read a horrible novel loaned to me by Randon and which I wanted to be familiar with because it passes for a masterpiece: *Bubu de Montparnasse;* author: Charles-Louis Philippe. Totally superior talent, to the point of giving one the sensation of *genius*, but what ignorance of God and what monstrous sentimentality replacing it! The reading of that book filled me with horror.

9. – Sermon by the Lenten missionary. Unbearable mediocrity. A need to toady to the audience: "I know that you assist the poor a great deal." That for the ladies of Providence or other groups of the same kind. What to do with such a cleric? That priest knows that he lies and perhaps believes his lie to be useful. It will serve at least to reassure the rich bourgeoisie who think about making alms by withdrawing one centime of a franc from their surplus.

While he was speaking, I imagined the choir of people dying of poverty saying: "You hear that man, Lord!"

10. – Jansenism continues to exist. The number is infinite of the so-called Catholics who do not know that quotidian communion is a rigorous consequence of the Lord's Prayer: *Panem quotidianum.*[34] Bizarre Christians who want nothing to do with it are forced to recommence, unbeknownst to themselves, the frightful Wickedness of Bethlehem. – I was a stranger, the Judge said to them, and *you did not give me hospitality.*

Our housemaid no longer shows up. Since we had taken the opportunity to speak our disdain for Godless people, that swine seems to have developed a hatred for us. The moribund of last week was interred on Saturday. One of the vicars came to find the body and, from our window, we saw the family in tears. Those tears and those prayers over that carrion of a renegade!

14. – This morning some young, pious girls gathered together at church, I do not know why, and sang canticles wherein heaven's impatience was expressed. I got the strong impression that not one of them had the desire nor even the hint of a desire to go to heaven. At the very instant when the refrain came around, I felt that the imagination of those virgins was filled with

---

[34] *Panem quotidianum*: Latin for "daily bread."

merchandise or filth and that only practical-minded and sentimental atheism was at the bottom of their hearts.

16. – I have such a disgust for the bourgeois people of this place that I come to fear going to the offices on Sunday where I am sure to encounter them. Sensation of being among *Scolopendra* and fleas.

17. Read the story of the miserable death of the Breton poet Quellien, nick-named *The Bard*, witness to my marriage, and my fickle friend for twelve years, crushed yesterday by an automobile. *Perhaps he was coming to see me*, and he will have taken the shortcut.

18. – Encountered, at the door to the convent, the famous mother Mary, the pretty woman of the house. That very ripe and beautiful face, judging it apropos to speak with me about Véronique, "one of the school's best pupils," she assures me, speaks to me incidentally about the *arithmetic* that that child is loaded down with. I respond that it is too much arithmetic for a girl whom we do not destine for commerce, but in whom, on the contrary, we strive to inspire contempt of it, given we want to make her a *Christian*... I leave her with that, without seeking to know the effect produced on that quasi superior of a house where the children are principally raised to become sales counter help.

19. – To my Jesuit about another Jesuit. It has to do with a father Milleriot, famous thirty years ago, who had turned me off from any project of retreat with the Jesuits, by speaking to me about money from the get-go:

> *I wanted to tell you this story because I had to explain certain thoughts to you, certain repugnances that have, in part, that origin and which I have never been able to completely get out of my system. I do not have the right to suppose that that father acted with harshness or villainy. People say quite beautiful things about him which I do not doubt. But, being used to blokes who did not resemble me in the least, he refused to pay me his attention and the consequences of that refusal have been such that I am authorized to blame him for a* homicidal *levity. The ill was great and irreparable. Several years later, in 1878, I actually went on a very long retreat at La Trappe, but the timing was wrong, the good moment had passed. I have the firm conviction that my entire life, for nearly thirty years, has been the* providential *consequence of that event. He who is not mistaken, as always, has extracted the good that I needed from a certain bad. It was necessary, doubtless, that I*

was put aside, completely isolated, that I did not receive any help from men. Otherwise, how could I have written The Desperate Man, *and* The Woman Who Was Poor, *and above all,* The Ungrateful Beggar, *considered by some as a unique book in its genre?...*

27. – To the same person who asked me for an explanation of the dedication of *Je M'Accuse* to Mirbeau...:

Nobody detests more than me the impiety of Mirbeau, author of several absolutely unpardonable books. That furious impiety, maintained and exasperated by a sort of rage against the sixth commandment, took into its service – while paying excessively dear for it – a militia or Varangian Guard of the most invincible commonplaces. Anticlericalism wants it like that. One cannot attack the Church except on all fours and while putting on a hideous face. You see what my sentiments can be.

But man is a complicated animal. That man, depraved as much as can be, does not lack generosity however and he sometimes has, in matters of art, a magnanimous clairvoyance. On the appearance of The Woman Who Was Poor, *that celebrated journalist whom I had never seen nor implored, wrote an article full of enthusiasm and* imposed *it* on *the* Journal *where I am detested. That article did not procure the success of the book, and there you have a bizarrerie added to many others, for that was a charge of the calvary fundamentally, executed with the most dazzling bravura, which should have, it seemed, swept away all resistances. To be honest, the Enemy wanted it to take place on the day of the Grand Prix, one of the days of the year when nobody reads anything.*

After that, be careful not to believe that the dedication, which surprises you, was a result of my gratitude. On the contrary, it is ironic. The Parisian literary world was not mistaken about it. But when one does not belong to that world, outside of which is salvation evidently, how to know, for example, that Mirbeau in '99 greeted the appearance of Fecundity, *that dirty novel by Zola, analyzed in* Je M'Accuse..., *with a prodigious article wherein the Cretin, I no longer say "of the Pyrenees," but instead of all mountain chains, was called a God (!) decidedly and resolutely?*

Immediately, and as if by a miracle, that publicity erased in me all affec-

*tionate memory of the article he wrote
on* The Woman Who Was Poor. *It
seemed to me even that that would in-
volve some prostitution if I reveled in
it, and as I was writing precisely day
after day the pamphlet against Zola
and his vile* Gospels, *the dedication
fell of its own out of my quill like a
drop of too-heavy ink...*

Dialog on the threshold of the church:

"How does it happen, Madame Bloy," said a
notions dealer, "that we never see you decorating the
altars, as all these ladies do?"

"It's because I'm not worthy."

"How can you say that? You, so pious a person, whom one sees every day at church!"

"It is you, madame, who is pious, because one
only meets you on Sunday, which proves that you
have need of God only one time a week. But we others, who have need of him every day, we are evidently riffraff."

Response to an imbecile, dictated to a benevolent secretary:

*... Léon Bloy, happy to learn that he is
your "confrere," is afflicted nevertheless to see that you have not read him.*
The Desperate Man *and* Léon Bloy
Before the Swine *say completely what
he thinks about dueling. He charged*

me with giving a response, according to his very ancient and very fortified conviction, to your two questions:

1. Dueling is a stupidity invented by bad actors;

2. In matters of honor, the only true and decisive response is several kicks in the ass.

Please receive the assurance of my confraternal sentiments.

Read several chapters by Mary of Agreda on the Passion. O the shining, the supernatural resplendence of the hurled at and slapped Face of Jesus Christ.

29. – Divine Office of Holy Saturday. Noticed this bizarreness that our deacon, so mediocre otherwise, gives to ceremonies, to liturgical forms. He read, without omitting one line, the Twelve Prophesies, each of which the curates of Paris generally limit themselves to reading the first verses of. Let us glorify this poor man.

April

1. – Thinking of the priests here, we deplore both our solitude and the vanity of hoping for sacerdotal assistance. In Cochons-sur-Marne, the act of going to find

a priest to speak with about God would be looked on as an act of dementia. How to dream of a friendship with one of those truly "useless" servants, dreadfully useless, who never come to see us and who are not interested in our souls?

With respect to the commonplace: "You cannot take it with you," I'm told of a woman in the countryside who insisted, on her deathbed, that someone put a 20-franc coin in her coffin.

3. – Terrible suicide of Dubut de Laforest, the sottish serial writer and corrupter of morals. He threw himself from the fourth- or fifth-story window, having carefully concealed his intent, exactly as if the miserable wretch had been precipitated by a devil. I vaguely recall that individual, in the past, at the *Chat Noir* cabaret... What an ignoble death! There would not have been enough windows in Paris nor the suburbs if every time life seemed insupportable to me I had decided I had had enough.

4. – According to a talkative seamstress, the bourgeois of this town, more or less without exception, would be criminals and evildoers. Adultery, incest, sacrilege and parricide would be their ordinary practices, to say nothing about their lesser horrors. Of course, I am disposed to believe all sorts of evil by the bourgeois, but I do not grant them so much style.

This morning, the Friday after Easter, the vicar who celebrated the mass at 7 o'clock, read yesterday's imperturbably. At communion and after communion, he picked up on today's prayers however. So he had noticed his mistake then, without apparent affliction, for he axed large portions of the Gospel in a sort of heroic fit, driven, one might say, by fanfare. The truth is that he is a musician and a cyclist. Such is our clergy. Whom to complain to? I would be taken for a bother, for an unsupportable arrogant person, for an enemy of the Church, and that would be absolutely all.

6. – Quasimodo Sunday. The deacon, giving a speech to his parishioners to exhort the latecomers as to their paschal duty, began with these words: "I would like you to note the *charming comparison* that the apostle *Saint Paul* offers us on this day: QUASIMODO GENITI, etc." It is universally known that that text belongs to the apostle Saint Peter. And there we have it, what is completely *charming*.

To Otto Friedrichs, the celebrated historian of Louis XVII, who writes to me that a path will be cut through the cemetery of Delft where Naundorff is interred, but that they will leave his tomb as a kind of protestation:

> *I think that they will not commit such stupidity to a monument over that deplorable dust. The "indignant protestation" that you mention would be quite eloquent otherwise, with that poor, completely bare tile, that lugubrious Calvinist tile, without a*

cross, with only the terrifying and phantasmic name of Louis XVII on it.

8. – Enormous work correcting the proofs for the *Exegesis*. I have high hopes for this book which is indisputably the most original I have done.

13. – The gospel of the Good Shepherd which is read at High Mass for the instruction of the pretty flock made me think bitterly of our priests. I heard rising from the bottom of my well, saying to our deacon: *Mercenarius es et non pertinet ad te de ovibus.*[35] For a year now that we are his most exact parishioners, he has visited us once at home. Ah! if he thought we were rich!...

Apropos of a misunderstanding that made us suffer considerably, Jeanne said to me:

"While two men full of loyalty and nobility are speaking of money, a *third* presents himself immediately to mislead them, to change their views, to denature their feelings. If it is to the letter that that comes to pass, the two men are absolutely in the hands of that invisible person."

14. – Confidences made to my Jesuit:

... Véronique's first communion fixed

---

[35]*Mercenarius...*: From John 10:13 of the Vulgate. Latin for "he is an hireling, and careth not for the sheep" (KJV).

for May 8, the Day of Ascension... You must think, my dear Paul, that the approach of such a day would move my heart, but I am afraid that that unique and extremely pure joy will be empoisoned. The truth is that we are in the hands of thieves...

I have spoken to you about the women religious and their carrots. The methodical extracting of small sums from the pupils, under a thousand pretexts and from start to end of the year, fills me with horror. The detailed breakdown, besides, is grotesque...

As for the parish deacon of our unmentionable location, he is a remarkable caster of nets. He passes for one of the most curious units of this clergy of the diocese of Meaux whose reputation is already established. I am told he sets up two or three works *per month, uniquely in order to bring people together in the sacristy, whose* door he closes by key, *and* slaps *them with a vigorous hand. What to think of a priest who gives rise to such gossip? I have never been convoked. He distrusts me, knowing me to be a writer and not easy to manipulate. Then again, I take communion every day,* the only one *of all the males in the parish, which is an unheard-of scan-*

dal. I pass for an extremely dangerous man.

One is informed in advance that each child, according to usage, is expected, in good conscience, to make a "gift" to that worthy pastor, so that it is a question of knowing whether a poor child who had nothing to give would be admitted to her first communion. I think we will have the honor of being taxed 20 francs at least. The women religious exact that sum, merely for the candles that do not cost more than 3 francs at the most rapacious of grocers... Our Véronique is pious and well prepared. I really do hope that those vile souls don't splatter her white dress with their rottenness.

16. – This morning, Saint *Fructueux*, so says rather ridiculously the [liturgical] calendar of my agenda. We needed to take, from the little that remains to us, 5 francs for the feast of the superior who is called mother Isidore (!!?) We have consented to that injustice, only so that our poor Véronique be not oppressed, humiliated, outraged perhaps.

16. – I am extremely sad. This morning, at mass, at communion, all the sufferings of my life passed before my eyes. I prayed to Mary to make that enor-

mous mass a marvelous benediction for our children and in particular for Véronique.

Jeanne having let the portress-sister of the convent see several good pages from the *Exegesis*, this latter reflected for a minute, then put forward this admirable question: *Is it approved?*

22. – The Body of Jesus Christ! What is that flame that traverses sometimes the heart, *nemo sciens unde veniat aut quo vadat?*[36]

23. – There will be in the next few days, the 27th I believe, a celebration at Véronique's school, for the fiftieth anniversary of the founding of the Order. On this occasion they have decided to ham it up. It is for that even that they ask 5 francs to participate. They will enact ridiculous comedies in the large hall above the chapel. I learn that they have hired workers to shore up the ceiling of that chapel. They are afraid lest it collapse under the weight of the multitude. The memory of the Charity Bazaar makes us decide not to send Véronique, this sort of divertissement, in a religious house, not appearing to us of a nature to make benedictions rain down.

24. – Véronique's teacher reads to her pupils *the list of girls having brought five francs*! Enormous.

---

[36]*Nemo...*: a slight adaptation from John 3:8. Latin for "Nobody knows whence it comes or whither it goes?"

25. – Saint Mark. Gospel teaching at mass: *Si ibi fuerit filius pacis.*[37] Nothing simpler than the moral interpretation of that Text. But the *other* interpretation, what a gulf!

26. – Our Lady of Good Counsel. Observed that the little swarthy vicar who says mass, and who has always disgusted me by his manner of dodging two thirds of the Last Gospel, has very strangely omitted the last two words, *boni consilii,*[38] which are spoken today in the Introit and at Postcommunion. All the rest was pronounced clearly, and I had my ears cocked. What would be the point of asking him what that omission means?

27. – Véronique attends, at the convent, a *rehearsal* of the play that is scheduled to be put on in two days. I accompany her to the door and with what emotion! The absence of faith among those who make a profession of a superior life, priests and women religious, and the thick unintelligence of everyone here, would it not be contagious? Something seen by Véronique. The play was a stupidity, absolutely second-rate when one saw Joseph sold by his brothers. *Jacob was represented by a girl wearing a* BEARD! At the end of the performance, she went to embrace, still wearing her beard, the superior, a foolish and base profanation

---

[37] *Si...*: Luke 10:6.

[38] Boni consilii: Latin for "good counsel(s)."

that gave rise to a delirious elation.

29. – Instead of attending the idiotic masquerade where the girls are disguised as patriarchs, Véronique visits Martyrs Hall, at the Foreign Missions seminary in Paris, with her mother; better preparation, doubtless, for the ceremony she'll take part in in one week.

May

1st. – To a certain ridiculous doctor who speaks only about vaccinations, serums, modern science, and Pasteur whom he believes to be a God: "Your scientific arguments or objections find me speechless, as I have not studied physiology and am very ignorant about it. But I know intuitively, I *see* that you are mistaken, that Pasteur was mistaken, and that your luminous path leads to dark abysses."

5. – A poor man, affectionate and devoted but disgraced by a caruncle, wrote some inane phrases on the occasion of Véronique's, henceforth so close, first communion. Several lines from my response:

> *Véronique is not an "angel of light,"*
> *but a poor little girl on whom weighs*
> *six thousand years of disobedience,*
> *who prepares, trembling, for an ex-*
> *tremely redoubtable act on which her*
> *life depends and who has a most inex-*

pressible need for prayers...

This morning, Jeanne ran into the mother Mary, the pretty woman religious who recommended to her with importance that she *pray for Véronique*.

7. – I know a so-called Christian mother, creature lacking any sort of spitefulness, able even to pass for a very good person, but sentimental, cramful of commonplaces, like a turkey stuffed with chestnuts, but capable of doing ANYTHING to avoid the *supernatural*. The abjection of those thoughts is frightening. An angel would renounce throwing light into that gulf.

8. – Ascension Day. With the emotion that God knows, I have seen my Véronique receive Jesus for the first time. Dear and beloved child! I did what I could, all that I could, in truth... The poor girl would have had need of meditation and peace. Having chosen to ask for alms at the church door, she only just collects fifteen francs, a considerable sum for the charity of this parish. Total, 25 francs, with what we put in the bottom of that purse. The ladies of Providence will be able to afford their garters. They can even offer a pair of them to Monsieur the Deacon. That thought fortifies me.

In the afternoon, confirmation. From the same location as this morning, I see Véronique at the moment when the bishop confers on her the Holy Ghost. May God hear me and may he fill this child of my sorrow with benedictions, at whatever price it takes for me to pay for the blessing! Such was this day of eternity – "the most beautiful day of my life" – to employ the famous commonplace that we have been served up on all sides for the last twenty-four hours.

9. – Mass of thanksgiving. Melancholic allocution by the deacon predicting that before too long his first communicants will have dropped everything.

Of course, but whose fault is that? Rigorously and absolutely, the faithful are worth what the pastors are worth. "The holy clergy make the people virtuous," said a great philosopher; "the virtuous clergy make the people honest; the honest clergy make the people impious." I have often cited this admirable foreshortening of contemporary history. But where is the curate, even the deacon, capable of understanding it?

10. – First news of the immense catastrophe in Martinique. Thirty thousand dead in several seconds, *at the precise hour of Véronique's first communion!* As chance does not exist, that extermination was indispensable in order for there to be a counterbalance, in the infallible Hand, to our child's prodigious act. Not one victim less was needed for that innocent, and the volcano, for centuries, waited for its signal.

11. – Mass atrociously celebrated by the aforementioned abbot Galette, whose indisputable merit, peo-

ple assure me, is to know about finance and even the lowest type of finance, like a stockbroker or a buyer of IOUs from the Mont-de-Piété. I would willingly offer a reward to the man who would tell me why the Deacon suffers that miserable man in his church.

Continuation of emotion with respect to Saint-Pierre Martinique. Read this: "Among the vessels at harbor, and almost all of which perished, there was an Italian one with this extraordinary name: *Sacred Heart of Pompei!!!*" God knows what he is doing.

12. – Bizarre visit by an old man accompanied by a young woman, his daughter, and a child. Those strangers apprise me that they are Belgian and that they come hoping to obtain from us information on the child of Apollon's whom we lodged. I understand that the latter, reduced to desperate straits, has laid hands on a rich woman, a theater director (?) whom he would have made believe that he is a great poet and a great prophet. He would have stood proudly before her as an apostle, as a *Biblical exegete* (!), and that idiot woman, as unknowledgeable about any religious notion as any literary discernment, would have been dazzled and subdued to the point of being unable to do without that companion who lived with her lavishly, the better to instruct her. He has her wearing scapulars, consoles her (she is divorced), and makes her glimpse the delights that a union of their sister souls would procure, in other words in marriage, after that man of God will have obtained a divorce from his current wife!!!

My visitor, who says he is the father of that nutcase, and his other daughter come with him are sure that our poet's overweight wife is an accomplice of her husband in that manœuvre of captation, as they simulate incompatibility or hatred, and that they really want a divorce in order to secure that monstrous marriage which would put a great deal of money in their hands. Almost incredible story and I barely understand. It is a passably suspect mixture of rudimentary wickedness, hypocrisy, and profound stupidity.

Truth be told we have the means not to believe a word of this serialized novel. Our visitors act like they are being served our heads, rather awkwardly. They declare – with an evident bad faith and a very false indignation, – to have hoped [to obtain] from us I do not know what revelation that would have served to enlighten that exploited person by unmasking the exploiter. The curious insufficiency of the explanation warns us to keep up our guard and not to forget to *fasten the security chain on our door*. I dismissed that riffraff assuring them of my most distinguished sentiments.

13. – Saint-Pierre again. Véronique, without a doubt, will later hear about that terrible event and about the extraordinary coincidence, when she will know what *a soul* is worth and hers in particular. At the moment when she received the Nourishment which gives Live, others, a very great number of them, children like herself, died a terrible death *for her*.

Newspapers' typographical grievances are of

a completely normal and satisfying abjection. There is mention of "the planet's caprices," of the volcano's "brutal anger," and some other things. Even among Christians, it is only a question of bodies, *never* souls.

14. – I cannot get over how inexpensive betrayal is and how always so humble, and so very low-priced, Judases are. The most hideous mediocrity costs absolutely nothing to anybody. Overheard a sickly-sweet Capuchin whose *sole* preoccupation appears to be pleasing the ladies.

The *Journal* publishes a miserable map of France and the colonies, giving an indication of the present political situation after recent elections. Almost everything is Republican with varying nuances. Among the *conservatives*, that is, I think, the Catholics or capitalists interested in maintaining the current order, I notice the second district of Martinique; *that of Saint-Pierre*. The deputy for Saint-Pierre was a CONSERVATIVE.

15. – The most heroic act on that day was the payment of a bill. The exegete of Commonplaces *honors his signature*. (See my book, p. 155.)

19. – Pentecost Monday. Funereal procession. A death that one of the vicars, the most virtuous doubtless, sought after. On the sill of the church, a large wreath placed on the ground and these incredible

words in glass beads: *Offered by the tenants!!!* The bier, moved difficultly by four men, seemed very heavy to me. Baneful presage. For the ten-thousandth time, we are taken for a ride by someone.

The "finger of God," it is the Holy Ghost, said the Venerable Mary of Agreda.

20. – Pentecost Tuesday. Twelfth anniversary of our marriage. Twelve years spent waiting for the mailman!

21. – Our curate – I want to say Deacon – who thinks of himself as a man of initiative, had the idea of a service for the stricken of Martinique. The mass, which I did not attend, was naturally followed by a collection. I would be curious to know the [requested] figure which should hardly exceed one hundred sous. I would not be surprised if that celestial man imagined shaking down his parishioners at home. In that case, I would respond that I give directly, *volcano notwithstanding*.

The stupidity of almost everyone is unprecedented and cannot be outdone except by universal infamy which disconcerts the imagination. Passing, this morning, before our butcher's shop, I heard these lofty words proffered from the back of the boutique: "One must be terribly imbecilic to go to mass."

The newspapers publish the numbers. They had collected nearly a million for Martinique. The unfortunate wretches will receive a fortieth of that maybe? I imagine the monetary assistance will go principally to some millionaires whose opulence has been more or less cut into by the volcano and who have need of *recuperating*. As for those dying of hunger, one will send them unsellable cod, rotting wheat, conserves in putrefaction, all the cast-offs and scraps from the warehouses in France or England. The suppliers will be swimming in joy and the tenant farmers of public Compassion will buy property situated at enormous distances from any crater.

22. – There is talk of a new indiscretion by the volcano. Question: Were crematory furnaces in use in Martinique? The eruptions would amount to this: You wanted to incinerate yourselves? Here you go.

Paris. Forced to pawn, for the twentieth time perhaps and with internal sobs, our marriage bands. When I was about to catch the train back home, obsessed by sad thoughts, I read the front page of the evening newspaper, in enormous characters: *Eruption of the Mont-de-Piété*. Naturally it had to do with *Mont Pelée*.

23. – To Georges Dupuis, Géo for short, already mentioned:

> *Rémond must have told you on my behalf that I would see you again with pleasure if you had the generosity of sparing me your frightful boorishness.*

While waiting for the effect of his approach, I imagine, wrongly or rightly, that you will be grateful to me for sharing with you that Véronique's first communion took place on May 8. The invisible Individuals who were witnesses with me to your abjuration and your first communion must have been saddened not to see you at that ceremony.

I add that we are in dire straits. Rémond having told us that you are fortunate at this time, I ask if you will absolutely not do anything for the poor who have done so much for you.

(No response.)

The *Journal* yesterday printed a letter by the wife of an industrialist, post-marked from Saint-Pierre and before May 8. She declares that they have "no idea what to eat" and that Martinique is a "satanic country." I will hold on to this monument of bourgeoise abjection. The sender must have perished. Would it have been possible, I ask it on my knees, to find in that country a single human being, clergy included, capable of thinking of the Justice of God? All *martyrs*, as at the Charity Bazaar.

24. – O the beautiful liturgy of Pentecost Saturday! *Spiritus ubi vult spirat...*[39] At the moment that the

---

[39] *Spiritus...*: Latin for "The Spirit blows where it will."

Lord of volcanoes manifests his wrath, those words strike my mind in a singular way and are not too far-away to move my heart deeply.

What is most repugnant to the bourgeois instinct is quotidian communion. The bourgeois eat *everything*, except God.

26. – Two beautiful things in the *Journal*:

1st. The text of a proclamation placarded in Saint-Pierre on the 7th (!) by order of the governor, which said that, *after scientific explanations*, "the security of Saint-Pierre was assured." It is the volcano which torched the placards. What a document that printed piece was, if only one could procure a copy!

2nd. An inconceivable article entitled: "Humbert-Daurignac Competition," containing a complete questionnaire on those crooks, unfindable to this day. There are 200 prizes for those who respond more or less correctly. It is a universal invitation to spying and informing. But in the there is the sum of 50 centimes that must accompany each competitor's mailing, without which one will not be allowed to participate. The total will be routed to the national committee of the ministry of the colonies to come to the aid of disaster victims of Martinique. I have never seen anything more beautiful.

Jeanne points out to me that the twentieth century begins in this way to take on a physiognomy, to constitute its proper physiognomy. We are, at the present hour, at the point of sentimental loutishness.

My soul is so distraught that I read some chapters by Montaigne.

27. – Having energetically dismissed a hussy in our service, I abandon myself to a meditation on bugs. It would be terrible to say or think, like the Manichaeans, that the devil was able to create anything. However, it is impossible to suppose bugs in earthly Paradise. They would be then, like so many other beasts or hideous and noxious plants, creatures particularly affected and *deformed* by the fall of man. See what Anne-Catherine Emmerich says about repugnant insects.

28. – Continuation, pure and simple, of enormous sadness. Nothing comes in, not even the hint of an expedient of any sort. Our poverty is crushing us. I spent the day as best I could, seeking assistance from Saint Paul and I don't know what others. Why does God not want to deliver us? That *Exegesis* which had given me hope and which does not appear! That miserable Dupuis whom my letter of the 23rd does not stir! So many other things, not to mention memories of the past that continue to return when one suffers and which are a hell of sorrows!

30. – To a man for whom God is dead:

> *I inform you that our friend Marche-*
> *noir succumbs. The anguish of these*
> *latter days can no longer be support-*

> *ed. He does not receive any news, any assistance, any sign of mercy. He barely eats, and when he does, weeping. His shakiness is such that he is at the point where he has a thirst for death, despairing to find a man and filled with the bitterness of this thought that certain people who have received the mission of* DELIVERING *him have disobeyed. I ask you then for a* consoling *dispatch for that miserable wretch, you understand me, a telegraphic dispatch. I would pay for it, as needed.*

31. – Requested dispatch: "Am with you." Alas! is he really with us? Is one with people so miserable?

June

2. – Post-scriptum of a letter to friends who wanted a picture of our poverty:

> *This letter costs our poor little children their morning meal, the leftovers of which we counted on for this evening. Effect of a too-great preoccupation. All is burnt and* irreplaceable. *Somber disaster, this ragout having been the object of a long and painful deliberation. Would that this detail enlighten you as to our panic and our*

distress which are something to sob
over.

3. – Lord, I weep too often.

Is this for the sadness of thinking of what I suffer?

Is it for the joy of recalling you?

How to untangle that and how not to weep in trying to untangle it?

4. – One believes in the reality of too many things. This diary is a proof of that to me. I consign here the least events with a meticulous attention. After a small amount of time has passed, I am surprised to have given so much importance to what contained so little. Events or incidents that had acted on my soul turn flat, are effaced at a certain distance, give the impression of returning to the nothingness from which they probably never exited. All that remains is what one did or suffered for God.

5. – Day without suffering, but pale and sad. One waits for your will, Lord! My thought is inert and my acts vain. After a lot of work, I have made a coarse table and two benches for our garden. We go there in the evening. The air is very pure at that height and the light of the setting sun seems gentle to us. After an hour or two, we half forget our difficulties.

6. – I would have need of 1,000 francs. I receive one hundred sous with the promise of a novena to Saint Anthony of Padua. It is how one becomes impious.

Procession in the convent's garden on the occasion of the Feast of the Sacred Heart. Jeanne conducts our dear little ones there in white dresses. Me, I stay home because of the ladies whom I prefer not to encounter. On sight of those pious and implacable bourgeoise women, I am plunged into hell's abyss. I go alone, to church, to sob in a dark corner.

7. – A dreadful secondhand goods dealer, judging my case to be desperate, pays me one hundred sous for a lot of old things that are not worth less than 200 francs.

8. – The *Journal* publishes the portraits of the new ministers: Combes, André, Pelletan, Trouillot... I do not think that the democratic, renegade, and Free-Mason villainy on the faces of those flunkeys, cretins, or bad actors can be exceeded. Such are our masters. At high mass this Sunday, listening to the organ, it seemed to me, as always, that I heard the infinite Battle of the cannons thundering, prefigured by all the battles of Napoleon, and which must precede the Consoler. What then will become of those miserable wretches?

10. – Words of a sorrowful soul: – I felt myself in the tenebræ, the terrifying and desperate tenebræ of the spirit. Every now and then, after waiting for an infinitely long period of time, the door half-opens just enough to let a hand enter, which throws a piece of bread in...

11. – Saint Barnabas. He is one of those from whom I have received a great deal. So great a personage that, by witness of the Holy Ghost (Act of the Apostles, 14:11), the inhabitants of Lystra in Lycaonia, believing him a God and the King of Gods, in human form, called him *Jupiter*, while his companion Saint Paul had to be content with being called *Mercury*. Surprising circumstance that seems not to have been noticed by anyone.

Barnabas, stunning apostle, prodigious in kindness, miracle of plenitude of the Holy Ghost, and of plenitude of the Faith, – deliver me.

Who believes in Prayer? To recite the *Pater* or the *Ave* or any other liturgical prayer, in whatever mood one might be, is like tossing a burning brand into a magazine of gunpowder. There are people who have been thunderstruck by their prayer.

Having been, this evening, at the cafe, to try, while reading papers, to forget for one hour my torment, I saw our old landlord pass, Le Bison of the cows, the old bull of the post office who afflicted us last year. Wearing a dirty cap, he walks like an old prefectural lancer in an immemorial pair of slacks worn for seven days straight, the bottoms of which hovering around the calves give the impression of a bulwark against the eventual artillery of the shoes striking the ground. Had there ever been a more hideous mask of a reprobate? O the abominable old man!

13. – A very poor and very ill man, an old librarian who hasn't even got the means to live, invents privations in order to send me now and again a small sum that I would not refuse without sending him into a fit of despair. Today, I receive a money order for ten francs. It is enough to make me cry. He declares that "his powerlessness to insure my material life kills him and has turned him, for a long time now, into an old man." His letter compared to certain friends who are less powerless has something of the supernatural about it.

Response to several questions:

> ... *You speak to me about Martinique and the Boers. My ideas about what happened at Saint-Pierre are little different from those expressed on the occasion of the fire at the Charity Bazaar (See* Mon Journal, *p. 52). You were able to read that in the booklet by Martineau. It is impossible for me not to execrate the wealthy who live solely for pleasure while not giving a damn for the poor, and it was the same in Saint-Pierre, city of delights and one of the most considerable ag-*

glomerations of slave-trading million-aires in the world.

As for the Boers, they have got, those Calvinists, exactly what they deserve. The idiocy of their donquixotism is huge and appears to have something infernal about it. When I think that those miserable wretches had England in the crux of their hands and let it escape; when I think of the unheard-of ascendant they could have taken if they had been men of the head and heart; when I recall their prisoners returned like so many bothers, when instead those fathers of family, whose women and children were murdered, ought to have, like Caesar, sent them back to England with their hands lopped off or their eyes gouged out like the Bulgar Slayer did; finally, when I see that triple extract of a sentimental cretin named Delarey giving an English general his freedom, without even thinking to demand in return for that pig head a single captive of his own nation, generosity for which he should have been punished with the death of a traitor; yes, of course, I am with you in concluding that detestable England has done well to walk all over that dungheap and crush that vermin!...

15. – *The Exegesis of Commonplaces* is on sale for three days now, and already I have lost all hope of its success. More than ever, I think that God does not want me to earn my living by my quill, that I receive in this way my recompense. He wants to act alone and leave nothing for men to do.

To someone:[40]

My dear friend, I ask you, for the love of God, not to speak to me about my book. I have spent my life, for nearly fifteen years now, hearing my praises sung, while I die in misery and fight against despair. I have had enough.

Dedication to our doctor: "To doctor N., the only doctor in Cochons who does not seem like an imbecile."

16. – Sizeable funeral. Sinister procession. Workers or peasants in their Sunday best can never be anything but grotesque. But the bourgeois, from the bourgeois stump! Ah! they are monsters of ugliness, of villainy, of cupidity, of stupidity, of infamy! The females above all. What a horror to stand in the midst of that vermin! The rain not allowing *thinkers* to stand outside in front of the church, as normally happens during funeral services, the nearby cafes had to

---

[40]Someone: Potentially René Martineau; see his "The Biography of Léon Bloy," wherein he mentions a similar story about this edition of Bloy's *Exegesis*.

receive them in large numbers. Of course, those were the most flagrant among them... I am dying of the need for Justice.

17. – Letter from a friend telling us angrily that he is doing everything that he can for us. One could simply respond to him: Why not *share* with us? But it has been a long time since that Hebrew was taught at school.

A money order that was announced three days ago does not arrive. Absolutely insupportable irony that one has no choice but to put up with. God requires us to move mountains and resuscitate necropoles.

> *There is only God and his saints who* assist, *Christians must share. A rich person can never be alone, as he is among the crowd of those who have assured him* of his daily bread. *Only misery isolates. Poverty groups men, misery isolates them, says Léon, for Poverty is from Jesus, and Misery is from the Holy Ghost.*

> *When everything is lacking, except threats and ignominy, there are moments when the breath is immediately cut short by indescribable anguish. Then one thinks of one's friends who are not in danger and one asks oneself: "All the same, how do they come to terms with it?"* – JEANNE

19. – Strange obsession with the idea of wealth, triumph, deliverance. No matter what I do, I cannot escape that dream. I see myself suddenly inundated with gold, acting finally like a free man, that is, as a master, for the service and glory of God, and seeing it come on its thousands of feet, the hideous multitude who would fawn on me finally.

Jan Lorentowicz wrote to me: "We others, the Polish, we are famished for the Absolute, and the word of Léon Bloy is particularly suggestive to us." If one was less unfortunate, that vote of confidence would bring more pleasure.

Read in the *Journal*, under the byline of Jean de Bonnefon, an article about an act of extraordinary malice and perfidy, apropos of a possessed person identified in a village in Aveyron. That hypocritical sophist, who voluntarily protests his respect for the Church and who wants to please the bitches and sons of bitches who consult him, decides that the possibility of possessions is in fact affirmed in the Gospel, but that one can always deny the particular cases. The infamy and baseness of that imposter has something surprising about it. He dares say, knowing the contrary, that possessions today are very rare cases. It is terrifying to think of all the poor so-called hysterical beings, countless numbers of them in the hospital, entrusted to the ghastly experiments of physicians, whom the charity of not a single priest would dare to assist.

20. – This extra-sorrowful week has taught us that in a case of grave danger we have nothing to hope for from humans.

Flashes of joy to be seen suffering.

The hours walk all over us with the feet of a bronze elephant.

22. – Monomotapa is located in Moravia. I have an inconceivable, extraordinary friend there, a very poor Czech who sends me a pint of his blood every time he supposes that I am about to die – *a wire of money*, o my admirers of France! It will be brought up at the Last Judgment.

23. – Card from our doctor thanking me for the copy of *Exegesis*. He spells my name "Bloix." Response:

> *On receiving your message, my dear doctor, I felt, once again, the emptiness of everything. Judge for yourself. About twenty-five years ago I began my life as a writer, a life which has been immensely difficult, having always preferred indigence and even discredit to the literary nastiness and prostitution that has led many of my old comrades to the Academy and Power. Eh, well, after a quarter of a century of often terrible suffering, I have not even obtained, at only 40*

> *kilometers from Paris, that an educat-*
> *ed man should know the four letters of*
> *my name!*

24. – Predilection of Napoleon for the imperfect sub-junctive.

25. – It is a rule without exception, since my distant youth, that I write long and important letters to which the response is several banal lines. It happens, I do not know how or why, that the first person to come along is always the one whose boots I have the duty of shining, respectfully.

26. – Horror of living in an epoch that is so cursed, so renegade that it is impossible to find a saint; I do not say a holy man, but a *saint*, healing the sick and re-suscitating the dead, to whom one might say: What does God want of me and what must I do?

28. – My dear André, several lines of response to your reproaches... Huysmans does not take pains to write the Truth, as you believe, but to Succeed, which is exactly the opposite. He seems to have never been able to sober up from the unexpected victory of *Là-Bas*, bad book that made him famous. From that day on, des Esseintes, haughty until then, began carefully to count his *print runs*. He understood finally the joy of shopkeepers who count the money in their register at the end of the day. From the strictly Catholic point

of view, his present profession is to throw bread to the dogs and to disgust souls. His previous profession, less lucrative, was preferable.

You speak to me about forgiveness. Being his judge, if not before men, at least before God, it is not up to me to forgive him. It is up to him to forgive me my misery which is, in large part, his doing and the famous rectitude of my feelings or my doctrines. But he will never do that.

(For people of goodwill who would find this judgment excessive, see the chapter on Huysmans in *Les Dernières Colonnes de l'Église*.)

The *Journal* has finally published an echo of three lines from *Exegesis,* echo paid for naturally by the publisher. What contemporary ignominy, that quasi impossibility of obtaining from newspapers merely the mention of a book without their requesting the salary of surgeons!

29. – Articles or correspondences touching on Martinique still continue. Evidence, greater each day, of a supernatural punishment. There are so many signs! I have collected all that I could, and I will keep this curious dossier in view of a future work. A certainly unexpected aspect in the history of these catastrophes is that not *a single* witness remained. Some individuals located at a more-or-less great distance saw something. But everyone who was alive in Saint-Pierre, man or beast, without exception, was killed in one minute.

July

2. – This day of the Visitation, I waited in vain until 10 o'clock in the evening for a certain visit. We are frightened by our suffering. For more than twelve hours, I have endured such a palpitation of the heart that anything would seem preferable to it to me. Henry Houssaye will never know that it was in such anguish that I read his very beautiful book, *1814*. When a soul is in torture, the things that one sees or that one reads make ravines in the memory. The historian of the Fall of the First Empire will never be forgotten. That agony of the power of Napoleon, seen thus, during my agony, is something terrible.

4. – I do not dare speak of my moments of awakening for some time now. That must be a pity for God and his saints to see a soul from the first hour of day suffering so much.

5. – One hangs on as best one can, but reason has been extinguished. One no longer sees. One is like an animal who moans, lying on the ground. This torture is really intolerable. If, at least, one had a sign, a feeble assistance, a word of kindness. Having gone to look for a soda siphon in the neighborhood, the old man who served me gave me a stem of a lily in bloom taken from a spray he had just cut in his garden. Those flowers were half withered, no matter. I had difficulty holding back the tears, because I had the illusion or evidence of an act of kindness.

6. – The introits from the last two Sundays express anguish. It is a cry to God for help. In the second particularly, the anguish is extreme: *Ad te, Domine, clamabo, Deus meus, ne sileas a me: nequando taceas a me et assimilabor descendentibus in lacum.*[41]

Today is the canticle of victory: *Jubilate Deo, in voce exultationis.* It is up to our hearts in agony to see in that our own mysterious story.

Found this in our mailbox: "Dear friends, here is a little money order on the part of a friend you have, but who cannot do all that he wants." Response:

> *I entreat you, please thank the person whom you speak of. I was on the verge of writing you to tell you that* it was all over. *The agony may last some time yet. You will be kept current.*

Today, national holiday, I do not know why. Enormous noise and universal drunkenness.

7. – Sent a copy of *Exegesis* to a colonel:

> *For my old friend L., these cheerful words by an artist dying of poverty, whose skin is torn off his backside after having been attentively scalped, and who is bound to be roasted over small faggots in several days.*

---

[41] *Ad te Domine...*: Psalms 27:1.

8. – A poet to whom I had made the same gift wrote to me that he was too drunk until now to be able to read properly what I had sent him.

9. – A famous individual, whom I will not name, is resolutely among those who want nothing whatsoever to do with the poor, receiving neither their visits, nor their letters, not even registered, as formerly the appalling Duchess de Galliera did, and as so many others do; – people whose door is inexorably closed to strangers, that is to say to God, so closed that when death comes, they themselves will be unable to unlock it in an attempt to escape.

To the secretary of the aforementioned individual who had one hundred francs sent to me:

> *I did not ask M. for a miserable alms, unworthy of him and me, and given without any tact. I made him the very honorable proposition of helping me to vanquish by means of important publicity the unjust and veritably homicidal silence that weighs, for so many years, on the author of some of the best books of our time, the which author searches for bread for him and his family at 56 years of age. It seems to me that that proposition had some grandeur and that it merited another response.*

Forbearance on the part of our landlord who

deigns to be patient. I am surprised. He is so old and he has so little time left to make people suffer!

10. – People ask of me what is not asked of anyone. They want me always to write about Léon Bloy. The day I write about Paul Bourget or Anatole France, they would say that I have gone senile. There are even some readers of meridional temperament who would certify that I write like a pig.

Despite everything, I cannot shake this thought, that old certitude that I must have my revenge on this world and that my drama, until now filled with darkness and sobs, must end with splendor. For more than twenty years, I count the days, *an unknown number of them*, which separate me from the great day when a powerfulness that I'm unaware of will be accorded to me. In the evening or in my sleep, I hear the call from deep places.

Also, what feelings didn't I experience reading a book like *1814*, which I just finished! From a completely superior point of view, Napoleon is the great Failure, the colossal Invalid. At a certain point, everything goes wrong for him with an immense crash, and he is no longer the man of any work, but the admirable instrument of the Prefiguration.

11. – Fifty-sixth anniversary of my amiable birth, according to the stars. Bizarre effect of my commencing old age. Several years ago, I could, entrenched behind a solid contempt, laugh at inattention or injustice. Not

today. I confess that I suffer in the end from so many infamies and that the daily reading of enthusiastic articles about books in which Our Lord Jesus Christ and his Mother are horribly outraged, without there being a single line about my own books, crushes me... Then again, there are souls for whom I earn bread, with infinite fatigue, and that bread of the poor, earned by a poor man, is intercepted by pigs. [Ernest] Hello died with this [same] dejection, but he had at least a very secure home and pittance – the possession of which things would seem to me like a foretaste of Paradise. I might add, with a strong desire to cry, that he certainly didn't have as much need for bread as I do, and that consequently there was less failure, less bitterness.

A statue of the Reverend Father Judas (Didon) in Arcueil has just been inaugurated. Speeches and merrymaking. It is surprising what advantages that must bring him *in loco suo*. Where then is Haceldama, and what happened to the good garbage of bygone days?

12. – Incredible document:

SAINT JOSEPH BOARDING SCHOOL

Under the Direction of

The Sisters of Saint-Joseph of Cluny

Cochons-sur-Marne, July 6, 1902

M.,

Given the immense mourning for Martinique which affects so great a number of families and our Congregation in particular, it seemed to us fitting not to give to the Distribution of Prizes its ordinary cachet (sic) of festivities; it will be deprived then.

The students are prepared unhesitatingly to renounce completely their prize books. The resultant sum of that difficult, but generous, sacrifice will go to disaster victims.

Please accept, M., the homage of our religious devotion.

– SISTER M. ISIDORE.

What to think about a distribution of prize money that will be "deprived," when no prizes will be given? What to think about the students "prepared to renounce completely their prizes," when not a single student has been consulted probably. Véronique knew nothing about it.

What to think about this lie, this hypocrisy, this inconceivable tactlessness? For a sordid economization, a rich congregation saddens the poor children and discontents two hundred families, when there are such menaces! As for the pretext of Martinique, it is truly shameful. But the injustice done to the children is certainly one of the most hideous aspects of this nastiness of the Devil. Poor Véronique who had worked so hard in the hope of that celebration! How many others? That decision is, moreover, so stupid that none of it makes any sense.

Noted on the occasion of a very small chastisement, the mysterious horror of the Devil for the *rod*, given it has, when children and even adults are involved, the power to put him to flight.

13. – A sort of friend, very sure about coming, is waited for seven trains in succession and does not come. It is in this way that I am treated by those who would qualify as my lowest domestics on the day after my success. "Certain people," says Father Faber, "must live in their souls as in magnificent caverns."

14. – So-called *national* holiday, anniversary of the victory of two hundred thousand men against four squads, victory followed by the murder of the prisoners on parole. Solemnity of cannibals now defunct. What a memory for me, that of the first July 14 in 1880! One week of national holiday. For seven days, nobody sobered up. This morning, my soul was completely bruised when thinking of the formidable suffering that was needed for me to get through these last twenty-two years, not to mention other griefs that had preceded that central period of my life around which I unwound my *Femme pauvre*, mirror of such great ag-

onies... I was thirty-four years old then and had im-
mersed myself in a supernatural splendor. My literary
life, is there any need to say it? had not even begun. Is
it over today, or how many years remain for me to
suffer still?

15. – To write to such a person and to hope for a response, whether it be a matter of mortal danger or not,
would be, on my part, an act of dementia. I am quite
certain that he made the vow never to respond to a
single one of my letters, under any circumstances.
And he is so faithful that nothing would bring him to
break that religious engagement. It is to the point that
if a billionaire obliged me to offer him, on both knees
and with hands joined, sixty million [francs] to meet
an impending due date of his, he would prefer to renounce it rather than write simply 'Yes' in response
to me. It is one of the most extraordinary *vocations* I
know.

The famous Belgian lawyer, mentioned previously, desires that we put our quarrel behind us, the
one from 1900 I believe, and I am having a hard time
remembering it. "There where your exceptional sum-
mit is," he wrote to me in his maternal tongue, "it
makes one forget the clouds encountered midway
up." It is a response worthy to be added to the *Exegesis*.

20. – Departure of the women religious of Saint-
Joseph, each day a little more probable. What a
hideous epoch and what a rabble governing France!

Truth be told, the victims, here or elsewhere, have really merited their fate! By victims I mean the men or women religious in general. There are others, the children, alas! on whose souls the atrocity of that persecution is borne. That there is a terrible mystery of pain and sorrow. *Everything revolves around the children.* It is impossible to commit a crime or consent to a turpitude, without immolating the children, without compromising the palace of heaven which they are the weakest columns of.

I no longer know how to express our misery, our solitude, our sadness. Prayer, reading, all is impossible.

For two days now, we purchase the *Authority*, a resolutely Catholic journal, the better to inform ourselves on the expulsions. What the Church suffers now is so much in harmony with what we suffer, and there were such promises for me, formerly, that I was led to believe in a near-future denouement of my destiny. My excessive tribulation concomitant to the Church's tribulation would be its prodrome. Ah! if one could understand what God understands, doubtless one would die of admiration. But understanding nothing, one dies despondent...

The *Authority* informs us that Combes,[42] the odious and imbecilic Freemason president of the Counsel, which deprives tens of thousands of children of religious instruction, is an old, defrocked deacon.

---

[42]Combes: Émile Justin Louis Combes (AD 1835-1901) who became minister of pubic education in 1895 and, as an anti-clerical Free Mason, was responsible for closing religious schools as part of an effort to separate Church and state.

The war on children! Such is the special character of the persecution of Judas, practiced in our time.

But what to think of a prime minister going humbly to receive, at the blow of a whistle, a cussing out or slaps by a dirty lout, a cobbler, or a cesspool emptier, and a bishop of the Freemasons who asks him, while treating him like a good-for-nothing, whether there were not any more children to eat!

21. – Our life is a monster of suffering. By dint of audacity, one subsists. But the pork butcher's wife and the pork butcher from whom I get our meals, treat me extremely poorly and I get the sensation, in their shop, of something very heavy in the air. It seems to me that there is something else than pork there.

My only resource in this agony has been the *History of the Crusades* by that old ass Michaud, re-read for the third time and henceforth as devoid of savourousness as rhinoceros blood pudding.

24. – Vallette informs me that the *Exegesis* is selling about as well as my other books. A thousand buyers in one year, very sure, very faithful clientele, but not growing. The publisher, neither losing or making money by me, publishes me for the look of it. I am an object of luxury, a bibelot.

The ancient hatred against the author of *The Desperate Man*, bequeathed by the dead to the supposed living whom I have never offended, has become invincible, inextirpable. In order to assure the success of my books, it would take the obstinate will of a millionaire, inflicting the most insolent and quotidian advertisement in public newspapers and on the walls of Paris.

25. – Feast of Saint Christopher, the Auxiliary Saint and Giant Martyr who died very particularly for me, 1652 years ago. At another period in which I am still unsure to what point he was my protector and without knowing too much what I was doing, I attempted to explain, apropos of Christopher Columbus, the extraordinary importance of that personage, above all from the prophetic point of view (See *The Revealer of the Globe*). Today I would have something altogether different to say...

What do the doctors think of the following simple story? Returning from Denmark in 1900, we spent a night in Cologne, several paces away from the cathedral. I did not fail, the following morning, to attend the first mass. I found a seat, not realizing it, beneath the traditional and colossal statue of Saint Christopher, which one is sure to find in the majority of old basilicas. Bothered by something, as if by an enormous weight had been placed on me, I finally raised my eyes and I received with all my heart the commotion of that presence of a friend of seventeen centuries. *Christophorum videas, postea tutus eas.*[43] I then remembered this Leonine verse, since then turned into an adage: "Look on Saint Christopher and

---

[43] *Christophorum*...: Latin for "Look at St. Christopher, then go in peace."

then go in peace." People believed, in the Middle Ages, that nothing could happen to a person during the day who had seen, in the morning, an image of Saint Christopher. That, for profound reasons which the present enfeeblement of Reason no longer permits understanding.

At the hour of our departure, the train we were counting on boarding did not appear, but in its place another one, completely extraordinary. We had nothing to hope for from that interminable convoy each wagon of which was taken in advance by a torrent of Germans drawn to the Exposition in Paris.

But we slipped a humble coin into the hand of an employee, exposing to him our embarrassment. Then voila. Without a second thought, that man led us to a non-smoking compartment where three pipe suckers sent by Saint Christopher were holding our seats. After a word by our guide, they welcomed us politely, descended with an air of satisfaction, like men whom one frees from a chain gang, and we arrived in Paris in the evening, almost refreshed and at a very decent hour, carried by that rapid train.

26. – What God asks for from his poor, it is the patience of Atlas who holds up the skies.

The distribution of prizes that was to be held today at the convent has been replaced by a solemn farewell. I continue not to understand the privation of the celebration inflicted on the poor children, which many of them will remember with bitterness, and whom the women religious are going perhaps to leave forever. Was it not, on the contrary, an opportunity to rejoice together for the last time? But what I buy less and less is the stupid thing about Martinique.

Véronique had, by exceptional favor, a minuscule bust baked by the founder and as for myself, I had the surprise of a little supplementary invoice for 12 francs.

27. – At any moment, I fear an eruption by the landlord.

31. – Distressing article by Rachilde on the *Exegesis,* which seems to have completely disoriented her. Impossible for me to imagine an individual, even well-meaning, buying my book after reading those dreary and discouraging lines.

August

2. – René Martineau who just sent me some assistance, tells me of a newly-elected deputy of la Sarthe, comparing his victory to that in the same place, in 1370, by du Guesclin. "One has no idea," he says, "of such similar loutishness."

4. – Letter received by our deacon:

Monsieur the Curate,

This morning, the mother of a family was found, by exception, present at your discourse. She heard you proffer this: "You tell me, ladies, that the poor are not interesting. It's true. Poverty is not interesting."

Eh! well, when a priest dares say such words before the Holy Sacrament, it means the hour of persecutions has sounded alright. He will become an apostate for sure after the first threat... Our Lord is not ashamed of poverty, Him, and you would throw him rudely out the door of your church if he dared present himself today, barefoot. After several hours, I am still boiling with indignation... When you are deprived of your wages, perhaps you will find out how "interesting" poverty is, as it is the door to heaven.
– A Christian from the Meaux diocese.

5. – I have a lot of esteem for Cassagnac, so devoid of talent but so loyal! His behavior seems perfect compared to all those who, when they are not sitting on the chamber pot, are drinking with the assassins of children.

To Georges Rémond:

... What do you think of what is happening right now and what seems to you to be the growing cowardice of

our Catholics? Do you not find that there is a feeling of something readying itself finally, of precipitating itself rather, something that I foresaw more than twenty years ago, and furiously announced? You thought you had triumphed over me, back then, considering me a bad prophet, as if a disparity of several months or several dozens of months invalidated the exactitude, when it is a question of so prodigious an upheaval. We will certainly see. I take this occasion only to entreat you to be attentive. The present events are certainly hideous, and vulgar as far as their tendency goes. What one absolutely wants and everywhere is the end of the Church, which cannot end. Only, if there were merely a single *Catholic* left, *it is a point of theology that the church would live in him with all its mysteries, all its miracles, all its power, all its fecundity... I think then, once again, that we are at the prolog of an unprecedented Drama, like nothing we have seen for twenty centuries, and I invite you to a certain degree of contemplation.*

6. – Saw the famous château de Ferrières, tiresome Italian Renaissance forgery from the last epoch. Nothing but in passing, two minutes scarcely, that's

enough. Wilhelm and Bismark were lodged there with honor, and it is there that the ignoble Favre, plenipotentiary of France, wept in despair on the Chancellor's boots. Beautiful forest possessed entirely by Rothschild. It is another shame that such noble demesnes should remain in the hands of shady dealers. Stopping for a drink in the next village over, I exhale my bile before a fat innkeeper and an individual with the lowly expression of a teacher, which seems to please and displease. But I have neither the time nor the desire to sort it out.

7. – The deacon is no longer anywhere to be found; he is, I believe, on the eve of a retreat. The letter cited earlier will have been an excellent point of departure for his sacerdotal meditations.

10. – Saint Laurent, whose feast day it is today, restitutes the Deacon to us, in top form, who gives a discourse that is boring to tears and pointless.

11. – The means to make certain souls understand that death is an act of mercy, the only means of salvation and, consequently, the most precious of all the graces? When a bourgeois family's young child dies, it seems to me a light should turn on. But there are plenty of other cases.

12. – The universal infamy unleashed for over a week

by the *Journal* is unprecedented. That ignoble paper has come up with distributing gifts to every reader on the street. The illusory gifts, I think, and even totally fictive, such as 500-franc bank notes in an envelope, etc. are *advertising* for countless commercial firms.

Bold attempt to lure customers which could be thought genial if it did not give one an irresistible need to vomit. And the stupid avidity of the public, snared each morning by promises and unbridled lies! France can never be more demeaned.

But wait, there's more. The same paper fit to wipe one's ass has once again invented the triumphal return of a rehabilitated galley slave, the pharmacist Danval, condemned twenty-five years ago as a poisoner, whose unfriendly militant Judaic mug it publishes. The *Journal* prepares at great expense a grandiose or rather enormous manifestation, scheduled for this evening, at the gare de Lyon. We ask ourselves what this new farce signifies when it makes a stink about *justice* and LIGHT, while at the same time hundreds of thousands of children's souls are condemned to perish in darkness.

13. – The said *Journal* is filled with the news of Danval and the reception that was given him at the train station by journalists and some other pharmacists who have not yet been condemned. One would think that he was Bonaparte come back from Egypt or from Marengo. Ridiculousness and ignominy beyond measure.

15. – The Assumption. The more I go, the more the public on Sundays and feasts is hateful to me. The thoughts suggested to me by the sight of those bourgeois are horrible. Those beings are more hateful, I think, on feast days than ordinary Sundays *because*, on those days, they TAKE COMMUNION. Shopkeepers taking communion! It is frightful...

That procession in memory of Louis XIII's vow, in all the parish churches of France, is bizarre in effect when one sees what is happening and when one knows what the faith has become.

17. – Our garden begins to become unsupportable to us. We wanted to escape people. Now look at us having become a prey to red insects particular to Brie where they pullulate and devour, completing thus in their way the abomination of the other vermin in this execrable countryside. One spends his life itching.

20. – Reading in *The History of the Consulate and the Empire*. What a sententious and gloomy cretin that Thiers is!

24. – Anne-Catherine Emmerich says that Saint Bartholomew must be invoked in cases of desperate illness and paralysis. It is the present state of France. If Catholics were men, pious and charitable sons, they would start anew, in a much more serious fashion, the

bloodletting that was so benign in 1572.[44]

For the first time since we live in Cochons, I hear the curate read the Gospel from the pulpit. That reading, formerly so recommended, is ordinarily replaced by an intolerable prattle which those gentlemen have the cheek to call *The Word of God!*

As a result, the majority of parishioners who do not even know what the word *Gospel* means and who do not come to mass on Sundays except by habit, lose thus the unique occasion to learn something. The holy Parables on which centuries have been built, they absolutely do not know them anymore.

29. – Apropos of a publication of letters by Barbey d'Aurevilly to Trébutien, I am counseled to publish those by the same d'Aurevilly to me. Is it possible?

31. – *Consulate and Empire*. I am at the death of the Duke d'Enghien and that of de Pichegru. There was that of Frotté. Those extremely obscure dramas, but completely clear for Thiers' limpid blindness, make me think, once again, about the emptiness of history. How crushing it is to tell oneself that one knows absolutely nothing more than the tip of the iceberg of events, the underside of which, the profound causes and the deeper effects, sometimes will never be known except on the Day of God! *The mysteries of*

---

[44]The bloodletting... 1572: In reference to St. Batholomew's Day, August 20, 1572, when thousands of Protestants were murdered in Paris, by Catholics.

History. I reflect that such a chapter would not have been an hors-d'œuvre in my *Son of Louis XVI.*

September

1st. – To Rachilde in response to her article on the *Exegesis of Commonplaces* (See July 31):

> *Dear friend,*
>
> *I expect that you will find me to be a bit loutish for not having thanked you for your recent article. That would put me at ease for admitting to you that that article hurt me. I had counted on you so much! Think on it! I have no one but you anymore, today, to speak about the things I write, and the* Exegesis *appears precisely to be the most impenetrable, the most inaccessible, and the most inexpugnable of my works, without question.*
>
> *What happened then? Tell me. You began that unfortunate article so well, and you threw me into the face of the public with so amiable an impertinence! "What a disconcerting masterpiece this latest book by Léon Bloy is," you said in the first line, "and what a beautiful dream he made by tearing out the tongue of all the bourgeois folk!" Ah! you had come out of*

the gate running, and two or three dozen maniacs, on your word, went out to buy it.

Then, suddenly, you shred your paper, – thinking that wealth does not make happiness, that I have no need of any-one, that one is not on earth to amuse oneself, etc. finally that "Nothing is eternal." For you wrote it, that phrase there, on the fourth to the last line of your article. I had forgotten or ne-glected it, just as I had forgotten or neglected so many other common-places, so that my book would not have the disadvantages of a phone-book.

Monstrously you write – to please whom? not yourself, I think, – that "Bloy is much closer to Ravachol than to Jesus." As much to say, with all due respect, that I dine more willingly on excrement than on a fattened chicken garnished with truffles. It's pathetic.

Finally, my poor Rachilde, admit it, I have no idea why, you invented the lamentable bit about pretending to have barely flipped through the pages of my unfortunate book, and above all not to have read the preface.

"Who cares!" you cried, "Bloy will think that being forced professionally

to read inept or filthy work, I am de-bilitated to the point where I can no longer discern a generous and excel-lent book, and lack the courage to speak about it as it deserves."

So, o Rachilde, this time, I am com-pletely vanquished. I had, for one in-stant, the vague desire of writing these things to you in a response to be pub-lished by the Mercure; *if it weren't for the disgust I have of advertising my-self!*

2. – I try to discourage a poor man from bleeding for me, telling him that my deliverance would cost about 50,000 francs if one really wanted to deliver me, as-suming the power to do so.

3. – Reading in the marvelous poem by that triple bourgeois Thiers, whose one-eyed and club-footed wisdom does not succeed in destroying the magnifi-cence of Napoleon.

4. – Reread d'Aurevilly's old letters, of such sad childishness to me, but perhaps of interest to many people.

A female inhabitant honors us with her visit. I see a mechanical ugly woman saying anticipated stu-pidities in a cut and dry manner; an unfortunate creature without education or intelligence, come very visibly to make an effect, perhaps to dazzle me, and who thinks only of herself. It is impossible to be so completely lacking in tact, simplicity, intelligence, and to be more antipathic.

After a few minutes, she felt the need to speak to me about the *Femme pauvre* which Jeanne had loaned her, and which she says she read the first part of. "It's nice, very nice, but it is serious, very serious," she pronounced. On top of that, she promised to give me her *judgment*, when she finishes it. Jeanne having spoken to her about *Sueur de Sang,* "Oh! military stories, they're too *dry*," she responded.

The enormity of that sottishness starting to suffocate me, I had to get away. I think that she must have despised me greatly for having so little enjoyed her presence.

6. – Napoleon's story intoxicates me. In that light, our dreadful situation becomes tolerable.

The dreadful Vignoble, the ancient curate of Ceux-d'En-Haut, has a successor worthy of him. Frequent visitor to his old church which I love, and not knowing the new pastor except by sight, I am persuaded that it would be the simplest thing in the world to borrow five francs from him, which I would return tomorrow, having to make a necessary trip to Paris tomorrow morning and not having even the money for the fare.

It did not take long for me to learn that nothing is simple with curates. It is always the way of the cross. What a way of the cross! Those meditations of seminarian sentimentality wherein Mary is called "poor mother" are hateful beyond expression. And then, what a passion they have, all those priests, to continue saying the prayers, such as the *Pater*, the *Ave*, the Litanies, etc. *in French.* What more could Protestants do?

After that *exercise in pity*, I go resolutely to find the curate in the sacristy and I receive one of the most beautiful mortifications of my life. As soon as he found out that I was asking him for a favor of money, his face, benevolent before, changes. There is no longer anything in front of me but a mask of hypocrisy and avarice, and there I am, in spite of my protestations, forced to submit to an elegy, dripping with acrimony, on sacerdotal poverty. He speaks to me about the indigents of his parish whom he must help to begin with, and of the certain infidelity of so-called borrowers, etc. Impossible to make him understand that I'm asking for the most banal favor and only for twenty-four hours. No matter what I do, he wants to see me as a mendicant and I effect my retreat, inundated with ignominy. I have no luck in Ceux-d'En-Haut, clearly. That servant of God goes by the name of Toudou.

7. – My visitor of three days ago has asked someone to communicate to me her appreciation of the *Femme pauvre*. Here is that very precious *judgment* that she promised me: "That monsieur is *like me*, he was not made to live in Cochons!!!..." Now I no longer have

the right to complain about being deprived of a salary.

9. – *Consulate and Empire*. Despite the author, this history is for me so lively that I really suffer for the abandonment of the project of the descent on England, just as I suffered previously for the evacuation of Egypt. Another punishment. How to express, in the sense of the *symbolism of history,* the absolutely *unique* greatness of Napoleon? It is discouraging.

Alfred de Vigny, whose *Dialogue inconnu* I just re-read, understood nothing, nothing at all.

10. – Rachilde responds to my letter of the 1st. It appears that there is a "good canon" who gave her the phrase "closer to Ravachol than to Jesus." Nice, the canon. Does he belong to the college of Priapus or to that of Bacchus?

The publication of Barbey d'Aurevilly's letters to me is settled. The person whom the poor Barbey, three-quarters destroyed already, set up as his legatee deigns to consent, but on the condition that everything that is not the text proper of the deceased – is to be submitted to her for review. The collection will appear then without preface and without commentaries. One could have had a book, instead one will have what was scraped together from a drawer. *Amariorem morte mulierem,*[45] said Solomon.

---

[45]*Amariorem*...: Latin for "... more bitter than death the woman..." (KJV), from Ecclesiastes, 7:27.

11. – I come finally to the campaign of 1805, after the horrible catastrophe of the forced abandonment of the project to descend on England.

Today even one learns that the Boer generals who had capitulated, counting on the good faith of the English, were abominably duped. Just payment for their stupidity. Those Calvinists offered some interest, weapons in hand. Now it is over. All that remains are imbecilic heretics to whom God does not wish to give the glory of demolishing the pimp of nations.

12. – The campaign of 1805 deprives me of any energy to occupy myself advantageously on whatever else there might be.

One can be an imbecile and practice the imperfect subjunctive all the same, that is clear. But hatred for the imperfect subjunctive cannot exist except in the heart of an imbecile.

15. – The *Matin* publishes an extraordinary letter by Cardinal Rampolla. "It was decided," the letter says, "apropos of a refusal of audience, which the Holy Father would say nothing about, and simple wisdom demands that he say nothing about it to anyone, nor even do anything that could elicit inopportune commentaries."

The Pope grows disinterested in Christianity! "Prudence," "wisdom" demand that he sacrifice his flock. At least that is what his domestics lead people to believe.

Question. Why can a man not say without ridicule, *I am a thinker*, whereas he inspires respect and even admiration when he says, I am a *free-thinker*?

16. – Surprising not to find in the Battle of Austerlitz the amazing strategical masterwork that I had dreamt of. To be honest the narrator is a miserable storyteller. However, he appeared awesome all the same when he was telling the story of Marengo.

18. – I wander around that abject and redoubtable Prussia of 1805 and 1806, which Napoleon would have destroyed if God had not needed it to hang around for France's humiliation.

I do not tire admiring the precision and fidelity of my friend Vallette, director of the *Mercure de France*, one of the most reliable and rare men I have met.

20. – Jeanne has waited pointlessly for a little couturier who has been coming on Saturdays for the last two or three months. The last time she came, she had deeply disgusted us by her display of a sublime sorrow. Having interred her grandmother the week before, she had decided to astonish us with the pomp of her filial piety and had served up for us, the entire

day, a weeping face, affecting to show, so that the beauty of her heart was indisputable, the worst humor to the poor children frozen by the frost of that affliction. Would that she stayed away forever!

21. – *Consulate and Empire*. Jena. One thing strikes me which could be the subject matter of a beautiful page. It is Napoleon's unprecedented *solitude*. Of course, he was seconded by his lieutenants, sometimes in an admirable way; the functionaries formed by him served with devotion and intelligence. But who would have been able, in all the universe, to be the companion of that prodigious Dreamer?

22. – Nothing comes but sadness. I am indignant at the mediocrity of my life, as discontented as possible with myself. Sanctity is at an infinite distance and always seems to be retreating. Then, the misery of the body, of this body, companion thus far robust and young, of a consumed and dolorous soul... I become very old overnight.

Eylau. Apropos of the *temple* project! in honor of the Grand Army, which has become the church of the Madeleine, mediocrity, total incomprehension of Napoleon *in art*. See the first pages of book XXVI by Thiers.

23. – My Jesuit sent me a small photograph of the unimaginable and terrifying crucifix venerated in

Uden, in a Crusaders chapel and which today I learn the existence of. The history of that miraculous crucifix is huge, and the image that is before my eyes, although insufficient, is absolutely terrible. I'm haunted. That vision pursues me into the deep recesses of my soul where I have rarely the occasion to penetrate. I tell the sender about the effect produced on me by that image: "It will make me into a saint perhaps. The continual sight of Catholics in Cochons-sur-Marne did not cut it. Disgust can accelerate a salutary flight, but vomit is a poor springboard for leaping into Paradise."

25. – Painful payment of our contributions. I do not hold back expressing my true feelings to the preceptor. Gracious likeness of his guichet to a hole in the latrines into which I would be forced to throw the bread of my children, thus become the bread of Trouillot, the aperitif of Pelletan, or the trousers of the abbot Combes!

Undertook with despair the reading of a handwritten collection of free verse submitted to me for my review. It is annoying. Free verse is, in my eyes, one of the worst modern aberrations, one of those that proclaim with loud fanfares the weakening of Reason. To replace the totally supernatural mystery of Rhythm and Number by lines and punctuation marks, that is not only stupid, it is perverse.

29. – Feast Day of Saint Michael. Death of Zola.

News of that happy event is carried, in advance of all information by the newspapers, by a neighbor woman who found herself in the vicinity of the pigsty. We are gripped by this idea that the author of the *Four Gospels*, the very filthy ending of which I announced two years ago, has died on the very day of Saint Michael, and in the morning. *Divina virtute, in infernum detrude.*[46] (See the *post-scriptum* to *Je M'Accuse...*) The sacrilegious churl was unable to finish his fourth Gospel. SOMEONE had enough.

30. – To the author of the manuscript of poetry mentioned earlier:

> *There would be a means of understanding between us which would be to* not *speak of* art. *I am a traditionalist, a man of the past. I have need of Authority, in other words of Obedience and of Discipline in all things. Absolute necessity. You are wrong to apply to me. I have written* poems in prose, *but not free verse. Never that. I become dangerous when someone brings it up. I have read as much as I could of your manuscript. Eh! well, because you insist, here it is: There is in the greater part of these pieces and above all in those which you hold dearest, not only the adoption of a horribly defective form, but, alas! the*

---

[46]*Divina...*: Latin for "By divine virtue, cast to hell."

absence of style and originality; worse than that, the absolute lack of thought, of central and generative conception. The morsel that you so highly recommended to me is annoying. But when you touch on religious things, it is a misery, enough to make a man cry.

One other thing, which you desperately don't know, is this: that art is not my goal, *but only an instrument that I learned to use like a sword or a cannon, and that I am, before everything and more than anything, a religious soul. I would trade all the artists and all the masterpieces of art in the world for the* Lord's Prayer *spoken by a mendicant on the edge of a grave. But do you know even what that Prayer is? No, right? Then what could you understand of a man who has written only to paraphrase the syllables contained in it, and who thinks constantly on death?*

There is, at this moment, on rue de Bruxelles, an "infamous decaying carcass" which will not be sung by any poet, deserted habitacle of a very dirty soul, which knows, for the last twenty-four hours now, what it means to rely on the Lord's Prayer...

The newspapers confirm the good news. According to a report, the Cretin of the Pyrenees would have died in his literature. He was apparently picked up out of the excrement... In the *Matin*, dithyramb by the brothers Margueritte, four-footed literary hacks, like the Rosnys or the Brothers Goncourt. There is mention of the Zola "way," which was a "calvary." In the same journal, interview of Huysmans declaring that Zola was "a brave man"!!! In the *Libre Parole*, interview of the same Huysmans, of an unbelievable cowardice surpassed only by Coppée, saying that "death purifies."

In summary, excrement superabounds in that death. Scatological gorgings. The *Écho of Paris* explains that Mme. Zola who survives her husband – considered as having lived – "owes her salvation to the fact that she was able to reach her bathroom." Émile, less blessed, was unable to run quickly enough to the latrines...

Jeanne, having had the occasion to see the women religious of Saint-Joseph, was well received by them, but she was made to endure a sort of interrogation tending to try to understand what our resources were, my earnings as a writer, the approximate capacity of our chamber pots, etc. "You put money aside, don't you, madame?" said one of the Mothers... All that accompanied by a miraculous unintelligence. One wants me to be a sort of merchant. After that ridiculous struggle, Jeanne comes home feeling dejected.

October

1st. – Continuation of vileness. The *Aurore* invokes the Pantheon. The *Libre Parole*, which does not stop invoking the sewer, publishes a German image representing Zola as Saint Michael, dressed in armor, holding in his hand a sword, on the blade of which is imbecilely written the word *Truth,* and striking down a Wagnerian dragon made out of papier-maché. In the margin: "Long live Zola, the avenger!"

To Vallette regarding Barbey d'Aurevilly's *Letters.* Response to the proposition of an explanatory preliminary note and its need to be *controlled:*

> *Deprived of freedom, what explanations could I offer? At fifty-six years of age, prostitution has no future, really, no benefit, and no excuse.*

2. – What do they do, the Guardian Angels whose feast day is today? In announcement: *Jules Barbey d'Aurevilly, His Life, His Work*, by Eugène Grelé (!!!?) vol. 1, in 8vo. That book would have been based on *the most serious* documents. Nothing is missing apparently. The proof is that I was not consulted, even though I lived in intimate friendship with d'Aurevilly, from 1867-1889. Is it not admirable that that publication, evidently inspired by the legatee, a work by one of her sweethearts and all for her glory I imagine, – that it should be announced at just the moment when I have need and thirst for a revenge?

3. – The publication by the *Mercure de France* of one of my first literary essays: *la Méduse-Astruc*, a sort of crazy poem about a bust of Barbey d'Aurevilly, is bizarre. It makes me look like a dead-and-buried writer that one scrapes the barrel to find work to publish.

The baker spoke to me this morning about my account, with an interior eloquence that was similar to how the first Christians formerly spoke about the kingdom of God.

It is said that Zola had an immense and panic horror of death. It appears that that cursed man sometimes fell out of bed at the thought of death, prey to an indescribable fear.

4. – Idea for a study on Barbey d'Aurevilly with respect to that Grelé whose existence was revealed to me yesterday. I say "existence" because words are lacking.

5. – Some words by the poet of l'*Ensorcelée* about Zola apropos of *Pot-Bouille* and the soirées of Médan: "Ah! how wrong he was to eat then! you will see the *result*."

As recalled in the *Écho de Paris* by Octave Uzanne, on the day itself of the Cretin's funeral.

6. – Article by Joergensen on Zola in *Vort Land* (*Notre pays*), the important Copenhagen newspaper.

That article, entitled ironically *A Martyr* and thought quite mediocre, is a kind of tour de force. Joergensen has succeeded in writing more than three hundred lines without naming me once. How could he do that? He had my book *Je M'Accuse...* open before him for the occasion and he delved into it at each instant. Among the dead, he names Barbey d'Aurevilly and Villiers de l'Isle Adam, Catholics the both of them, whose two names invoke my own with desperate cries. Among the living or presumed living, he names Anatole France and Remy de Gourmont, two declared enemies of Our Lord Jesus Christ. Those there are the *virtuosos of the language*, the ONLY ones he knows. What would have made him resist at this point the imperious injunctions of his conscience! Joergensen, whom I thought to be "a man sent by God" (see *Mon Journal*, p. 156 and following), is a journalist then like the others and, believing me to be dead, he tosses, he too, onto my casket, his handful of Scandinavian dirt. How shameful! Me who loved him like a brother and who made him known in France, speaking about his work like nobody will speak about them again! Ah! will nothing be spared me? But he knows just how abandoned I am and how unjust my contemporaries are to me! He knows it better than anyone in Denmark, and the book that he had under his eyes while writing that article, he told me it was a masterpiece. How could he act like that, not mentioning my name, and why? So that is how they are, those Scandinavian Catholics!

7. – René Martineau loans me a copy of Grelé's book

in which I am not mentioned, he says, except at the end where I am mentioned in passing as a "common friend" who went to find a priest, an act, moreover, without importance.

Our life is the supernatural prize of a daily, furious combat. I have chosen to follow Jesus and behold what he plants for me in the desert, *in terra deserta, invia et inaquosa.*[47]

8. – One will say what one wants, I cannot accept having friends or admirers living in abundance. I was barely ten years old when I read, in a poor book that I won as a school prize, a story entitled naïvely *The Sensitive Son.* I must believe that there was in that infantile story a divine virtue, for the memory of it has stayed with me all my life. It had to do simply with a little boy crying at school before a sumptuous meal and refusing to eat it while recalling the very poor table his parents had. After forty-five years, I continue crying, me, the old *pamphleteer*, remembering that so humble and so distant thing.

9. – We empty the poor piggybanks of the children in order to survive another day.

10. – Nothing to report but a very mellow, almost springlike weather, which seems to thumb its nose at

---

[47]*In terra*...: Psalms 62:3. Latin for "in a dry and thirsty land, where no water is" (KJV).

our troubles... I die of sorrow.

11. – Is it possible that in all my earthly life I should never obtain a bit of justice?

12. – *Consulate and Empire*. I reach the great insurrection in Spain. The reason for that uprising of an entire people, that act of Bayonne, so virtuously blamed by Thiers and, of course, because of that, worthy of praises, is to be studied, at least in its consequences which frightened the world. That war in Spain having been the beginning of the fall, is it not infinitely to presume that it is there that one must look for the key to the mystery of that unimaginable Prefiguration?

13. – Found a nice page in Thiers on the capitulation at Baylen. So it is a kind of prodigy. What that mediocre general[48] needed was the Empire's military glory deep down in his heart! I copy:

> ... *M. de Villoutreys, having returned to his general in chief, is told to take the road to Andujar to meet the general Castaños in order to ratify the truce consented by his lieutenants. The unfortunate general Dupont, until then so brilliant, so fortunate, returns to his*

---

[48]Mediocre general: In reference to the French General Pierre Dupont (AD 1765-1840).

tent, crushed by moral issues that render him almost insensitive to the physical pains of two serious wounds. So goes fortune, in war as in politics, as everywhere else in the world, an agitated world, a changing theater where happiness and misfortune are bound together, succeed one another, efface one another after a long succession of opposing sensations leaving nothing but emptiness and misery!

Three years before, on the banks of the Danube, that same general Dupont, arriving out of breath to offer assistance to marshal Mortier, saved him at Diernstein. But other times, other places, other spirit! That was in December, in the north; it was old soldiers full of health and vigor, excited by a rigorous climate instead of being beaten by an enervating climate, habituated to all the vicissitudes of war, exalted by honor, never hesitating between dying and giving themselves up. Those there, if their position became bad one moment, there was time to run to their aid and save them. And then fortune was smiling still and repaired everything: nobody showed up late, nobody was mistaken, or if someone was mistaken, someone else corrected his error. Here, in this Spain, where things had started out so poorly, they

*were inexperienced, weak, ill, over-
whelmed by the climate, new to suffering. They stopped being lucky anymore, and if they made a mistake,
someone else made it worse. Dupont
had come to the assistance of Mortier
in Diernstein; Vedel was not going to
come to the assistance of Dupont except when it was too late.*

16. – Undertook the reading of Grelé. It is a ridiculous book and, as far as I can tell from the first pages,
the book of an *enemy*. The person who inspired it and
who is certainly not an idiot, would have been then
and would continue to be an enemy of d'Aurevilly,
and even the most dangerous. A completely simple
assertion that will sound excessive.

17. – For the entire day, read Grelé whose stupidity
interests me, but I continue to think that there is
something other than stupidity. I make this remark
once again that d'Aurevilly never spoke to me of his
youth, unless it was in an extremely vague manner.
He never went back earlier than 1840, avowed nothing earlier than that. It would have been beyond his
courage to say that he had been a young man in 1825.
How old is he now, over there, in the Abyss?

20. – *Nationalist campaign*, inept book with apologetic pretensions by that Jules Soury, a disciple of Re-

nan, who twenty-five years ago found, I believe, the secret to going further than his master in villainy of thought and in blasphemy, being one of those Excluded men in favor of whom the least whim of pardon seems forever impossible. It appears that he also, like Coppée or Huysmans, has become a *column of the Church*.

22. Masses at seven o'clock and eight o'clock. This won't be the first day that we notice the difference between those two masses. To start with, there is a certain grace, inherent in the first, in the mass at dawn, in whatever country it might be. Then, in Cochons, it is the only one where three or four people might be found praying. The mass at eight o'clock is said for M. the Deacon's flock, in other words the ladies who have every intention of honoring the church with their presence.

Those pious servants of the devil necessarily create a dangerous atmosphere that I have felt on multiple occasions and which Jeanne has greatly suffered from. I resist it better, having a stronger soul than the souls reunited by those miserable creatures who cannot inflict their ascendant on me.

24. – I come to the end of Grelé whose inexactitude, sottishness, and perfidy clearly grow, the closer one gets to the conclusion, in other words when the female inspirer appears on the scene.

26. – Patronage of the Holy Virgin. Of the four poor people that we are, three have received God this morning, their living God. Jeanne is ill. Who to consult in this countryside of imbeciles and how to give her the nourishment that she would have need of?

27. – There is, above Cochons, a phantom that would strike fear in Edgar Allan Poe. An old woman of the theater, formerly jumping around and making a racket, but after having acquired wealth, continually resides in I do not know what cave at the back of a park that nobody penetrates. Around a group of houses uninhabited by formal will of that ruin of a person who bought them, expressly so that negligence and meteors might make them into ruins like herself, pitiful ruins that stink and cause horror. The proprietor had need of silence, fearing perhaps the least noise might stir up memories. Unable to obtain that silence from neither birds nor thunder, she tried to realize it in that way. The poor or homeless vagabonds who pass by those boarded-up and dead houses, which the four seasons devour, must have thoughts or feelings that the most frightening Angels register attentively.

29. – In an hour of enthusiasm for her husband, Jeanne writes a very fine note that does me the greatest honor. (It was published several months later, in the VIIIth volume of the Mariani album. I care to reproduce it here, not imagining a writer capable of doing better.)

Léon Bloy

Judged by his Wife

*In these times of Americanism, femi-
nism, outrageous snobism, when everything is done by group or herd, it
would be perhaps good to rest one's
eyes by contemplating a painting by
the Primitives which exists, living in
our midsts, in the recesses of a sublime attic where only the sun and the
sound of bells penetrate.*

*A man, of fifty some-odd years, "hair
white by the foam of the cataracts of
contemporary Turpitude," subsists as
he can, outside the world, outside the
society of men, by his own choice or
by the choice of that society that no
longer loves Art. That man is a solitary contemporaneous with the Van
Eycks or the Cimabues. He is a wor-
shiper of the Cross and an inhabitant
of the Dream.*

His name is LÉON BLOY.

*Invested with a magnificence of imagi-
nation, completely unique, he never
ceases turning out images, sometimes
fierce, other times naïve or delicious,
in his books which keep cropping up
at the moment when one thinks him
vanquished, always* published, *be-*

cause there exists a group of people, more and more numerous, who want them; always buried in silence by the loathsome press; and rising, all the same, and always to the surface of contemporary literature like the sublime wreck of an old pirate ship that one wanted to sink, but whose captain has the gift of keeping afloat.

There you have, in several words, that man of another time, that writer of the first order who will never leave you without a response – by a completely prophetic intuition – if you should think to ask him for counsel.

Read the Femme pauvre, *his work of maturity, then read* The Desperate Man, *the book that made him famous, fifteen years ago, and compare the sorrowful suavity of the first with the storm of the second. You will find the same man, in great part because he loves, either in the eye of the storm to save his soul, or in peace to save others'.*

When your mind, shaken by the emotions contained in his work, desires to rest without descending from the heights, then take his Salvation Through the Jews, *written with all his art for an elite group of thinkers and which forces you to get down on your knees. With a steady and tranquil hand, his mind in heaven and his heart on fire, he bends the Word to his will and impresses you with his thought, which wants action in the calm, war in peace, and adoration under the cuirass.*

But to have heard him read his truly inspired work, only the few friends who have remained faithful will remember! The sonorous but supple voice, which the great soul that supports it loans extraordinary accents of love or anger to, could not be forgotten, once heard. The intensity of his gaze under the two serious folds of his forehead melts into infinite tenderness when a friend speaks to him. One feels that the artist and writer in him, however great they might be, will never give more than his strong and tender Friendship which knows how to make sacrifices, to the point of depriving himself of everything, to the point of joyfully wearing the mantle of ignominy that all those who control or withhold public opinion today cast over him, mantle made of calumny, deceit, envy, and a hatred for Beauty. The man who had given everything he had was called a beggar!

LÉON BLOY *persists. They wanted to*

kill him by silence, the most cowardly and murderous of weapons against a writer. Why? Because he is not like others; *because he has a horror of selling out his thought; because he has taken Christianity seriously.*

Without wishing to, they have facilitated his life which cannot take place except in solitude. It is there where he finds the living water of prayer, and it is there that he desires to be left alone. Age of money which is ours, all that was needed was your abject frame around that picture of a solitary weeping for Love, who hates you because you have stolen his Glory!

Do you want to know the words of reprobation that Léon Bloy *utters against the world, that is, against the Bourgeois, who are the kings of money and the enemy of Beauty? Open his* Exegesis of Commonplaces *then, and you will spend gay moments seeing with what justice and bonhomie your neighbor acts.*

Variety is one of the most remarkable aspects of Léon Bloy's *work. His place is, by that fact alone, entirely indicated in some great journal whose success it would make, for the source of his genius is inexhaustible, and while one after the other our so-called great men fail and dry up, he remains standing, master of his thought, sometimes tragic as in his memories of the war of 1870, in* Sueur de Sang, *and sometimes amusing and satirical as in* Histoires désobligeantes.

Finally, his Mendiant ingrat *initiates us into his everyday life, life of sorrow and joy, which he shares with his family, and which he is not afraid to recount. We encourage all those who do not find enough to nourish themselves on in the literature offered them today, – to knock on the door of this little-known author who invites them to accompany him through his exceptional existence in that book made of sunlight and tears.*

– Jeanne LÉON BLOY, *née Molbech.*

Thiers. The taking of Madrid. I find myself freed of the prejudice from my childhood as to the heroism of the Spanish against Napoleon. The great man despised them like a vile and cowardly rabble, and he was right, with an exception made for Saragossa. But what to think about a heroism that has a need for walls?

30. – I see two bourgeois, a man and his wife, having spent half a century together, without having said

anything other than commonplaces to each other, without having said a thing. If God wanted them to see each other in the Light, *they would not recognize each other*.

31. – The newspapers tell how the king of Portugal, on a visit to Paris these few last days, conferred on the ignoble Combes the Grand Croix of the Order of *Christ*!

November

1ˢᵗ. – All Saints. I ask, once again, for independence to be in a state to do my work which is to combat the spirit of the century, to crush it terribly, for the honor of God and the glory of all his Saints.

Véronique repeats to us the surprising words of her teacher, speaking about a girl of thirteen who has not yet taken her first communion. "In general," that woman religious said, "it is better to take it as late as possible." Must one wait until one's deathbed? We explain to our child the thick ignorance and the inconceivable lack of faith supposed by such words.

The *Mercure de France*. Very mediocre article by Remy de Gourmont on Grelé in which he limits himself to transcribing his affirmations and ideas. Another article by Quillard comparing Zola to Socrates!!! The *Mercure* never ceases to be young... Half the issue is filled with an inquiry into German influence apropos of a discourse by Wilhelm. Frightful boredom. Everyone has been consulted, except me of course.

2. – Day of the Dead. The consequences of evil that one has practiced continually return to their source, – torment of the damned and of the souls in Purgatory, – unless one has interrupted the current and cut the cable by becoming a saint.

Spirits don't have a place. Nevertheless one can say that certain souls are kept in a certain place, Purgatory for example. But that is meant in a spiritual way, in other words that certain indispensable things are hidden to them. Their ignorance constitutes their captivity.

4. – Another registered letter containing no money order, and I have given the mailman our last sous! I will pray to my correspondent, when he feels inclined to write me by registered letter, to warn me several days in advance so that I am not caught off guard too much.

5. – Someone loans me a surprising book: *Politesse et convenances ecclésiastiques*, by the abbot Branchereau, an authority, in which priests are taught how to behave at the table and elsewhere, code in 323 articles. (Here are some of my notes taken during the course of reading it, which occurred over several

weeks.)

Sanctum Canibus

Saint Paul "professing *to adapt to all exigencies."* Page 10. *People profess-ing to read that Apostle's Epistles could have come away with the oppo-site impression. See the famous* Nolite conformari huic sæculo. *Rom. XII.*

Ideal of a polite priest. *p. 10.*

"No one will say that an honest man who pays his debts performs an act of politeness." p. 12.

According to this extraordinary doc-tor, "the act of resisting temptation has nothing in common with charity." p. 13. Just the opposite of what is read in the common run of non-pontifical confessors: Qui potuit transgredi non est trangressus,[49] *etc.*

And this prodigious maxim, on the same page: "Politeness is an extra, charity is what is strictly necessary."

He sees in the liturgy "a perfect code of courtesy." p. 20.

As for PERFECTION, *it consists in*

---

[49] *Qui potuit...*: Ecclesiasticus 31:10.

"putting oneself in unison with men, with their mores and habits and doing the same things in the same way, or risking singularity.*" p. 29. The entire passage is to be read.*

It is exactly as if one said that a mountain's highest peak is not to surpass by a hair's breadth the droppings of ruminants on the lowest plain.

He who could measure the ecclesiastical world's hatred for singularity, *for two or three hundred years, would know, like the angels, why there are no longer Saints in the Church.*

Recommendation to "change one's socks every day when one's feet smell." p. 31.

"Above all, no perfumes." p. 35.

"When smoking tobacco in company, do not offer any." p. 47.

"Act in such a way, when smoking your tobacco, primarily when you are outside, not to blow smoke into your neighbors' eyes." p. 48.

"Those who pinch snuff will do well to change their handkerchief often." p. 49.

"The act of blowing one's nose. Guide for the young priest." p. 49.

"Clothes are the most apparent thing of one's person"!!! p. 51.

The clothing material that a priest wears does not have to be rich or precious. It can EVEN be poor, *provided however that it not be coarse." p. 54. Translation: Jesus can be born in a stable. He can, at a pinch, provided that the Bethlehem bourgeois who refused hospitality to his parents are not displeased or scandalized, provided above all that there is not satirical or allegorical intention on the part of the bull or the donkey who are the coarsest of animals.*

"According to M. de la Motte, bishop of Amiens, a tear in one's clothing is less reprehensible than a stain." p. 55.

"In the Life of Saints, *there are certain details that it is not always expedient to imitate." p. 57. – You don't say! said in chorus the seminarists of the twentieth century.*

"Do not blow your nose or dribble on the rabat." p. 68.

"Full dress is a must when one visits rich people." p. 74. When one visits poor people, shitting in your pants,[50]

---

[50]Shitting in your pants: in French, the expression is "chie-en-lit," literally "shit in the bed," a stercoracious play on words with "chienlit" which means masquerade or costume.

without being a must, *is completely acceptable.*

"Never, under any circumstances, is the meal to be served in the kitchen." p. 77. Only in times of bloody persecution will it be allowed to eat in the loo.

"It is an impoliteness to make honorable guests enter into the kitchen area," p. 77, in other words, the mayor, the notary, the bailiff, the tax collector, the brigadier of the gendarmerie, the superintendent of bridges and walkways and preponderant merchants or capitalists.

"As for furnishings, the wisest rule is to do as everyone else does." p. 78.

"It is not suitable for a priest to have furnishings that are so poor that one cannot tell him apart from the lowest class of people." p. 79. It is a matter of knowing whether the furniture of Saint Simeon Stylite would be suitable for a vicar of Sainte-Clotilde, or if the abbot Olmer, curate of Saint-Laurent of Paris and a famous Yid, could advantageously swap his furniture for that of Saint Alexis, who lived with pigs for thirty-four years.

"No artistic curiosities." p. 80. There must be some exceptions. Surely there are some district curates who collect

stamps or postcards. I heard tell of a humble head priest who surprised his diocese by the stuffed frogs that one saw fighting, sword in hand, on his fireplace mantle. A subjugated missionary, considering the infinite multitude of those bactrians in the neighborhood of the presbytery, counseled him recently about the siege of Port-Arthur. Finally, people whom I could be the intimate friend of have known a deacon who works for thirty-five years now on the shipwreck of the Medusa or on the Last Judgment by Michelangelo, in corks. Artistic curiosity, if one wishes, but governed by patience and tempered by chastity.

"At the table, pewter place settings are a no-no." p. 82. But one manages quite well with leaden *guests, as in Huysmans' novels since his conversion.*

"What goes on in high-society salons, is not obligatory *in a 'presbytery salon'??? p. 83.*

"Let's point out certain loud movements that politeness prescribes to be checked or moderated." p. 100 The word movements *is a totally exquisite instance of ecclesiastical modesty.*

"Hunting is forbidden to priests, but

fishing is not forbidden"??? p. 109.

"Card games tolerated"!!! p. 110. Except, I imagine, in the case of transparency.

"Let us remain physicians of the soul and leave the profession of physicians of the body to those who bear the name." p. 118. Saint Mark poked in the eye. The last chapter of that evangelist is struck by Branchereau. As for Saint Peter whose mere shadow healed people, it would do better to keep him carefully at a distance from the ministry.

"It is improper to stand in the window or at the door of a house to chat with people who are on the inside. People do it, but a man of polite society never permits himself that." p. 121. Very good, but when one is on the inside, can one flatter oneself to belonging to polite society still if one hails passersby? The first apostles, who certainly did not belong to polite society, have left us too much in the dark on this point.

Visits. — "Do not present yourself before the ladies have done their toilette." p. 153. It would be unfitting, admittedly, to witness a pedicure, and it is rather difficult to imagine an ec-

clesiastic, even an eloquent one, visiting a lady in the process of having her hair curled, etc.

Why is this work addressed to priests, given the author never seems to distinguish them from other men? The infinite superiority *of the Sacerdocy is not even noticed. Ah! how far we are!*

"Do not place your hat on the ground nor on a lady's bed." p. 158. Apparently it would not have the same disadvantages on another bed.

"When one receives a visit, it is not polite to offer the seat that one is sitting on nor that which another visitor is seated on*"!!! p. 170. Let's take the ladder and get to the chapter on meals.*

"Do not sit too far away from the table." p. 179.

"At table, as elsewhere, always observe the order of dignity; *a village curate, for example, needs to defer to a subprefect or a canton mayor, as being less dignant." p. 200. What would be the place of the tenth leper in the Gospel, and where would one put those crippled beggars in the Parable whom the father of the family sends out into the street in order to force*

them to take part in the feast?

Ah! Lord, all these worldly customs, all these rules, all this etiquette of the Devil put forward, recommended, to the priests of Jesus Christ!

"Ecclesiastics are dispensed, in general, *from having to give their arm to ladies in order to pass into the dining room." p. 201.*

Among the various formulas for refusing one plate of food or another, the author forgets this: "Thank you, madame, I'm full!" Or if one allows: "Permit me first to unbuckle my belly-band."

Here is another excellent piece of advice: "With respect to domestics, do not be impolite, but avoid being respectful. *" p. 210.*

Gambling. "A priest must not cheat"! p. 232. Excepted, naturally, are the Greek priests.

"Gambling debts, debts of honor." p. 233. In other words, if a curate who has the honor happens to lose at gambling a sum earmarked for the poor, the poor must go pound sand, honor demands it.

"It is not proper for a priest to give

his arm to another man," p. 235, even, I imagine, if that other man has need of some assistance.

Horseback riding. "The place of honor is on the right. If however, as you keep to the left, you should happen to incommode your superior on the right by kicking up dust, change sides with him." p. 237. If he was an inferior, it would be no big deal kicking up the dust, mud, or horse shit for that matter.

"Do not visit a museum where one might be exposed to encountering some indecency." p. 238. That which is conventionally called Art having absolutely no interest, or if one prefers, the taste for painted or sculpted images being fully satisfied in the boutiques along rue Saint-Sulpice, what motive could there be in exploring a museum if not the need to see some indecencies? In that case, it would be better for an ecclesiastic to content himself, at home, with an album of captivating photographs.

"Let us be friends of the truth, but not be uncivil." p. 241. In other words, there are times when one must know how to flat-out lie.

"Carefully avoid all that could bear

the cachet of singularity or originality." p. 274. See, earlier, the citation from page 29.

"One of the most appreciable advantages that a sojourn in a chateau offers to a young ecclesiastic is to be able to acquire, better than in any other place, the knowledge and experience of knowing how to live." p. 322. The conclusion is obvious. It is too evident that frequentation of the poor is the most dangerous thing of all for an adolescent who is called to drink the Blood of Jesus Christ at his altar.

Pronunciation. The author teaches how one must pronounce the words Mosieur, taba, estoma, almana, por[51]. *p. 262.*

Discourage liaisons. Encourage people to say "interesting discourse, an exact rapport." p. 365.

"Do not say slap *or* joker, *etc." p. 380.*

"In general, do not risk any figurative or proverbial expression of speech without being sure that it is acceptable in polite society. However, that would be to push delicatesse too far as to exclude from conversation the words

---

[51]*Moseiu... por.* Mista, taba, tumtum, etc.

pork, snout, vomit, etc." p. 382. He forgets to say whether the word Cambronne[52] is admissible in polite society or only in impolite society.

Extreme defiance for the imperfect subjunctive. p. 383. Well, damn! I've had enough of this huge bore...

Ipse Spiritus postulat pro nobis gemitibus inenarrabilis.[53] One asks for Priests.

6. – We think that Contempt would be the sure tincture, the true electuary for the health of the soul and body. But what is meant here is complete contempt, contempt of others, contempt of oneself, finally and primarily contempt of contempt which liberates.

Sin is the door to heaven. *Felix culpa.*

7. – It rains inside our church. Torrents of water escape from the vault in certain places. Is it the fault of the deacon whom everyone accuses of avarice and who would employ too few workers for the reparations? Would it be that the church is irreparable?

Discontentment. Here it is several days or sev-

---

[52]Cambronne: a general who fought under Napoleon Bonaparte and is reported to have said "Merde!" (Shit!) when his company was outmaneuvered at the Battle of Waterloo. It is probably more legend than verisimilitude.

[53]*Ipse Spiritus...*: Romans 8:26.

eral weeks now that the mother Mary, the ex-pretty woman, general supervisor of the school of Saint-Joseph, seems to have taken a dislike for Véronique, weighing into her for a minute or two for being late when the little girl is completely innocent, as that delay is caused by the necessity we are in to plan every minute difficultly so as not to miss mass. But mass is nothing to that religious who has to con-temn us greatly for liking it and for not *having a busi-ness*. One knows that we have no maid, which doubt-less appears to be the last degree of abjection.

8. – I am fasting, but the paper imbibes. One does what one can.

I have, today, reasons to believe that the old pretty woman is one of those women religious who have need of being hit on.

Neglected *Politesse* in order to read Wagram instead.

9. – Article by one Pierre Gay in the *Salut public* of Lyon. It is said that I am the equal of Ezekiel or Jeremiah, which does not prevent me from being "malicious" or even a "perfect bourgeois"!!!

11. – Surprising obstinacy by Thiers who is always speaking about Fortune, always writing the word *Fortune* in place of the Word of God, as if he truly worshipped it.

13. – Martinique again. Has anyone noticed that the recent and notorious catastrophes by fire happened in May. Comic Opera, May 25; Charity Bazaar, May 4; Saint Pierre, Martinique, May 8 and Ascension Day.

16. – My day is spent reading successively *Politesse* and Soult's Campaign in Portugal. It is possibly the same thing in the Infinite.

It is with a fine dose of bitterness that we think of the Feast of Saint Catherine in several days. On that occasion, we will infallibly be cadged and by a firm hand. The sisters have instituted a profitable trick of regaling the girls by means of a payment of 2 francs a head for lunch, 5 francs for two meals, which makes, considering the little that suffices for children, and their number, a profit of much more than half. No means to get out of it, the poor girls who *would not go along* having to be taxed with ignominy.

17. – It has been a long time since we have had to suffer so rudely in our souls. It is that constricting feeling so well known by us, that suffocation, that internal agony that does not allow for any hope. To have felt that so often and without dying from it, how is it possible? "We are suffering for someone," Jeanne tells me.

Battle of Talavera. What a heartrending story that war in Spain and what "affliction of the spirit" that crumbling to pieces of the colossus!

20. – The faithful have no need for the light. Such is evidently the thinking of our deacon, literally and figuratively. The snow having obscured the stained glass windows of the small chapel where mass during the week is held, the darkness would be complete if not for the two candles on the altar. There are gas lamps but the deacon, *economizing*, does not want to light them. Impossible to follow the liturgical prayers, which leaves that venerable pastor deeply indifferent. He already only just recites them, himself, because he cannot get out of it, but the faithful have nothing to see by and nothing to do but pray with the Church. In turmoil and indignation, I ask Jesus to have pity on his priest.

I become popular in the diocese. I learn that the priests or seminarists of Meaux read me with more or less satisfaction.

22. – Huge bill from the convent, 88 francs for the trimester ending January 1st. They are really pressed, the miserable wretches! They had the nerve to raise the prices. There is, in the breakdown, 13 francs of unjustifiable "furnishings." We have already given 3 francs for the lunch on Saint Catherine's Day. They ask still more for a tombola, for a group photograph, etc., etc. Those merchants fill me with disgust. Despicably they have calculated, doubtless, that being poor, we must be overwhelmed, and that our known piety would recommend resignation. In which they are mis-

taken.

23. – *Consulate and Empire*. The Divorce. On this occasion when Napoleon wanted to give himself an
heir, it seems to me that he engendered the modern
Bourgeois primarily.

25. – Saint Catherine's Day and our present situation.
I would need 20,000 francs, but I would receive 0 fr.
50 with tears of joy.

26. – Terrible morning, horribly aggravated by indignation. The children have given us details on yesterday's divertissements, at the convent. They put on
two plays. In the first one, a girl blows kisses to her
cousin from the window! In the second, of loftier
character and, by consequence, of more intense fool-
ishness, one is in Lyon, at the time of the Martyrs.
Saint Blandine and Saint Pothin! are represented, this
last one by a silly little goose wearing a beard! and a
miter!!! and giving *her benediction* to the Martyrs!!!
Véronique tells us that at that moment the audience
burst out laughing... So here we have the Martyr Pontiff, *in other words Our Lord Jesus Christ Himself*,
handed over by the women religious to the laughter of
the little bourgeois riffraff, the little future bitches
whose villainy they flatter by aggravating their sottishness. As Christians, the father and mother of
Christian children, it is enough to make one weep for
shame and grief.

27. – Thiers. Continental Blockade. Ignorance, ineptness, and bad faith, insofar as regards the affairs of the Church.

29. – To two priests, friends who dreamt for one instant of interesting Paul Bourget in me:

> ... *What you don't know then is that, for twenty years, I have been the enemy of that individual and that he has always and methodically been on the receiving end in my books or my articles, apropos of anything whatsoever. The most famous of my books,* The Desperate Man, *is primarily against Paul Bourget. I add that I will never let him go. He* takes communion *now, you say. That horror is all that was missing. Terrible aggravation that would make me detest him a little more if that was possible. "A good man," you wrote. Ah! if only you knew! There is, for the longest time that I know him, that I know his infernal mediocrity, his villainy of heart, his cupidity, his avarice, his lack of a spine with respect to those in power, and his hardness of heart towards the weak or those inferior to him. He becomes today, I am told, a column of the Church, one of the last with Cop-*

pée, Brunetière, Huysmans, and several others. Ah! the last cut and the most mortal wound that could be given to the Church, it is assuredly the conversion of litteratasters...

December

1st. – Letter from a friend persuaded that everything is going very well and who congratulates me. I know nothing more bitter than the irony of those felicitations to people who suffer, at the moment when they are suffering the most.

3. – I begin no longer to be able to take a step outside without passing under the view of some creditor.

Idea for a book that would be called: *The Poor Master*. Protagonist: Jules Barbey d'Aurevilly.

(I decide, after two years, to publish the first page – the only one that exists – because it sheds some light into two or three obscure corners. The book could be important, the author being one of those who have the need to say all they know and all they think. He renounced it for fear of giving too much pleasure to certain demons, perhaps also so as not to break his own heart. Consult on this subject the *Mendiant ingrat*, pp. 420-424.)

Unfinished introduction to *The Poor Master*, with this epigraph: "*Flammeum gladium atque* VERSATILEM, Barbey d'Aurevilly in person."

The worst misfortune for a great man is the admiration of imbeciles. A heavy volume entitled JULES BARBEY D'AUREVILLY, *His Life and His Work* has just been published by a Monsieur Eugène Grelé, with a preface by M. Jules Levallois (?). In that juvenile work by an autochthonous pion, informed by an old cosmopolite demoiselle, what I found most agreeable is the preface by M. Jules Levallois, which is absent. If the *rest* was only stupid, one could understand it. I do not hate the simple idiots who often consoled me as men of wit, but I willingly pound on the crafty and the venomous. Now, Monsieur Grelé's concern seems to have been to make Barbey d'Aurevilly into a grotesque and even something more.

God knows that I have renounced the old plan of writing a book about d'Aurevilly. Having been, for twenty-two years, the intimate friend of that deadman and remained the *only* person capable of speaking about him with any competence, it pleased me that the noble artist who had such fine hours of pride has become once more, on his way to blessed Eternity by way of Purgatory's torments, the grandiose *Unknown* man that he was five hundred years ago.

But can I stand idly by as the swine of vanity or the flat-headed and short-tailed macaques of the literature of complacency leave their droppings on his grave?

"I am counting on you," he said to me, "to ensure that I am respected when I die."

Barbey d'Aurevilly has nobody but me to defend him. If I did not speak, there would be no end to the profanations and stupidities. Ah! I do not forget that I speak for a small number of people and that the ignorance of literary things is more and more universal. Who knows, for example, whether M. Doumic is a sot and whether M. Ledrain is another sot? As for myself, it is enough if *I* know it, having all the trouble in the world to remember the names of those prigs, which continually escape me.

How many times, when I thought I was young still, didn't the author of *The Bewitched* say to me: – "My dear Bloy, you are the only one to whom I would like to confide the publication of my works, when I am no longer here!..." One person knew how to relieve me of that legacy. Barbey d'Aurevilly was not a difficult fortress to scale, especially at eighty years old.

I had [dreamt of something] better than that. Was it not to me whom, several weeks before his death, he asked to have a priest come to prepare him for it, telling me, the poor devil, that he did not know anyone else to turn to for such a service. Knowing him well, I had the joy of finding almost immediately the priest that suited him. He was a very humble Franciscan, a confessor of indigents and illiterates. I knew that the dying man, never having habituated his old stomach to the toads of penitence, would have been disgusted to the point of despair by a *distinguished* ecclesiastic. Grelé who believed to write what he believes to be the life of his character, mentioned at least that circumstance, – for him, moreover, so secondary in importance! – on the last page of his massacring biography. I was named, on that page, for the one and only time, and mysteriously qualified as the *common friend...*

(Having then, once again, renounced, provisorily at least, to discourage the assassins of the dead, I think that some of my notes on the book that has just been honored with a mention [of my name] will not be judged without interest. I have included them here, all rough around the edges, such as they were written – like those on the prig Branchereau's book – during a reading that disgusted me. Eugénie de Guérin's charming expression about d'Aurevilly is well noted: "A beautiful palace in which there is a labyrinth." The Minotaur lost in that labyrinth assuredly does not find Theseus' sword. The great statuary to which the present work is dedicated often told me that there are people, much more numerous than I thought, whose vocation is constantly to solicit kicks in the pants and who die of consumption when they don't get them. Grelé appears to me to belong to that crowd.)

"Ante Porcos"

Old Barbey's "Antigone." It is, I believe, Séverine who invented that. The Poor Master, disguised as blind Œdipus and led about among the publishers or merchants of autographs by a forty-year-old demoiselle... And to say that no man could have, more than d'Aurevilly, the preoccupation and fear of ridicule!

"The sister of charity of genius," said the tender Coppée, speaking about the same person. It is surprising how that poet is gifted in writing phrases all the words of which, without exception, are inexact. Sister of charity *on the one side,* genius *on the other, it is the height of stupidity or dementia. It is above all the height of commonplace adopted by senility.*

"For want of talent," admits Grelé, "I put all my soul into it." All Grelé's soul! There must be some room left. Grelé represents posterity. p. 8.

Hanotaux and a dozen personages of that same importance, nearly all presented by me, of whom never a word is mentioned. p. 10.

D'Aurevilly's Protestant ancestor and consequently a "good fellow." p. 15.

"Barbey's woolen stockings." p. 17.

"The best things have one time only." p. 17. One can believe that the worst have two times or even three, like the waltz.

Grelé's base hatred for nobility apropos of d'Aurevilly's, which he considers ridiculous. His reflections on buying one's way into the nobility *are a fine instance of loutishness.*

Adjectival lyricism. "The febrile over-excitement of a contagious enthusiasm that became unhealthy by force of being violent." p. 29.

"He (the young Barbey) was more inclined towards that sort of latent paganism, immanent naturalism...." *p. 32.*

"The pretty *name of d'Aurevilly, that* graceful-sounding appellation." *p. 61.*

He shut himself up in his ivory tower." *p. 62. When will people stop using that sacrilegious cliché?*

"D'Aurevilly's sadnesses and despairs of a Byron, What Never Dies, The Story Without a Name, *etc." p. 94. My extreme disgust for all that.*

Why did d'Aurevilly not become a democrat? The unpacking of Grelé's generous ideas.

"His vanity, his only goddess *from then on." p. 104. D'Aurevilly's incredulity. pp. 109-111.*

Grelé's comical attitude recounting a crisis of melancholy that d'Aurevilly had, – crisis which he was not the witness to and which he is not quite sure about. That historian resembles a nurse who is full of solicitude, contin-

uously offering the chamber pot or a tisane.

Grelé speaks of d'Aurevilly's Irony which "characterized" him. p. 122. False and stupid.

Barbey d'Aurevilly passes his days "babbling, getting dressed and undressed." p. 123. Platitude and perfidy.

Complaisant reminder of that "ancestor whom the Beloved was the father and godfather of." p. 129. When a person has been cuckolded or born a bastard by any ordinary individual, it is an enormous shame. When that happens by a king, it is an infinitely honorable memory that is preserved in the family papers. Poor Barbey who was not a stranger to that vanity, sometimes spoke to me, stamping his feet with glory, about a great-grandmother who would have passed down to him, in a way, the abominable blood of the Bourbons. Grelé wallows in that filth.

Our Grelé's mark of style: "The clouds of revery and the solid platform of the earth"! p. 126.

"The press disgusts me." D'Aurevilly's phrase seems to Grelé the effect of an ill man's bad mood. p. 128. It

won't be him who would be easily disgusted. He has an excellent stomach.

Grelé knows better than d'Aurevilly what comedy is. p. 142.

Barbey d'Aurevilly, merchant of chasubles. The great artist had hoped, for one minute, to earn, in this way, a little money. He never spoke to me about it, and I don't know the details. But how could he not have been odiously duped? The thing was so well hidden. What was needed for this misery to be found out was the sense of smell of a truffle searcher such as MM. Anatole France and Jules Lemaître possess. Grelé naturally very keen on vileness, mentions those two individuals "our finest critics." p. 179.

Barbey d'Aurevilly's high life. "One cannot keep pouring out twaddle in the salons and boudoirs." p. 180. This tone on the part of Grelé is unexpected.

The chasubles again. Joy of Grelé representing to himself the effective and material sale, by the admirable writer, of those church ornaments. He has gone off about it enough already, the dirty reptile! p. 187.

His indignation at the thought that d'Aurevilly treats contemptuously such pedants as Jules Simon, Vacherot, Saisset. p. 193.

Barbey d'Aurevilly did not know how to make himself loved by the crowd, he took it badly. Nobody tells it to him straight to his face. p. 199.

The workers of 1848 did not find in d'Aurevilly the "sister soul" they had need of.

D'Aurevilly having, at that time, desired to escape the world, to close himself up in a monastery, the sage Grelé thinks that he would have needed a monastery like those before the Revolution where one lived it up all the time. p. 216.

Grelé, the just Grelé, rejects d'Aurevilly's anti-liberal doctrine applauding the Coup d'État. p. 222.

He does not support the Credo *with regards to criticism. p. 233.*

He calls Baudelaire: the "fantastical poet." p. 240.

The one happy expression by Grelé apropos of Trébutien who spent a fortune on the publications of his friend d'Aurevilly: "His friendship alone has need of the making of a fortune." p. 241. He must have stolen that very modest gem from someone.

Imbecilic ideas by the same on the occasion of a plan of marriage by d'Aurevilly. It is just the opposite of what he says or rather what a certain person told him to say – so stupidly besides. p. 261.

Grelé does not forgive d'Aurevilly for wanting "to lead the world back to a former time, etc." p. 282.

The name of B d'A. not figuring in the edition by Maurice de Guérin, in exactly the same way as mine does not figure in Grelé's Life.

Long perfidious note on the Forty Medallions of the Academy. *p. 299. Why would anyone want that gentleman to disoblige other gentlemen of his kind who succeeded?*

The triple cretin Grelé explaining the Right of Providence apropos of Un Prêtre marié. *p. 308.*

Ever that ridiculous word of "individualist" to characterize d'Aurevilly's independence!

Grelé's Ignorance. He says not one word about the journal The Tenth of December, *in 1869 and 1870. The skirt who feeds him his documents never heard of it.*

"When he returns to Paris, in the spring of 1873, he no longer brings his former warlike ardors to the task of journalism. His critical faculties be-come finer and suppler. He cultivates the beautiful flower that had never, un-til then, germinated in his soul: *the virtue of tolerance and charity." p. 347.*

The word TOLERANCE *is evidently the only word that Grelé can understand.*

"The truth is that a sixty-five-year old man would not know, in good faith, how to share the intolerance of a neo-phyte. What else would the test of time serve for?" p. 348.

"You'll come around!" said an old, despicable priest to a seminarist full of enthusiasm.

"Having grown old, he is always inde-pendent, but he understands better *that the independence of every writer has its limits and that that rare virtue must not be confused with the spirit of in-transigence." p. 356. Without a doubt, there would be no more possible chaos then.*

"After Léon's death (his brother), he lies low in his modest room. He runs

away from the world." *p. 358.*

For twelve years, from that epoch forward, November 15, 1876, I saw just the opposite, every day.

Enormous inexactitudes. p. 363.

Forever "the individualistic d'Aurevilly, his battle munitions, his musket blasts, his punt gun, his rutilant panache, *his well-fed fusillades, etc." What style of a pion!*

D'Aurevilly's panache "rallying" individuals who never set foot in his home. p. 370.

"His Germaine, *he adorns it like a bride ready to receive the nuptial ring of* public favor." *p. 374. That phrase alone merits the Monthyon prize.*

"Renan, the suave iconoclast of the life of Jesus." p. 388.

Grelé, like a good bourgeois, calls life "the universal lottery." p. 391.

"Barbey d'Aurevilly," he says, "wanted to die a quill in hand"! p. 392.

Such is the idiot made responsible for writing the biography of one of the greatest Christian writers of the last century.

6. – The death of a Christian is nothing but a huge act of humility. – JEANNE.

Read an article with neither light nor heat by Lucien Descaves on the subject of church bells. I understand by it that the ignoble Combes, who actually seems to be possessed, has just prescribed by circular an incredibly strange inquest. The jackass would like to collect all the complaints by inhabitants whom church bells or religious communities prevent from sleeping. The administrative interdiction of bells!... *L'Invitation au voyage!*[54]

"… If we did not live in the thoughts of an overwhelming beauty," writes Jeanne to a friend, "where would we be? May God have pity on those who eat and who keep warm."

"Provided we possess Eternal Life, what does the rest matter to us who would like to follow Jesus Christ in his ignominy?..."

7. – Thiers. Andalusia and Torrès Védras. What a pity to see Napoleon waste his strength like that!

We spoke of the compass whose magnetic needle continually points to the North, that is to say to the Enemy, to the Devil. Thus does the Fall want it, for one must see in him a figure of the crucified Man. Turned to the North, it suffices for him to stretch out his arms and touch the Orient with his right hand, and

---

[54]*Invitation au voyage*: French for "Invitation to the voyage." In reference to a poem by Baudelaire, of the same title, included in *Flowers of Evil*.

the Occident with his left.

9. – Admirable correlation of events or incidents in this life, the which cannot be seen except in succession, alas! and which revealed in that way God's designs, if one could fix them simultaneously in the Light! It is like the letters of the alphabet, which are nothing in isolation, but which, brought together by intelligence, have the power to give life or death.

It is many years now that Jesus forces me, by the blows of a whip, to walk before him on the waters... He is the Truth, and the truth has need of Saints, Martyrs, – it has no need at all of writers. I confess that I have often hoped, because of a certain power of the word, to lead the multitudes toward God. What has that dream achieved? Several souls only, several poor and dear souls who were conquered. But that is not huge, and who can say how many is huge?... Be patient and gentle with yourself. It is infinitely probable that God will do nothing about what you dream. He will do *better*.

Thiers. Masséna[55] still in Portugal. Lugubrious and terrible story.

13. – Simon the Cyrene helps Jesus to carry his Cross. Modern Christians place their cross on the back of Jesus.

---

[55]Masséna: Marshal André Masséna (AD 1758-1817), a French general under Napoleon.

Read Bossuet's panegyric on Saint Theresa. There are beautiful passages, but what a detestable ending! "Abandon riches, macerate the body?? No, I do not say to you, *Christians*, that you should abandon your riches, nor that you should macerate your bodies by long mortifications... etc." It just at our deacon's level. Christianity is good for louts. The truth is that Bossuet preached before the court of Louis XIV, while our deacon addresses himself to the barnyard of M. Ménier. It is probably the same thing. One goes to the devil with all the words that are a derision of Christianity, and if one is Bossuet, one becomes schismatic at fifty-five years old.

Thiers. Fuentès de Oñoro. Since Tilsit and the Bayonne incident, I endure the anguish, ever building, of witnessing the most monstrous waste of strength, beauty, greatness that has ever been seen.

What man was so manifestly blind as Napoleon? The inconceivable inertia of that Hannibal – perfectly available however after Wagram – obstinately remaining in Paris, then when his presence would have been so profitable in Portugal, is a stupefying proof of it.

17. – After a large number of days of an atrocious poverty, the details of which cannot be expressed, we receive finally an assassin's response. A rich man, previously my friend and even *obliged* to me a little, declares the absolute impossibility of his being able to do whatever it might be and protests his devotion. I sense the faint breath of death.

18. – I have had many friends who have passed through my life as one passes down a dark and dangerous street and who have grown distant so as never to be seen again.

19. – The seventy-year-old mailman who serves us declares in an apologetic and sepulchral tone of voice, with regards to the eventuality of death, which he spoke about, I don't know why, that *there is nothing to reproach oneself for*. God forfend that we should contradict that admirable man!

Thiers. *The Council*. It is here primarily that the old Voltairean umbrella must be deployed. "Sanctity does not always mean Wisdom." The entire chapter is summed up in that sentence, like a wad of excrement picked up in one single scoop by a vast shovel for manure. I have had enough of hearing people speak in my childhood and youth of that wisdom of the bourgeois!

To say of someone, were it of an illustrious person: "One cannot get any stupider" is assuredly an act of malevolence. Why does the opposite, "One cannot get any *less* stupid," sound even ruder?

20. – A character trait of the bourgeois is the fear of any heroic determination in others, as well as in himself.

To a priest:

Tell the "good poor person" who gave 10 francs that I placed it with you in my heart and that he will see me, one day, among the beggars, at the feet of his Judge.

22. – The place that I occupy in the hidden Plan is such that I cannot be assisted, even materially, except by those who love me *supernaturally*. Those who love me naturally cannot do ANYTHING.

    A poor person exists who would willingly deprive himself in a complete manner, and have himself be spit in the face, if that could deliver me. He can do something, most certainly.

23. – Admirable story touching on the incomparable mercantilism of the devotion to Saint Anthony. A novena of masses is requested of a curate whom one vaguely informs of a temporal advantage to be obtained. On the tenth day, the devout person comes for a mass of acts of grace which the saint, it appears, sorely won. "A relative," she says, "from whom I was to inherit something died yesterday, just when the last mass was finishing."

25. – Noel. High mass very painful because of that old ass of a deacon who cannot dispense with yammering for half an hour. He would do better to economize his words and be more generous with the coal.

His church is never heated. I return home frozen to the center of my soul and to the bone.

26. – *Deus Caritas*. Text for the exclusive and constant usage of those who hate God with all their heart.

It is nice, the new exegetic school, insofar as regards the interpretation or only the reading of the Holy Texts. There are some priests who think, in contempt of the Council of Trent, that there is better than the Vulgate. I know one person whom the tail of the dog of Tobias prevents from sleeping.

27. – Way of the cross at the convent. Let us speak about it, it is worth the effort. The meditation, the parochial and fetid meditation in French, was read by the mother Mary, the old pretty woman who for fifteen or twenty years now makes the decorations and fixes up the boarding school, a person full of sweetness whose speciality it is to be perfect in all things. Even though fairly habituated to the venality of Pharisaism, that superficial person's manner of reading surprised me. She had a *divine* voice, one of those voices of an angel, by turns broken by emotion and reinvigorated by holy bursts of passion. She has a way of exhaling "sweet Jesus" at you that reminds me invincibly of the – however frightening that might appear – "ma'am!" of prostitutes. Right afterwards, the Lord's prayer and the angelic Salutation, always in French, were grunted, if I dare say so, in the mother superior's voice of a cleaning woman. Fourteen times in a row, that. Rough test of my piety. The event in

Martinique could be the consequence of a way of the cross of that sort, executed by the women religious of the same institute.

28. – Nothing, and here is the joyous New Year's Day right around the corner. If God permitted this distress to last several days longer only, we could no longer hide our indigence and, in this vile town, that would be our death.

29. – Agony. More than ever, this world appears hideous to us. The merchants, the women religious, the greater part of the priests are really the enemies of God. A house like the Saint-Joseph convent, for example, with all its outward appearances of piety and its professional edification of innocents, is most likely a habitacle of demons. If one circumstance like the divulgation of our poverty came to chip away at the varnish of benevolence or politeness that the basest interest has extended over all those faces, their look would become, instantly, frightening.

30. – I had carried the lamp into a dark corner. Suddenly, in that light, I see on a shelf a small pile of sous placed there and completely forgotten. *There are 35 centimes*. It is as if Jesus said to me: "It is all I can spare at the moment. Patience and courage! Do not be angry with me. I was crucified..."

To him for whom God is dead:

You say to me, and this is not the first time: So many changes over the course of two years! *I scarcely know what you mean by that. But let me tell you what I do know. In matters of religion,* what one does not do absolutely, one absolutely does not do, *and it is something to fear that one never does it. A Christian who would take communion three hundred times a year, but who* DELIBERATELY *would not take communion* every day, *would be with all the "good Christians," that is to say with all those lukewarm, good friends of the devil who "effect their salvation" and who, for centuries and centuries, will not draw any closer to God. Priests who say otherwise are Judases or homicidal Christians. I didn't stop obeying Herod and cutting the throats of Innocents until the day I decided to take communion every day. Until then, I was in every way a bastard and a lamentable idiot.*

That, not in my imagination of a writer, but in substantial reality. I beg you to pay attention.

The day that you do what it is your duty to do, under pain of death, not only for yourself, but for your family, *that day then you will see, you will hear, you will understand, you will feel, you will cry, and you will be able to. Then you will deliver me, if there is still time to deliver me. I have told you so. But the ability will certainly not be given to you beforehand... I have suffered so much that I am without strength. I cannot offer you for your New Year's gifts anything else than my signature. There are more banal gifts.*

31. – HOW GOD TREATS HIS FRIENDS.

Ideo ecce ego ad vos prophetas, et sapientes, et "scribas," et ex illis occidetis, et crucifigetis, et ex eis flagellabitis in synagogis vestris et persequemini de civitate in civitatem. – Matth. 23:34.

Is that all, Lord? No, it is added that that will last until the time when all the blood spilt on earth covers the hypocrites and the accursed. But that flux, that rising tide is from an infinitely large ocean whose swells have receded from the bottom of the Heart of Mary, whose ebb is incalculable. While waiting, the friends of Jesus get by as they can, with the patience they find. As much as that is permitted, they are killed, they are crucified, they are flagellated, they are persecuted, and the consolation that they obtain, – I will tell you about it. It is that of the damned, who have no other refreshment than the sight of the frightful faces of demons. The friends of Jesus see around them modern Christians, and it is like that that they can conceive of hell. Such is our case in Cochons-sur-Marne.

Jesus said: "My yoke is easy and my burden light."[56] One is forced to suppose a mysterious meaning, for it is clear that in the direct sense, nothing is more terrible than that yoke nor more crushing than that burden.

Before everything and above all, Jesus is the Abandoned One. Those who love him must be abandoned, but abandoned like him, abandoned Gods! Behold the torment that has no name.

---

[56]My yoke...: Matthew 11:30.

1903

> *I affirm point blank that the modern Catholic*
> *world is a reprobate world, damned,*
> *absolutely rejected, irremediably, a vile world*
> *that the Lord Jesus is sick and tired of[57] in the*
> *most complete fashion, a mirror of ignominy*
> *where he cannot see himself without feeling*
> *fear, as in Gethsemane.*

January

3. – I am locked inside the darkness where I hear those whom I love weeping and bleeding, almost without seeing them.

4. – We suffer *at the table*. Question, as of this fourth day of the new year: does God want our hides?

René Martineau instructed by me, in October, to inform Joergensen of my feelings on the subject of his incredible article in the *Vort Land*, finally conveys to me his response. He wanted to forestall the Danish public from not reading his article by not naming me. So my worst suspicions are confirmed. Johannes Joergensen, whom I believed to be a man of the most admirable character (see *Mon Journal*, p. 156 ff.), is

---

[57]Sick and tired of: in French, the expression used is "soupé" from "souper" which means to dine or to take supper. For a powerful development of this trope, see Léon Bloy's *Blood of the Poor* (Sunny Lou Publishing, 2021).

simply a journalist. He explains away my laments as an extreme "vanity of a man of letters" and a "furious desire for notoriety." The notoriety of Copenhagen! The poor poet has fallen so far down the stairs that he cannot understand that after having tried to lift up his heart, I am sorry to see it so low.

Our poor children ask for bread before going to sleep.

5. – How is it possible, o Mary! that you resist so many tears? If my beloved little girls prayed to me on their knees and wept, I would be incapable of resisting them.

Here is something that is as astonishing as it is sorrowful. Véronique has *composed*, one can call it that, to the insignificant words found in a child's collection of stories, a melody of sadness, of an incredibly powerful sadness, and Madeleine, ravished, sings it all day long. I cannot express what I feel. Is it possible that my Véronique has received that particular infusion of the Holy Ghost which is the genius of music?

6. – Epiphany. At seven o'clock in the evening we are anguishing. Jeanne and the children suffering from HUNGER, I ran to the pork butcher who consented once again to give me credit for some morsels. Never, even in '95, have we been so low.

8. – Help arrives. Before continuing this terrible journal, and as we have been given an instant to breathe, I want to say one thing that fills my heart and which will remain there like a testimony to be read with emotion, ten years from now, by my beloved little girls.

The poor children were hungry, that is certain, and their laments could have been for us an occasion for despair. But the dear ones, by the effect of an intelligence and a resignation much greater than their age, made not a sound, limiting themselves to often asking for bread, the only aliment that there was in the house, the baker not having withdrawn his credit from us.

May God eternally bless them as I bless them!

11. – Thiers. Continued the grievous reading of 1812. What attenuates the pain is the thought that Napoleon was, if not the father, at least the uncle by inheritance of the contemporary Bourgeois, and that one must see in him, decidedly, an imbecile of the most striking genius.

12. – Moscow, the Battle of Berezina. Everything becomes insane, desperate.

13. – I will need other readings before I can form a personal idea of that atrocious war. Thiers condemns Napoleon in an absolute manner and his blame seems

plausible. But his name is Thiers, and by consequence he must be mistaken. In Spain, and above all in Portugal, there is an inexcusable error, I think. It is the *absence* of Napoleon. But he was present in Russia, having to submit to, with others, a prodigious chastisement... Moreover, History is, in essence, inconjecturable. Events other than those that are accomplished cannot even be imagined without stupidity or madness. Napoleon without Berezina or Waterloo would be a face without eyes, an indescribable monster. Then, the incomparable beauty of the Battle of Borodino, for example, what triumph could equal it?

14. – Undertook the reading of *The Cathedral*, by Huysmans. Repugnant, but necessary. Who would speak the truth about the *converted* Huysmans if I didn't speak it?

Apropos of that man, read in *Paris Echo* an article on the Académie Goncourt which Huysmans is the president of. I already knew that the ten academicians each have a salary of six thousand francs, but what I did not know was that there is an annual prize of five thousand, destined to encourage the young and poor writers of talent, in other words not me. It would be amusing to see how that mechanism functions.

15. – Continued *The Cathedral*. Nothing can equal the unintelligence and the sumptuous asininity of that book, unless it is the baseness of heart, the total lack of generosity that characterizes the author.

The crow of Saint Anthony the Hermit whom the Church honors on this day visited us. We continue to live.

16. – Spoke of Huysmans to a priest who knew him a little. I told him what I thought of that academician who treated me with such injustice and who will perhaps treat God in the same way, when his fantasy of Catholicism has passed.

17. – Still Huysmans and his book. If I didn't have to write about him, usefully, a little later on, no employment of my time could be stupider.

18. – *The Cathedral*, has a single person read it in its entirety? I do not believe that there exists in France a single so-called literary work whose boredom is more suffocating.

19. – Success, with a huge sigh! 488 pages without encountering a single idea, that is flooring. Ah! his success explains itself! But I think that one buys it to be fashionable, out of snobism, not to read it. One would have to be, like me, a galley slave of criticism to swallow that.

In a recomforting manner I pick up Thiers again whose mediocrity at least is confined to grandiose or terrible events. Began the XVth volume,

Spain in 1812, Wellington, Salamanca, the surprising disunity of leaders and the homicidal ill will of some, finally and above all the agony, in that other extremity of Europe, of the sublime soldiers whom Napoleon had not condemned to the terrible extermination of the Russian campaign.

20. – Finished correcting the proofs of *Letters by Barbey d'Aurevilly to Léon Bloy*. Ennui and sadness in this remembrance of a miserable period of time without the means to lift up my heart by notes and commentaries. Some of those letters, among the last, are quite good, very generous, and avenge me greatly for the calumnies and humiliations [I've suffered].

Poor Barbey deserved better then that period towards the end of his life, it seems to me. If *The Desperate Man* had appeared ten years earlier, in 1877, I believe he would have done something important for that unfortunate book, the fate of which could have been greatly changed. In that epoch, he didn't know Antigone, and he hadn't been frequenting so very long the terrible Jews who vilified, as much as they could, his old age.

Continued Thiers. Miserable aspects of Napoleon on return from Russia. His lack of moral greatness, so far as it seems. And yet what strength was needed by that lightning-struck man so as not to descend into despair!

23. – Yesterday I had read, in *Paris Echo*, the inter-

view of a centenarian Italian woman living in the vicinity of Rome, who is said to have held Leon XIII as a child in her arms more than ninety years ago, and whom one was going to see in pilgrimage on account of that. That ruin of a woman had very little to say. But one spoke of a long interview that she was supposed to have had, in those days, with the Pope, mysterious conversation on the subject of which she observed a singular discretion.

Now I learn that yesterday morning, at the moment perhaps when I was reading the interview, that old woman died, burnt alive by accident...!

Interrupted the Campaign of Saxony in order to begin *Saint Lydwine* by Huysmans.

24. – *Saint Lydwine*. Huysmans is brought by his subject to Holland; restituted thus for a bit of time at his origins, he has done a little better. But what a misery and what miseries! What to say, for example, about the ten pages on the *army of saints* of that period, with the employment of all the technical phraseology of military art? It is enough to give the poorest among us the illusion and pride of wealth.

25. – Sadness on Sunday, once again. It is, on this day, above all, when God is disdained, and it is on this day, above all, when we sense our solitude.

26. – Finished *Saint Lydwine*. The life of a saint, the

history of it studied in great detail, ought to be beneficial to the soul, ought to give joy, enthusiasm for
God. This one gives only lassitude and disgust.

Ah! how am I not, me too, a column of the
Church in my condition, a column of silver!

28. – The preceptor's invoice. That changes for me
the Bulletins of the Grand Army.

I learn that the ignoble apostate Combes, pro-
scriber of congregations, has inexplicably declared
before the tribunal I do not know what feelings or
what *spiritualist* views, which had immediately
caused a tempest among the enraged sectarians who
had given him their confidence. Will he also become
a column of the Church? A column of shit!

My readings of Huysmans have so depressed
me that I pick up Thiers again. Lutzen. The grandeur
is over, ever since Moscow. In 1813, 1814, and 1815,
one can feel the coldness of those three or four hundred thousand heroic soldiers' cadavers, absurdly sacrificed in Russia and Spain, and whom children had to
replace. Napoleon does not ever appear to have re-
pented it.

29. – Bautzen. The bitterness of this story is in harmony with my excessive sadness. Evening prayer at
church, said in French by a vicar who speaks through
his nose. That bias, in all the parishes, to say prayers
in French, obstinately, when everyone knows them in

Latin, appears *diabolical* to me.

30. – A friend spoke to me about my poverty. – Would to God, I said to him, that I were *poor*! I would be then the companion of worshiping shepherds. But I am *indigent*, absolutely indigent, living by miracle alone, incurring debts while counting on God to pay them, in a word practicing what all honest men would call fraud, an abuse of confidence, – in God. And that has been going on for years, and no one suspects anything, and I have yet to be pinched...

31. – While waiting for the effect of a dreadful step, I drag myself over Thiers, the dragging of a desperate man... Towards evening, I have the assurance of being able to breathe for two or three days. Then God will let loose again.

I am a miserable man who inflicts divine torments on himself for money, and who will perhaps die in twenty-four hours, having poisoned everything.

February

1st. – What afflicts us most is the succession, the law of Time. Being resemblances of God, participating in divine Nature, Gods ourselves, we have the need to see everything, to feel everything, *simultaneously*. The fall, it is to have fallen from Eternity.

3. – Saint Joseph's Convent. – *Lessons in courtesy*. Véronique tells us that she received this instruction: When a person sneezes, you must not say to him: *God bless you!* That was fine in the past. Today, nobody says it any more!!! You must say: "That's enough!" or "Be quiet!"?

5. – Here is what Jeanne gave me:

"All the Jewish people will rise up and make a bloody Way of the Cross. Their enemies will throw themselves at them, at each station, in order to crush them, there where they will have humiliated Jesus."

6. – Unpublished article:

Christmas Mystery

I just read Huysmans The Cathedral *and* Saint Lydwine, *one after the other. I cannot continue. That literature of tribulation which always gives me the feeling of having been drawn out into the light like a tenia, with the precautions of a pharmacist, had completely depressed me. The schoolboy of Médan, the author of several little impurities prior to his conversion, whom I took so much trouble to scrub clean about fifteen years ago, and who recently discovered Catholicism in order soon to become one of its columns, had overwhelmed me in twenty-five thousand lines with his "rare epithets," so laboriously extracted from diverse lexicons with a view to serving up silly and centenarian appreciations – on matters that children are all doctors of.*

It was in the middle of this distress when the good postman brought me a copy of Christmas Mystery *by Jacques Debout. (Gabriel Beauchesne, publisher; Paris). I hasten to confess a very hostile first impression of that small book, in which I was expecting to see one of those homicidal excogitations of sanctimoniousness by which one makes imbeciles of youth in Catholic circles or institutions.*

Soon, however, I changed my mind. This Jacques Debout – obviously a pseudonym – was not an unknown person to me. I had read a novel by him in which not all the ideas pleased me, but which had appeared generous to me and written with a robust use of the language. One would have to see.

Before going any further, I must warn the reader that I do not like the theater, whatever genre it might be. I consider it anti-literary to the point of deploring, for example, that Shakespeare didn't write the history of England in an epic poem instead of writing dramas. From a Christian morals point of view, I think like Bossuet, who followed in that the Church Fathers and Tradition, that the theater is essentially bad, absolutely indefensible. So one sees what is possible to hope for from me, when it is a matter of a play of any sort destined to be represented on the stage by young people, so-called Christians. Divertissement that the Jesuits are said to have been the inventors of, and which is practiced more or less everywhere, since the faith has died and is buried. But if some supposed piece has the pretension to be one of those Mysteries *as the Middle Ages understood them, oh! then, I rear up completely.*

At a celebration that took place, last year, in a convent in Cochons-sur-Marne, I saw, in the guise of a mystery, the unpardonable grotesque of a Joseph Sold By His Brothers *played by the daughters of shopkeepers or pen-pushers, one of whom having been dressed up as the patriarch Jacob and fitted out unthinkably with a beard! which took place in the vicinity of the Holy Sacrament among the women re-*

ligious who do not believe themselves to be disagreeable to God.

On another day, in the same house, the same artists offered the no less unexpected spectacle of the Martyrs of Lyon. There was, this time, a saint Pothin, bearded, him also, miter on head and cross in hand, giving episcopal benediction *to the Witnesses of Jesus Christ!!! The room writhed [in laughter] at the appearance of that pontiff... That occurred, I repeat, in a house where one is persuaded that God is believed in.*

The ridiculousness of those ploys is assuredly perceptible, even for retailers in the canton seat. But the perfect ignominy and sacrilegious horror of such masquerades wherein childhood is profaned, – who could have suspected it among the beasts of commerce, the stinking and incomestible livestock of the sales counter?

I know, right? Strange preliminaries to an article on that poor Christmas Mystery *which I have decided to speak about. It's the least I could do, as it consoled me, one day of sadness. After what has just been said, the praise that I would like to make does not seem very easy. But, to begin with, I have treated thus far only of ordinary stu-*

pidities, and the Christmas Mystery *is, on the contrary, a touching and beautiful thing. Then I persuade myself, as best I can, that that play could never have been represented* unadulterated *in any Christian school or boarding school. In fact, a troupe of actors of both sexes being impossible in those places, it would necessarily require either girls to play Saint Joseph, the Shepherds, the Three Wise Men, or a boy to* play Mary! – intolerable monstruosities. All that is left is the marvelous expedient of marionettes.

God forfend that I should forget the Mystery of the Nativity *by Maurice Bouchor, at the little Théâtre des Marionettes in the Vivienne Gallery, in January '91, the roles being read in the wings by Jean Richepin, Raoul Ponchon, and two others. Yes, veritable marionettes as big as ten-year-old children, defective and poor like figures cut out of humble calvary scenes.*

"Nothing surpasses," I wrote, several days later, "the sweetness of that poem where the important roles were played by the Bull and the Ass, after the archangel Gabriel accorded them human speech. The infinitely humble joy of those sinless animals, who can no longer do without knowing that Je-

sus will be born, is penetrating like the light. The muddied soul of the spectator is clarified by them. What happens then is the rain of Lilies, large pale lilies, dazzling and silent, of the purest Adoration. The mellowness of that moment is inexpressible. An effluvia of reconciliation and love which one might believe eucharistic, positively emanates from those cardboard beasts, charitable and rudimentary, who holily dialogue through the touching voice of invisible narrators."

Jacques Debout's Mystery is worthy of those marionettes, and that is the most affectionate and most profound praise [one can give]. May he obtain, one day, that interpretation, the only one he deserves! That humble poem is beautiful in its form, more beautiful in its tone, its author being one of those monsters who really love the poor and whom the Poor [Christ] fully burning with Glory visits amorously. He is, perhaps, the last or the penultimate friend of the poor, more and more detested in a Society that will one day be completely Godless.

Many people whom his Mystery would make weep are precisely the devourers of the poor. I recognize the athropophagy of sentimental people.

"I was hungry and you didn't give me anything to eat," the Judge will say. "Forgive me, Lord," they will answer, "We bled a poor person that day, and we had prepared him to honor you. All that was needed was for you to take part in our feast."

Jacques Debout has another manner of reading the Gospel. He has the manner of the Saints which is irresistible, and I know nothing better to say about that almost infantile book that touched my heart...

Excessively bitter reading of the Campaign of Saxony, a veritable disaster. That ruin of the greatest of men is intolerable...

There are days when one could believe God to be burning with anger against those who love him. *Deus noster ignis consumens est.* Hebr. 12:29.

9. – Read the terrible battle of Wachau, near Leipzig. On seeing Napoleon's impassive calm before, during, and after those immense butcheries, his gaiety even, sometimes, in the middle of the most terrible catastrophes and his absence, at least apparent, of any remorse, on Saint Helena, I am reminded of that troubling detail, true or false, given in I do not know what memoir. Napoleon having been auscultated one day, the doctor discovered that the beating of his heart was *absolutely imperceptible.*

Something in Thiers is very sweet to me. His furious and constant hatred for Bernadotte.

11. – Finished the terrible Campaign of Saxony. Napoleon is brought back to the Rhine. Enormous convulsions of his power. The Battle of Leipzig, it alone, cost the lives of 120,000 men... Why is that reading so painful to me? The word patriotism, at a distance of one century, does not mean much. The truth, I think, is that I cannot come to terms with the *lost forces*, – which is, from a transcendent point of view, one of the most afflicting forms of injustice.

In 1814, Napoleon made an effort to save France with several tens of thousands of men, the majority of whom were children, having lost *pointlessly*, in Spain to begin with, then in Russia, finally in the fortresses of Germany, nearly five hundred thousand soldiers of the best troops in the world. The guardian angels of France must have sobbed.

Have learnt of the birth of a little Lutheran, one more soul for infernal mediocrity, barring a miracle. I dream, with a great sweetness, of a man of God, of a prophet invested with his power, who would strike heretical nations with *infecundity* – while waiting for their abjuration or their extermination... EGEO GLORIA DEI (Romans, 3:23).

12. – Question. Why didn't God have need of anyone to create the world? It is quite certain that God created the world all by himself, by his own Hand, and it is

something one does not think enough about. God had no servants to create all things in his stead, etc. But when he wanted to "reform the dignity of the human substance," as it is said in the sacrament of the mass, he could neither be born, nor die, on his own; the almighty being, he could neither slap himself, nor spit in his own face, nor flagellate himself, nor crucify himself. He needed to be served, and the most horrible riffraff were the only ones able to be called on to collaborate thus in the Redemption. The executioners of Jesus Christ, could it be that, in that way, they were the veritable workers of the eleventh hour?

13. – Began the enormous XVIIIth volume by Thiers: 1814. The branches of that tall tree fall, one after the other. It is always the same suffering for me who am such a contemporary of the men of 1814. That miserable historian, that sententious mender of old umbrellas, uncovers such great things for me all the same! Oh! Napoleon's two discourses, the first at the Legislative Assembly (p. 179) and the second before the Senate (p. 182)! The first above all!

"When, for the first time, I met Léon Bloy, and I asked: 'Who is that man?' I was told, '*a beggar*.' Then and there I felt that it was fate. Six months later, we were married." – JEANNE.

14. – This morning we read here, in honor of Saint Severin, the mass *pro abbatibus* wherein it is said:

Centuplum accipiet.[58] Related to which, Saint Catherine of Sienna whom we are studying affirms that the number one hundred is that of the Holy Ghost. For a moment we think that all things divine are rumbling around us.

A Jesuit affirms to me that there are saints in his Order, contemporary saints, but hidden. Response: Is it possible to hide a fire?

15. – I am persuaded to write to a Mother Mercédès, illustrious and powerful woman religious whom one supposes capable of changing my life, if she wanted to, and of whom I've heard speak about for a month now. I wrote a letter to this religious that I defy her to forget. Among other things: "I would like to complete my task. I ask that like a pious child who asks that he be permitted to complete his prayer before going to sleep. I ask that and nothing else."

Exurge, quare obdormis, Domine?[59] says the liturgy of today, Sexagesima Sunday. Jeanne reminds me of the following surprising thing. In '95, in that dreadful house in Petit-Montrouge where we were so miserable, Véronique, just recovering from an illness that had nearly killed her so short a while after the death of her brother André, said, one morning, to her mother, while pointing out the crucifix to her: "Mama, tell him to wake up!" *It was the morning of*

---

[58]*Centuplum accipiet*: Latin for "[he] shall receive a hundredfold." Matthew 19:29.

[59]*Exurge...*: Latin for "Rise up, Lord, why are you falling asleep?"

Sexagesima Sunday.

16. – Elementary geography. What is Cochons-sur-Marne? It is a hole filled with vermin.

17. – Letter from Mother Mercédès to one of the friends who convinced me to write her. "She understands perfectly that she has the duty to act and understands that with a man such as myself, one must see things through to the end." Such are her expressions. Formal promise, if I'm not mistaken.

Thiers. At Montmirail now, I undertake a parallel rereading of Henry Houssaye. It is tiring to pass continually from a lively expression to a dead one, from Lucifer to a manufacturer of candles!

18. – Began the *Last Columns of the Church*. It is time that the truth be told. There is a little too much mocking of Jesus Christ.

19. – Spoke about Bossuet to a friend who is a priest. We compare that great bishop to Fénelon who wanted the director [of conscience] to give his own feelings or thoughts to the penitent rather than limiting himself to putting him on guard against deviations and divergences. I clarify by observing that the director must be a tactician and not a strategist, that latter role needing to be left for the Holy Ghost. With this expres-

sion, I express the idea, which I have had for so long a time now, that the death of God, for the result that we see, after nineteen centuries, does not make any sense, which seems to be approved unreservedly by the confabulator. He agrees that a priest's ministry, in our society given over to the demon of impiety or the demon of stupidity, is almost always in vain, an occasion for extreme sadness. We speak also about some imbecilic devotions, propagated for some time now, the devotion to Saint *Expeditus*, for example, in order to obtain a *prompt* response. That holy martyr, whose existence appears uncertain, is represented with a cross on which one reads this: *Hodie* (today) while stepping on a crow that cries: *Cras!* (tomorrow). Built up around this exceptionally comical devotion is an important commerce of medallions, images, ex-votos, statuettes, etc.

20. – A soul that God besieges with all his power! Try to imagine something more beautiful!

21. – *Last Columns*, chapter on Huysmans. The more I think about it, the more I despise the rigid and so profitable Catholicism of this confidant of dictionaries.

23. – Fat Tuesday. To two priests who remember the Passion of Jesus Christ:

Dear friends,

I profit by these days when Jesus is so particularly tortured, to supplicate you to remember me before his exposed Body. You know the hope that I have been given. It seems to me that I am a little more miserable than before, because of my fear of a new disappointment after so many others. Then there is the length of waiting *periods. One will have needed to endure the torture of the rack, applied by somnolent executioners in a lethargic solitude, in order to know that waiting periods and above all* unknown *waiting periods can make a miserable wretch suffer, who would have need of being succored or expedited instantly. Ah! the blessing by itself is not enough. It must not come too late, and there is room to fear that, by dint of being desired in torments, it does not finish by losing its savor or its effectiveness. That last observation cannot be applicable to the present case, but I am, all the same, obsessed. You know what my old friend Ernest Hello often said, who suffered so much by desire and by unanswered prayer: One would like to see the hand of God, and it is promptitude alone that shows that Hand.*

You know our lovable children. Imagine something more heart-rending than hearing those little stricken innocents asking us for what they need or what is very useful to them and our being unable to give it to them. We have already had that enormous suffering which threatens to return. Then, all the rest which you know quite well. Old and new creditors, impatient and shouting suppliers, the daily searching for expedients and the nearly insurmountable difficulty for a writer, plunged in such a hell, to contemplate, to sufficiently recuperate. Where is the galley slave who would want a like existence, and how could I support it if I did not have, each day, the crucified Body of Our Lord? This morning I felt the first breeze of spring, so delicious, and that caress penetrated my melancholy. I was dreaming of a small, very humble house, with a garden where my poor girls could run and play while I worked in peace. All that, in our neighborhood, o my dear friends! And at the same time I said to myself that that was a vain and dolorous dream, that those things, however easy, were not meant for me. Console me, if you can, but more than anything else – pray for me, pray like God's Princes of the Blood which you have the honor of being...

P.S. I occupy myself, as best I can, on

the Last Columns of the Church, *a book that no one, except me, thinks to write and that the success of the apostles of Camelot renders more necessary with each passing day.*

24. – Fat Tuesday. Jeanne returning from church: "Reminding Jesus of our extreme destitution, I said to him: Give me what is in your Hand, open your Hand. Then he opened HIS HAND, and *I saw that It was pierced!"*

I have found nothing more beautiful in any mystical writer.

1814. Thiers and Houssaye. That story is truly an agony for me. From beginning to end, there is nothing but mistakes or crimes. Augereau, Marmont, Ney, Soult, Napoleon himself who thinks only of Paris, instead of resolutely marching on places and summoning from there the formidable garrisons of Anvers or Hamburg, which would have put him at the head of 150,000 soldiers of good troops; everyone is mistaken or falters, and miserable France is eaten. Napoleon, alas! who could have acted like a reckless poet, and who would have saved everything if he had, seems to have been put off balance by the bourgeois desire to reign at any price, to reign in Paris itself rather than reign over the world while telling himself that, from then on, wherever his general headquarters was would be the capital of France.

28. – No response from Mother Mercédès. She is too busy, someone says. When God comes, without a doubt he will find his servants too busy to receive him. *In propria venit...* Does she know who I am, that woman who seems to want to give me nothing but hope, and who has perhaps not yet moved a finger to come to my aid? She is warned, however, and I imagine that her negligence will not attract very abundant benedictions over her *works*. But try to make a woman religious understand anything, who believes she is doing something!

March

1st – Formerly, more than twenty years ago, when I was not yet a writer, I looked forward to this first day of March with amorous impatience. Merely thinking about it, my old heart thrills. Since then, I have been so cruelly abandoned by Him whom one calls the "Guardian of the Treasure of Heaven" and who was the *first*, the most pitiless of my abandoners, that all that glory of my past falls in ruins around me, and I feel a sort of sorrowful distraction on seeing arrive, one more time, the terrible month of that terrifying Patriarch to whom I have given all that a man can give, without receiving anything in return except torments.

That Mother Mercédès! From day one, I counted on her as one counts on a man. She waits perhaps until I am dead before acting. One would surprise her by telling her that the friends who solicit her on my behalf do her the greatest honor... Ah! modern Catholics and their execrable works!

... Jesus has his Cross passed from his shoulders to ours and from our shoulders to his, so that one is continually weeping for sorrow or for compassion.

2. – Capitulation of Paris. Napoleon's admirable constancy. His infinite superiority over all contemporaries in whom I see the eternal riffraff unleashed against Jupiter's children.

3. – To someone who sent me a ridiculous image:

> *Ary Scheffer's* Saint Monica *is totally worthy of that painter. It is a Protestant and sentimental canvas, what I call a latrines painting. Your incertitude on that point proves that you have never read me.*

4. – When I am waiting for money in the mail, things like the following ordinarily arrive: A subscription form to the *Nouvelle Revue d'Égypte*, a paper consecrated to the "intellectual and artistic lifting up of the Egyptian people." The Director, by the name of Braun, who talks about his "apostolate," seems to me somewhat of a proud, cheeky fellow.

I am told that Mother Mercédès' delay is explained by the enormous burden of her responsibilities. She organizes the *charity sales* and other rubbish of the same sort. It is she, perhaps, who lifts up the Egyptian people.

5. – "I give myself to you, Mary, praying that you might give me to Jesus, so that he might give himself to me." – JEANNE.

7. – To weep is to be alive. Anniversary of the cruel day in Rendebanen. (See *Mon journal*, p. 350).

8. – Received Huysmans' *l'Oblat* which just came out. That new book of 448 pages is followed by a page of advertisement for each of his preceding books. I suppose that Huysmans is the author of it. Apropos of *Saint Lydwine*, it is said that he is the greatest Christian writer for many centuries. That is evidently his opinion. Who knows? He is perhaps consulted respectfully by the person who has my wife's and children's bread in his hands.

At mass, the deacon announces that at 3 o'-clock there will be a *Te Deum* in honor of the twenty-fifth anniversary of Leon XIII's coronation. Remains to be seen whether that *Te Deum* will be heard in heaven. The orator informs us that one must praise God for the length of that glorious pontificate – how glorious! Who could say? – and to ask for its indefinite prolongation. I would have thought that it was urgent to ask for just the opposite.

11. – Dream. I see myself as a soldier in I do not know what war, but separated from my regiment, isolated and ready to sell my life very dearly, for it was a kind of diabolical and pitiless war. The enemy appearing, I fought with superhuman energy. After having massacred a great deal, I was locked up in a prison, awaiting death, I do not know what terrible death. But I put my trust in Mary. Immediately I was able to escape effortlessly; I opened the doors extremely easily and I returned home barefoot, my soul steeped in delights.

I am again told that Mother Mercédès had been approached at a very bad moment. I have my doubts. If she had an atom of sanctity, she would have told herself that I was sent to her, perhaps *in order to save her*, and she would have dropped everything for me. Not being a saint, but only a saintly woman, it is very likely she does not give a hoot.

12. – I ask Mary if she has – She too – *works* to do that prevent her from hearing me, from delivering me, as I have been supplicating her with my tears for many years.

14. – Mercédès is seen by a friend who has put himself out with heroism. He is received by her like an enema and obtains merely two hurried words that prove that my goose is cooked. I deliver that Pharisee to Him who does not pardon.

Here are my thoughts on Fontainebleau. When Ney, Oudinot and others wanted to impose the law on Napoleon, to force him insolently to abdicate, in spite of the goodwill and absolute devotion of the army; what an unprecedented spectacle, what a prodigious shock if the great man, calling his guard, had had a half dozen of his marshals arrested and shot within the hour! What a terrible ascendant over his old soldiers who spoke only of betrayal! What a feeling of uneasiness for the tsar and his mediocre allies! What a possible return to fortune!

16. – Second-rate sermon on Joan of Arc, whose Cause for Beatification will be judged. There are lofty and magnificent things to say about Joan of Arc, but nobody realizes it and, moreover, who could hear them? Joan of Arc *prefigures* the Holy Ghost, like Christopher Columbus, but in a more precise way, given *she is a woman:* what is more unintelligible for the sentimental folk who vilify her with their admiration? Having worked hard in the past, – and how in vain! – for Christopher Columbus' Cause,[60] I confess that I am without enthusiasm for a cause that does not interest the Congregation of Rites except because it is a matter of money. There is hardly anything that costs more than the process of beatification, except turret ships.

---

[60]Christopher Columbus' Cause: See *The Revealer of the Globe: Christopher Columbus and his Future Beatification* (Sunny Lou Publishing, 2021).

17. – Another discourse on Joan of Arc by the abbot Galette, a priest interested in money and the afore-mentioned faller of masses. A tisane of common-places.

18. – Thiers. Read the first Restoration with horror. All those marshals, generals, and functionaries who received everything from Napoleon and grovel at the feet of the pig put in his place![61]

19. – Véronique's teacher said recently to the young shopkeepers in her class that, of course, it would be good to be closed on Sundays, but there is no harm in opening until noon. And there you have it, the women religious who don't give a fig for La Salette! They will see whether that will have a good return. The Chamber voted just yesterday for the *closure* of all teaching congregations.

20. – Two avaricious priests, just for this hole of a parish!

21. – I pray like a wounded man asking his absent mother for something to drink.

22. – An already ancient difficulty: *Non sumus an-*

---

[61]Pig put in his place: a reference to the French King Louis XVIII and the Bourbon Restoration.

cillæ filii,[62] said Saint Paul. *Ecce ancilla Domini,*[63] said Mary. All I find is that Mary would be an *ancilla* until the advent of the Paraclete and *liberated* immediately thereafter. That, of course, is for pure exegetes. But all the same, I think that it is not very convincing.

> *Maria Immaculata Conceptio, quæ sursum es Jerusalem, mater nostra, da nobis lætitiam tuam* HODIE.[64]

Sermon by the preacher of Lent on the Love of God. That preacher, come from afar, I imagine, is, exceptionally, a priest without a winding mechanism, an alive priest of sorts and appears to have some consideration for the poor, which greatly displeases. Feebly inspired today, it is the love of God within reach of grocers and the spouses of employees that he proposes to us. A corvée, one might think. At one moment, he spoke about the Love of God compatible with *commerce!* The walls did not stand back, happily... By that time, I no longer heard anything else but my dream. Dream of a book that would be a series of sermons on each of the Gospels of Lent, but sermons for the lower middle-class, and terrible, where that riffraff would be beaten like dogs. A nowise *practical* Lent, of course, but where the preachers of goodwill found perhaps some ideas. I was singularly assisted

---

[62]*Non sumus...*: Latin for "We are not the children of a bondwoman" (KJV). Galatians 4:31.

[63]*Ecce...*: Latin for "Behold the bondwoman of the Lord."

[64]Maria...: Latin for "Mary Immaculate Conception, who art risen above Jerusalem, give us your joy today."

by the neighborhood, getting the feeling of being en-
circled by filthy animals. The infirmity of preachers is
that of no longer daring to speak the truth: "You other
impious people, you other hypocrites," etc. "My
brothers and sisters, we are all the dead, and we stink
frightfully," etc., etc. Obviously the *Great Lent of
Father Marchenoir* would not be without interest.

At a certain moment, the preacher reminded
us of these strong words: "*Qui non odit patrem suum,*
etc." while following it with a seminarian's interpretation, when it would have been so easy to shed light
on it by Saint John's text: "*Vos ex patre diabolo es-
tis.*" What a misery!

There is, on the Church's door sill, never participating in any office, a miserable man, whom his
landlord has just closed the door and window on for a
debt of several francs. Naturally that landlord is rich.
He is a killer of the very aged poor who will probably
die himself tomorrow. I think that the Deacon will
confer on him a passe-partout to Paradise.
"LANDLORDS NEED TO EAT!" explained to us a genial
shopkeeper.[65] A pithy summary of all human wisdom.

23. – Will I ever have the chance to write the book on
Napoleon that I have so often dreamt of? It is scarcely
possible, the oil of my lamp being already nearly used
up. And I have many other books to do. It seems to
me, however, that I have received some light on that
Precursor and for a long time now. But I would need,

---

[65]Landlords need to eat: See also Chapter 10 of *Blood of the
Poor*, for another, perhaps fictionalized, account of this anecdote.

before anything, to be freed from my current prison, and never has a prison appeared so strongly locked to me.

24. – Visit by a son of a bitch server of constraints, bringing to me a commandment which is neither from God nor the Church. 1 fr. 60 centimes for the ass-wipe.

25. – Annunciation. And soon it will be two thousand years now that you bleed on me, o Jesus! and I am entirely dripping with your Blood. Look at me and have pity on yourself.

The holiday (4th after *Lætare*) is of an inexpressible sweetness. *Vidisti eum et qui loquitur tecum ipse est.* To see Jesus! To speak with him, my God! That man born blind is *evidently* me...

26. – Jeanne heard, yesterday, at church, about an old lady whom she knew to be ill. This morning, she learns of the death of that person who was unable to be at church yesterday nor even the day before yesterday as she was already dead or agonizing. Here then is a soul asking her for prayers. I have often thought that many people whom one apperceives, here and there, are actually dead, dead and *exhaling an odor of the grave, having the habitudes of a cadaver.* How many are there who are alive in the Ministry or in Parliament? One of the least observed inconveniences

of universal suffrage is to constrain citizens in putrefaction to leave their sepulchers in order to elect or be
elected. The President of the Republic is probably a
decaying carcass.

Read passionately the Return from Elba Island,
in Thiers, grievous attempt to repair the irreparable,
unique poem in the history of the world. It is noted
that Napoleon marching on Grenoble and nowise assured, until then, of his success, passed through
Corps, at the foot of La Salette.[66] There has got to be
something there to say.

27. – Continued silence from the saintly Mother Mercédès. Someone who knows her informs me that she
is *united* with God in a way that does not permit her
to think of riffraff.

28. – A friend whom many enemies will approve of,
wrote to me that my sufferings must be explained by
God's Justice which punishes me for my wickedness.
Apropos of the *Last Columns of the Church*, whose
design he is familiar with, this friend deplores that I
am ever the same impetuous "young man," incapable
of forgiveness who has been unable to grow up, since
The Desperate Man.

29. – Our preacher who improvises too much, speak-

_____
[66]La Salette: location of the apparition of the Blessed Virgin Mary
in 1846. See *She Who Weeps* (Sunny Lou Publishing, 2022)

ing of family and divorce, embarked on a phrase in which the woman performs acts of... Then, realizing that he was on the verge of saying an unsuitable word, he stopped for several seconds and finished by jumping on the first word that came to mind. So the woman performed acts of *agriculture!*... On hearing him, I was thinking of that frightening preacher who would be a sort of prophet, announcing the divorce of Jesus Christ and his Church. But who could understand?

30. – "On earth we see the Invisible through the Visible. After death, we will see the Visible through the Invisible." – JEANNE.

31. – Paris becomes insupportable to me. When I am there without friends and now that I have renounced the sensual life, what to do in the middle of bicycles, automobiles, electric tramways, in streets everywhere ripped up or barred on account of works related to the metro. What has become of the lovely city of forty years ago?

April

2. – The most discreet mention of the prayer for the dead, without any attempt at ministry, is enough to excite the most vivid indignation in Lutheran Protestants. We have just had, once again, the experience of

that. That practice is, in their eyes, an insufferable blasphemy. In effect, all Lutherans, without exception, leaving this world only to enter Paradise immediately afterwards, what insolence to believe that they might have need of help reaching it! I have often noticed the latent ferocity under the so-called gentleness of those heretics.

3. – To Henry Houssaye:

> *Do you want to send to me through your publisher the two volumes of* 1815, *the which are indispensable for me for a work of historical exegesis [that I plan to write] on Napoleon, undertaken for several years now already. Having read* 1814 *twice, and extremely attentively, I see in you the most excellent historian of that unique Man. I would like to show the place he holds in the Invisible Order – the only order there is. Now, I have the honor of being poor and the greater honor of* begging. *If you know my name, a very uncertain thing, it is probable that you know it only through my enemies, an equitable and proud multitude, whom I have never undertaken to count. That encourages me. Yours....*

4. – Extremely painfully, I write several lines on the

manner of envisaging the history of saints, apropos of Huysmans. Enormous difficulty to interest *intellectuals* in that. Even greater difficulty discerning or perceiving a Huysmans of any sort in the vicinity of Saint Lydwine.

Consulted Saint Augustine on the resurrection of Lazarus in his *Treatise* on Saint John, in view of leveraging his authority against Huysmans who spoke ridiculously of that miracle. I find nothing. Ever the moral exegesis, as in the majority of Fathers. The other exegesis is not noticed except in some visionaries and still so feebly!... This knowledge, such as I have conceived of it or invented it, departing from this point that the *Scriptures* – that is to say, the Vulgate – is nothing more than a divine *Autobiography*, can and must be defined as: THE ILLUMINATION, a place of departure for all theological and mystical teaching.

Thiers. The last act. Sadness and misery. Fall of the greatest of men clinging to a Benjamin Constant in order to reign a little while longer, instead of disappearing proudly with this: World empire or nothing!

6. – Holy Monday. Our preacher who has no shame, really, loving the poor and who will end up paying for it dearly, spoke this morning about the Holy Family wandering in Bethlehem and, in a beautiful fit of emotion, he showed the Savior exposed to being born in the street. Unfortunately, it didn't have the immediate effect that it should have, doubtless because he hadn't thought it through. – What is that to you, Mi-

ladies, who would not have acted like the women of Bethlehem? Hadn't they a thousand times more reason to repulse the poor and vagabonds [than you have]? etc. Ah! what a beautiful discourse to make if one had enough energy and precision not to give those Pharisees any outlet for escape. When will he come, the man of God, wielding the Word like a hammer?

Response from Henry Houssaye. He says he knows me by my books better than by my enemies, and he sends me *1815*.

7. – Holy Tuesday. The *Ave Rex Judæorum* of the Jews echoes the *Ave gratia plena*. That word "ave" so full of mystery, that anagram Eva[67], *mutans Evæ nomen*, is in this way at both the beginning and the end of the Redemption. I would like to speak to the preacher about it, thinking that this idea could serve him for his sermon on the Passion. I didn't encounter him. I would have spoken with him about Saint Joseph of Arimathea as well. I knew a very humble abbot who thought that priests would obtain very particular graces if they were devoted to that saint who was the first *reponens hostiam super corporale*.

8. – Read, this evening, at the cafe, a sort of tale in which Richepin miserably imitates the *Diaboliques*, citing d'Aurevilly even. Behold then the only trace left in souls by that poor, great writer. Always the

---

[67]Eva: Eve.

Diaboliques! I hope for a more consoling baggage for myself.

10. – Holy Friday. Attempt at an explanation of chapter 5, verse 15, of Saint Matthew. The Light is Jesus and the Bushel is the Law, the *measure*. Jesus must be put on the candlestick, in other words on the Cross where he must shine without measure, in order to be loved disproportionately.

Our little Véronique writes with much clarity and expression about a dream she had. She saw herself among the followers of Jesus and became witness to the third collapse and the help given by Simon of Cyrene. "It seemed to me that I was a virgin," she says with a delicious innocence, wishing to express a form of sanctity.

Completed the nineteenth and penultimate volume of Thiers. Strong impression. The author, so often miserable, insists, as if he had a soul, on Napoleon's sadness, fallen from so lofty a place. Page 628 appeared beautiful to me. From Porto-Ferrajo to Paris, triumph, because he was in the presence of Bourbon mistakes. But in Paris itself, difficulties, bitterness, somber presentiments, because he found himself then in the presence of his own mistakes.

13. – Met one victim of Mme. Frusquin's, the comical proprietress who paid me so delicious a visit on June 10, 1901. The unfortunate renter recounts to me the pretty existence that the landlady made for him, try-

ing to retain him in her house which he had resolved to quit and not even attempting to hide from him the poor strings she undertakes to bind him by. That woman, fortunately resistible, is enrolled in Paris in courses of dull and lifeless literature expectorated at the Sorbonne by that distinguished cretin who goes by the name of Deschamps. I had a friend in the Naturalistic slurry who had called that "sipping from the drain pipe of sinks." She goes there, it is said, regularly, with her two giraffe-like daughters, the ugliest two creatures, – the most stupidly ugly – ever seen. Aside from the fact that she herself is an indigent to make a person weep, she would like the poor to be labored with blows of the whip and drowned in the sewer like poisoned rats when it is impossible anymore to squeeze anything out of them. That student of Gaston is, moreover, a pious Christian and probably *a Lady of Providence*, the society of love patronized by our deacon.

16. – Letter from the Prior General of the Carthusians to our scoundrel of a prime minister whom he summons to appear before God:

> ... *So, no more blackmail, no more eloquent artifices, no more operations of the court, nor parliamentary maneuvers; no more false documents nor complacent majority; but a calm, just, and powerful judge, and a sentence without appeal against which neither you nor I can raise a protestation! See you soon, monsieur the President of*

*the Council. I am no longer young,
and you have a foot in the grave. Be
prepared for the confrontation that I
announce to you holds unexpected
emotions for you...*

17. – A Schwarz, publisher and director of the *Assiette au Beurre*, asks me for my collaboration. Why not? Léon Bloy at the *Assiette au Beurre!*

Waterloo. When I write about Napoleon, I will mention my strange anguish every time Waterloo is mentioned, by no matter whom, and the impossibility, eternal for me, of consenting to that disaster. There are mistakes and crimes that Napoleon committed, yes. But there is something else as well, and I feel, from the deepest recesses of my soul, that never, on any day, was so enormous an injustice perpetrated.

21. – Article sent today to Schwarz (and published in the *Assiette au Beurre* on May 16, under this title: *Journalists.*)

The Aristocracy of Pimps

*People, singularly informed, come and
pester me in an unsavory canton in order to ask me what I think about Journalism. I have said and written a great
deal on the subject. I have even gar-*

nered a pretty reputation as a result, and, if I dare say so, a joyous existence. "The French spirit," I wrote in '85, in the first issue of my ill-fated Pal *which lasted so few days, "the French spirit, at this end of the century, invincibly recalls the horrifying* Charogne[68] *by Baudelaire and the journalists are its vermin. Innumerable, they press up against that unburied cadaver and precipitate its putrefaction which is bound to empoison the universe."*

That image of an exactitude to make one bellow, I have trotted it out for twenty years, with a greater fidelity each day, and a bitterness that has not stopped growing until it becomes something unspeakable.

A woman of great spirit – why would I not mention her name? – Marie Krysinska,[69] said to me, not long ago, that she saw in me a man who has most amused himself, wishing to express that she could not think of any prince who had given his contemporaries a better thrashing. "You have paid the price," she added, "that is

---

[68]Charogne: French for "Decaying Carcass," a poem by Baudelaire.

[69]Marie Krysinska: Marie Krysinska (AD 1857-1908), the "mother of free verse." See Émile Goudeau's *Ten Years a Bohemian* for more on her.

*certain, but how you must have en-
joyed it!" She was right, I have enjoyed dying, literally, because of it.*

*As ill luck would have it, that begins to
grow tiresome. By dint of vilification,
journalists have become so foreign to
any feeling of honor that it is absolutely impossible, from now on, to make
them understand that one grows sick
of them, and that after having vomited
them up, one swallows them up again
with a fury in order to defecate them.
The corporation [of journalists] is entrenched at this level of ignominy
wherein the conscience no longer dis-
cerns what it means to be a swine.*

*Ah! well do I know that it was already
beginning to lose its luster, this pretty
world, thirty or forty years ago, that is
to say before the Dreyfus Affair, before the Panama scandals and
Boulanger, before the Franco-Prus-
sian war, above all, but all the same
there was then the means by which to
dishonor oneself. It was still possible
to be a person who didn't give a damn
and pass for a scoundrel. Today, it is
exactly the opposite. So much the better if that leads us to the desirable upheaval in the end. The day when there
will no longer be the means to do a
good deed or make a good work of art*

without risking forced labor or at min-imum the pillory, it is clear that the world will be governed by journalists and that the Deluge of Shit will be on the cusp of beginning. There are mo-ments when it seems to me that we are already there.

It is difficult, however, to accept that it should be like this! When one is old enough to have lived in an epoch where it was possible to encounter in the editorial offices something other than scum, it is hard to be the witness of a like disgust, and complete solitude appears to be a sacred delight.

I am not speaking exclusively about political journalism, it goes without saying, the infernal stupidity and arid-ity of which are beyond my strength. I have in my crosshairs literary journal-ism only, or so-called as such, institut-ed fifty years ago by the late Villemes-sant,[70] for the delectation of cavalry officers and the employees of diverse administrations.

That Villemessant, famous formerly and now unknown, was one of those burly men such as one runs into on the way to the slaughterhouse. He partici-pated in the piacular massacres of the

[70]Villemessant: Hippolyte de Villemessant (AD 1810-1879), a French journalist and founder of numerous newspapers.

*dreadful year, having exalted, like no-
body else, French frivolity. I'm not
quite sure whether anyone today is
able any longer to understand that dis-
embowelment, arson, grillade, can-
nonade, fusillade, and machine gun-
ning are the necessary and prosaic
consequences of that bit of fun. But
Experience, that iron god adored by
men, pronounces that that is how it is.
Rochefort was launched by that Bar-
num, does that not say everything?*

*In those days, however, I repeat, the
German invasion, the German boot
not having kicked all the derrieres yet,
there was, even among practical jok-
ers, a certain literary bearing, an appreciable need not to be solely imbeciles guarded over by swine. Those
days are long gone.*

*To be fair, it seems proper to add that
everything does not tumble down immediately after the Column. Ten years
later, one still finds some washed individuals here and there whose hands,
feet, and conscience even seem to be
clean. It is not absolutely impossible,
in 1880, to read articles of criticism
and even novellas or novels that were
not written in bordellos by adminis-
trants of suppositories. There were
still Barbey d'Aurevilly and two or*

three others who wanted, all the same, with more or less discernment or in their old age, art and justice.

But Gil Blas *had just been born and the reign of pigs was inaugurated. Then it was all over. Everyone can see where that brought us. Pornographic literature and pornographic journalism are asked for exclusively. The text disappears even, in order to make way for illustrations of the flesh. One does not yet dare, completely, [to publish] flat-out obscenity, attracting the eye with its vermilions and crimsons, but we are a hair's breadth away from it, and one can truly say that it is a done deal. What is more, the ardent high-school student or low-level employee, deprived of women, can find recourse, by means of one sou, on the 6th or 8th page of important newspapers. From that point of view, the* Marriages col-umn *and* the Letters to the Editor *col-umn leave little to be desired. I would recommend the "high-society ladies who have suffered setbacks and who give language lessons." There is also the barely veiled proxenetism of rental offers and sales of every sort. Finally, it is an illecebration without any risk, quasi chaste, economical and without damages. I know an erotomaniac na-tionalist, converted by disgust, who*

*was so horrified by that idiotic and
frenetic oblation of sexual parts that
he does not stop showing his indignation in a* transparent *fig leaf which has
need of some fortification for the elections.*

*You think about what other literature
becomes and what the pretty destiny of
a writer in love with Justice as much
as with Beauty can be, lost in that
American forest of advertisements and
prostitution. When one has the enormous misfortune of being that writer,
the height of disaster is obviously to
turn, with an imploring eye, towards
the consumers of evacuations who de-
tain publicity.*

*If one has amassed millions [of
francs] in the slurry of Louis XVIII or
the incestuous gonorrhea of the Duke
Decazes*[71] *and has been* diarrhetically
evacuated *like the presumed count
Robert de Montesquiou in the loos of
poetry, one can still with the thread
worms of meat, extracted from its authors' fundament at the cost of an immense labor, sufficiently astound a
multitude of readers regaled beforehand. But a poor novelist, even if he*

---

[71]Duke Decazes: Élie Decazes (AD 1780-1860), a Royalist during
the Bourbon Restoration. As the Minister of Police, he was
responsible for repealing the censorship laws of the press.

had the genius of three hundred Ti-tans, – how do you expect him to make himself heard?

So, ass and cake then,[72] *such is the diptych of contemporary journalism. Great artists, indigent or disgusted, if they can still be found, have nothing else to do than die of hunger, unless they be taken by a great despair which brings them to murder, and which would give them some notoriety in the courts of assize.*[73]

I did not wish to name anyone and, until now, I do not believe I have des-ignated a single contemporary who possesses a semblance of organic life. But, frankly, it is impossible for me not to go off on a tangent *in favor of the celebrated Félicien Tagueule, author of a famous thing entitled I do not know what. I caught a glimpse of that individual at the* Chat Noir, *twenty years ago. The last time I heard men-tion of him, I believe he was employed au gratin, at night. Where does it blow*

---

[72]Ass and cake then: with a reference to both the French "let them eat cake" quote (misquoted for "bread" seemingly) and the more distant Roman political strategy of pleasing the demos with "bread and circuses."

[73]Murder... notoriety... courts of assizes: for example, see Pierre François Lacenaire (AD 1803-1836) a failed writer, who did just that.

from today, the furious mistral, the simoon, the sirocco of advertisement that envelopes that notorious imbecile, that filthy cretin who will never be surpassed? It is certainly not for the quality of his merchandise that he was able to debauch the press and fix automobiles by inattention... A critic, important doubtless, whose slightly unusual name resembles an ablative, *said of that twirp that his book would have been "Balzac's masterpiece, if Balzac had been able to write it...!!!" I ask a historian – Spanish if at all possible – about the conquest of that ablative.*

And now, what do you want me to add to that? I have spoken, how many times! of the horrible abuse of the word, of the infinitely profaned vestige of the Word. If I was foolish enough to repeat it, who could understand?

Modern intelligence, drunk on the filth of its pride, takes a tumble down the Staircase of the Giants of Cretinism and the Sewer Maximus opens its gob at the bottom of that staircase.

22. – To my Jesuit, who seems greatly to appreciate that I do not contemn his Institute:

Assuredly, you have the right to a response about the Jesuits. After what happened, it would be rather difficult for me to have either defiance or contempt. I cannot have but a great tenderness for some, like you, and an immense pity for all the rest.

Sometimes it happens, you write to me, that you "make large alms in order to oblige the Lord to make a declaration of his love for you." Alas! isn't it too late? As far as I'm concerned, if your Company had done fifteen years ago what the Assumptionists, so well informed nonetheless, did not wish to do; if your fathers, considering that the Church was without soldiers, had decided to arm me completely, employing for that purpose a feeble amount of the resources that the Institute disposed of at that time, – who knows what the Benediction would have been for that act of justice?

At that period of time, that of the The Desperate Man, *I felt as strong as Bonaparte at Marengo, capable of winning every battle. An irresistible current could have been set in motion by me. Not having to fight, every day, against hunger and all the horrors of poverty, being assured of the material and moral support of a powerful Or-*

*der, what would my force not have be-
come? To think that the poor Huysmans has become a sort of leader of a
school, an oracle rather, acting with
certitude on many souls, – Huysmans!*

*Instead of that, I will have become, by
the monstrous negligence of all
Catholics without exception, a huge,
squandered force, just the contrary of
what God wanted, I think. You know
these things, my dear Paul, and you
understand that it is impossible for me
to think about them without excessive
bitterness.*

*Regular and secular Catholics can tell
themselves that they have merited
what has happened to them and what
will happen to them yet. Note that I am
an example among many others. "Nobody budges," you say, "we are fond
of remaining within legality." In 1880,
– I often said it, – two or three hundred armed men, lined up on the sidewalk of the rue de Sèvres, before the
house of your fathers and determined
to kill or be killed, would have been
an insurmountable obstacle to the execution of decrees. Never would the
weak government of the Republic have
dared risk that.*

*My ancient comrade, Hanotaux, hav-
ing become since then so pale a*

scoundrel, but who was at that time nothing but a little flunkey of Gambetta's, made a confession to me. As I was exposing to him the clear idea earlier articulated, he said to me: "Without a doubt, you are right, but one is quite tranquil. One knows quite well that one can get away with anything with you Catholics!..."

What do the Catholics of 1902 say, led by the Muns[74] and the Gayrauds[75]? If a single warrior soul had shown himself, several months ago, all Bretagne was up in arms, setting an example to all the provinces that have remained Christian. The vile government ministry was lost. Far from acting, one talked instead, as in '80, of legality, *and the nineteen centuries of tradition ended in several scatological protestations...*

God wanted that, of course, in order that his glory might shine by some ineffable miracle, for his Mother's France cannot perish. He is Master and he can dispatch Someone *tomorrow morning or tomorrow evening...*

---

[74]Mun: Albert de Mun (AD 1841-1914) a French politician and academician.

[75]Gayraud: Hippolyte Gayraud (AD 1856-1911) a French priest and politician.

Consulted on drawing, I respond with this:

*Universal Tradition and Reason say
that the study of the human face has to
be at the beginning of all instruction
on drawing. If one does not know how
to make an eye or a nose, one will never be able to draw a landscape, or a
flower, or anything. On the contrary,
when one knows how to draw the human face, one knows how to draw everything. Why? Simply because the
Son of God,* in quo omnia constant, *in-
carnated the Human Face.*

The sister portress told Jeanne in a mysterious
tone of voice that they were entreating me no longer
to attend mass at the convent, that from now on they
would keep the door closed in order not to give any
foothold to persecutors. What do those miserable
women religious hope to accomplish by so shameful a
prudence? One gets what one deserves, once again.

24. – Read, in large part, the last and so painful volume by Thiers. Napoleon did not appear to me in any
epoch of his life greater than then. Napoleon resigned,
a second time, to lose the empire of the world like a
thing of no value, too resigned. But what immense
and magnificent satiety of men and things, in that inexplicable being who did not know God and who
died, it is said, without knowing him! What a pity,
those ignoble intrigues that swarm around him, before
he is vanquished even! What ignominy, all those un-

grateful and filthy domestics teeming behind Fouché, without knowing, any more than their leader, why they teem and embarrassed by the results of their betrayal before it was even consummated.

The history of Napoleon is the Face of God in darkness.

28. – Another article for the *Assiette au Beurre* (published on May 9 under this stupid title: "Let's Colonize!").

Jesus Christ in the Colonies

> *... Went down to hell.*
> – Symbol of the Apostles.

One of the stupidest men of our time and, perhaps, of all time, my old comrade Hanotaux, admirer of Abdul-Hamid and Paul Bourget, undisgustable servant of all powerful people – pimps or emperors – whose crumbs one can sweep up; academician on the other hand and a man of State ready to serve, has recently published a rather joyous piece of fun under this title: The Choice of a Career. *God help me from an analysis of that feeding bottle! I do not ambition the Institute enough to bother my contemporaries in that way. I have another ambition which is otherwise recompensed.*

But having to write I do not know what on the colonies and the genial colonizer of our affable fatherland, it would have been difficult for me not to think immediately of Gabriel, who has so often spoken about it since having seen his ancient patron of Tunisia and Tonkin die in glory, he who had so handsome a face for a lupanar's maitre d' or dishwasher. Recall his enthusiasm for Algeria, where his trip preceded that of Loubet's[76] by only a few months. Those were some fine days. Two times a week, the Journal *caught on fire with the prose of that traveler. Through him, we learnt finally that what is past is past, that a person should not put all his eggs into one basket, nor throw money out the window; that the height of blindness is to mistake bladders for lanterns; that where there is smoke there is fire, that laziness is the mother of all evil, that one must learn how to play both ends against the middle, etc. Finally that political man, that so original writer, did he not whisper to us his most intimate secret, to wit that one does not catch flies with vinegar*

---

[76]Loubet: Émile Loubet (AD 1838-1929), President of France 1899-1906.

and that cobblers often do not wear shoes.

From that intellectual pinnacle, what extraordinary views, what teachings, and what counsels! Through him alone, once again, everyone could learn about the irreprehensible beauty of our colonial institutions, the lily-white candor of our functionaries and their probity of antediluvian patri-archs, the unmitigated joy of indige-nous peoples of all color subjected to the tutelary domination of the Repub-lic and the paradisiacal future of their godforsaken places.

But let's move on from this domestic whom I mentioned merely while think-ing about the atrocious and imper-turbably renewed derision of the most homicidal advert. It is with the same telescope that earthly Paradise had al-ready been discovered in the Sudan by the late Zola, a short while before he exhaled his generous soul into the ex-crement of his dogs. The subject is se-rious beyond what can be expressed.

"Great Lady," said Christopher Columbus to Isabelle, in the Atlantide *by Verdaguer, "give me ships and, in good time, I will return them to you with a world in tow." He obtained them, those little ships whose debris*

could have been kept as priceless treasures, the wood being the most precious artifact on earth, after that of
Christ's Cross, and for the same reason. He obtained them, as one knows,
after eighteen years of supplication in
all the countries of Europe, and it was
death that he brought to the Indian
world, in his ineffably paternal hands.

They changed his mission from day
one. They made darkness out of his
light, and what darkness! They got
drunk on the blood of its innumerable
sons, and what remained of that blood,
what the jackals of pillage and the
dogs of vomit did not want any longer,
they gathered it up into the hollow of
their hands, into the miners' shovels,
into the boatmens' bailers, into the
cups of debauchery, into the two
plates of prostituted justice, into the
chalices even of the holy altars, and
they were covered in it from head to
toe! That amorous Columbus was
forced to tread, like a crow, on the
charnel ground of assassins. The orgy
of avaricious and sanguinary men enveloped the mountain of his supercil-
ious spirit like a tempestuous tourbillon, and there was a most unprecedented solitude on that pile of sorrows.

Christopher Columbus had asked that no Spaniard be permitted set foot on the new lands unless he was truly Christian, stipulating the veritable goal of that enterprise, which was for the "aggrandizement and glory of the Christian religion." They emptied the prisons and galleys for him. There were swindlers, perjurers, counterfeiters, robbers, pimps, and assassins who were responsible for bringing the example of Christian virtues to the Indies. He himself was accused of all crimes, and the hideous riffraff that was sent to him was allowed to testify against that angelic Pastor who wanted to defend his flock, the principal error of his being an attempt on the freedom to pillage and murder.

He was dispossessed finally, expropriated of his mission, and for several years he could witness, bound and powerless, the destruction of his work. His illegitimate and rapacious successors immediately replaced Paternity with the Ergastulum and peaceful evangelization with the cruel system of repartimientos, *which was the death warrant for those unfortunate peoples.*

Such was the aurora of European colonizations in modern times. Nothing has changed for four centuries. The only difference – extremely appreciable, truth be told – is that in that precise epoch of the discovery of the New World, there was a man, great like the Angels, immolated by the multitude of riffraff, and that immediately after him there was nothing but riffraff.

Ah! the evangelization of savages, the dilatation and growth in them of the Church, things so passionately wanted by the Christ Bearer, how far we are from it! Not even a semblance of rudimentary equity, not a quiver of human pity even for those misfortunate peoples. It is enough to make one tremble from head to foot, telling oneself that those beautiful American races, from Chile to the north of Mexico, represented by several dozens of millions of Indians, were entirely *exterminated, in less than a century, by their Spanish conquerors. That is the ideal which can never been imitated, even by the English, as colonizing as they are however.*

There are moments when what goes on in the world is enough to make volcanoes vomit. One saw it in Martinique last year. Only, the progress of science prevents understanding, and the horrors do not stop for a single minute. To speak only of the French colonies, what a clamor if the victims could cry out! What howlings come from Algeria and Tunisia, favored, at this time, by the carcass of the President of our amiable Republic! What sobs from Madagascar and New Caledonia, from Cochinchina and Tonkin!

For as little as one follows in the apostolic tradition of Christopher Columbus, where is the means to offer something other than a volley of grapeshot at the knackers of indigenous peoples, who are incapable, in France, of bleeding the least pig, but who, having become magistrates or sergeants-major in very distant districts, calmly quarter men, cut them to pieces, grill them alive, give them as fodder to red ants, inflict on them nameless torments, in order to punish them for having hesitated to hand over their wives or their last sous!

And that is arch-banal, known the world over, and the demons who do that are very honest men who are decorated by the [National Order of the] Legion of Honor and who have no need even for hypocrisy. Revenues with pleasant profits, sometimes with a large fortune, accompanied by a long rivulet of black blood that flows behind them or beside them, in the Invis-

ible – forever and ever on end; they have crushed at most several bugs in bad places, as happens to all conquerors; and beautiful mothers, who are charmed, coddle and prepare their virgin daughters as future spouses for them.

I have before me documents, that is to say such and such cases. One could add millions more. The story of our colonies, primarily in the Far East, is nothing but grief, immeasurable ferocity, and indescribable turpitude. I have heard stories to make the stones weep. But the example suffices of that poor, good man who had undertaken to defend several Mois villages, which were terribly oppressed by the administrators. His account was soon settled. Seeing him without support, without patronage of any sort, they laid simple traps for him by which generous people are infallibly taken in. They led him as if by the hand to perpetrate violent acts categorized as rebellion, and here it is twenty years already that he languishes in a penal colony, if he is still alive even. One day I will speak more vigorously and with greater precision about that naïve man who believed in the law.

It is an article of faith that Jesus, after

the last supper, descended to hell in order to bring back the sad souls who could not be delivered except by him. All divine things being perpetual, it is therefore always the same unique hope for the same infinite desolation. But it is really unique, and it is what, above all, I want to say to the colonies, that there is nothing to hope for from men.

The official reports or banquet discourses are masks over frightening louts, and one can say with certitude and without documents that the condition of uncivilized autochthons in all conquered lands is the last degree of human misery able to be seen on earth. It is the strict image of Hell, as much as it is possible to imagine that Empire of Despair.

Every Christian leaving for the colonies carries with him necessarily the Christian imprint. Whether he likes it not, whether he knows it or is ignorant of it, he has on him Christ the Redeemer, Christ who bleeds for miserable wretches, Christ Jesus who dies, who harrows hells, who rises from the dead, and who judges the living and the dead. He is, that Christian, he also, and no matter what happens, a

Christopher,[77] like Columbus, but a Christopher with the head of a Medusa, a Christopher of horror, of howlings, of twisted arms, and his Christ has been halfway annexed by the demons.

The good young man raised by good Fathers, and filled with saintly intentions, piously embraces his mother and his young sisters before traveling to distant lands where he will be allowed to sully and torture the poorest images of God...

It is in this way that the mission of the gentle Columbus from the XVth century continues, and it is like this that the Savior of the world is brought to the colonies.

May

8. – Jeanne returns home, exasperated, in the month of Mary, having been condemned to hear the reading of an intolerable meditation. One might say that the curates strive hard to chase away their parishioners from the church. With that impression, she wrote to the Deacon:

Having been unable to attend, until

[77]Christopher: etymologically, from Latin, Christ + bearer, or the bearer of Christ.

now, in the month of Mary, I have just participated this evening. I very humbly submit to you my reflections, sure that you will not be indifferent to them. Why not choose a lively, vibrant reading, instead of those intolerable meditations whose terrible ennui chases, – I know for a fact – people of goodwill away from your church? You have habituated us, monsieur Deacon, to such heartfelt discourses. I entreat you, have pity on your flock and deliver us from that quarter of an hour in which ennui stifles the most fervent resolutions... I cannot resign myself to being bored to that point. It is impossible that you do not feel the same ennui. So why inflict it on your parishioners?

12. – To a man condemned to death:

... It will not be said that I did not have a word of thanks for the very precious hours you spent with me yesterday. God shows me in this way, from time to time, his mercy, above all after several months and, more and more, as if a desert had been crossed, an immense desert that I would have had to cross slowly with excessive grief. We had to meet only yesterday, for the first time, by virtue of divine decree

*made well in advance of the creation
of our days. That, for certainly admirable reasons, in view of an unknown fulfillment, whose hope inebri-
ates Heaven.*

*No less than an eternity will be needed
to admire the absolute and inexpressible beauty of things that* we did not
make ourselves, *and you know we never fashion our own destiny. It is for
many years now that I am the panting
spectator of my own life, as if I was
the spectator of a supernatural
tragedy. Being as much of a coward as
all my brothers, I have complained
about not being comfortably seated. I
continue to complain, and it is a great
pity, I know, not to acknowledge
God's gift better.* Si scires donum Dei!
*said Jesus to the Samaritan. Ah! yes,
of course, if one knew that there were
no* little things *and how much everything that happens in life is great, one
could die for ravishment.*

*Do you consider, poor Marchenoir,
that when you pronounce the name of
Jesus, everything bends a knee, in
heaven, on earth, and in the hells, and
that it was the Holy Spirit that said
that? When you perform a good or
bad act, remember that there are innumerable souls, living souls or souls of*

the so-called dead that correspond mysteriously with your own – all your spiritual kinship that will not be visible to you except in the Light – souls of slaves or emperors having been able to animate bodies, five thousand years ago, or animating them at this moment, the which have an infinitely great need of you. If then your deed is bad, that multitude is pushed down; if your deed is good, you lead it as if by the hand. The catastrophe of Martinique, for example, could have been determined by a refusal of obedience, or a venial transgression that, in half a century, a miserable creature eter-nally *designated will be made guilty of in order, in this way, to shed a glimmer of light at the bottom of that gulf. And it could also be that such and such a savage of Tasmania or Angola who abstained from an atrocity in the previous century has caused the fortunate crisis that will save, I do not know when, such and such a moribund in a hospital in London. When de Grouchy's exasperated lieutenants pressed him furiously to go help Napoleon, I imagine quite vividly the millions of invisible arms holding back that imbecile who had become, for one instant, the pivot of the world. All that is what one calls the Communion of*

*Saints, the ninth article of the Symbol,
the Solidarity of all creatures, of all
worlds, and all time, – Infinity!*

*So it is not possible that we met in
vain, and that event which was wanted
and planned since the beginning for a
certain point, adorably calculated, in
time and space is, without any doubt,
far and away more important than
what we could possibly imagine. From
our very desultory conversation, as it
had to be between two pilgrims meeting at the back of a dangerous cavern,
I came away with this impression that
you are one of those whom the Three
Persons have a thirst and a hunger
for, and that They call for you impa-
tiently. So see what a blessing [it was]
for me to have become, if only for a
few hours, the friend of a man whom
God can no longer do without!...*

14. – A person who knows Mother Mercédès informs
me that that woman religious, totally *secularized*,
lives in a sumptuous apartment and goes out dressed
luxuriously. I am informed, in addition, of something
that I had – after that – little need of, that *she never
keeps her promises.*

15. – I read, in the newspapers, that my old prophecy
of the universal upheaval of the Church appears on

the point of occurring. Already, in recent days, the church of Aubervilliers was profaned in the middle of a ceremony, invaded by scoundrels on the orders of Charbonnel and Tailhade. The audience, women and children for the most part, were struck, and the curate himself, beaten after having attempted a protestation, was *punished*, almost immediately, by the loss of his wages. It is reported that those scenes are going to re-occur throughout France. They no longer hide their desire for the destruction of Christianity, and it is probable that they will succeed given that Catholics are too cowardly to resist.

17. Very solemn high mass. In accordance with the usage established by our deacon, I believe, one Sunday, every year, around this time, is dedicated to the *French souvenir* (sic), a kind of Briardism or dialect signifying that one will pray for France alone, exclusive of Switzerland and Belgium, for the French living and dead. The church is filled with flags and fanfare, and look at me very moved by it. The curate of Ceux-d'En-Haut brays a pompous discourse made of all the patriotic commonplaces. The one reality in all this is the *mass* which, I imagine, nobody thinks of.

18. – To Mother Mercédès:

> *Very reverend Mother,*
>
> *I understand that you are planning to visit Cochons-sur-Marne and to see me on that occasion. I entreat you not*

to follow through with the second part of that plan. It would be extremely painful for me to see you. Must I say why?

You have caused me much harm, infinitely more, perhaps, than you can understand or believe, and I have confided the secret to God asking him for justice.

That you left my letter of February 15 without a response, so be it. The greatest writer in the world, if he is indigent, has no right to anything, not even to the most rudimentary considerations, I know; and persons gifted, such as yourself, by exceptional intelligence, know that I am not the greatest writer in the world.

But to deceive the Poor, to promise them a deliverance and not to give it to them, to intoxicate them with joy for NOTHING, *at the risk of hurling them, soon afterwards, into despair, is it possible to imagine a more malicious act, a crueler injustice? To mock the Poor is tantamount to stepping on the Heart of Our Lord Jesus Christ, do you know that?*

Ah! how easy it would have been for you not to have promised anything! You had merely to run away, like so many others. But to promise *and to promise that much, and so in vain, to such and such a miserable wretch and in such circumstances! That is dreadful!*

I entreat you then not to come and look for me, unless that be in order to humiliate *yourself. It would be beyond my strength to remain calm. Moreover, we are going to die, the both of us, tomorrow or the day after tomorrow, and it is the* Father of the Poor *who will judge us...*

Accept, very Reverend Mother, the assurance of my respectful compassion.

19. – There is someone here for whom Mother Mercédès is a *saint* all the same. Long live Cambronne!

20. – To my great astonishment some Catholics seem to be waking up. I am told that several of Charbonnel's hooligans were knocked senseless.

21. – No response from the saintly Mother Mercédès. Someone told me: "If I received such a letter, I would drop everything then and there and go see that person whom I would have offended in order to ask his pardon." Eh! well, it is not like that at all. It is, on the contrary, that admirable woman religious in a satin

corset who is offended and all the Catholics, all the Charity Bazaar, in her person.

23. – The weather has become very warm and my sadness is great seeing our poor children suffer in this miserable apartment instead of running around under the trees and among the flowers. Why do we not obtain our grace? Why are such humble wishes not fulfilled?

24. – There had been talk of a plan of invasion of our church by Charbonnel's hooligans and the cyclops of urinals. But the scoundrels, already thrashed in Paris and other places, are discouraged.

From René Martineau:

Here is an anecdote that you will not fail to appreciate and use on occasion.

Mgr. Renou, archbishop of Tours, on a confirmation tour in the environs, was invited to dine at a chateau on the banks of the Cher, a week ago. He was received by a very young family. Addressing himself to the mistress of the lodging, he said this in substance:

"Now that you are the chatelaine, Madame, I will point out to you your Christian duties. To begin with, you must visit all the poor and all the sick..."

*The woman interrupting him immedi-
ately:*

"But Monseigneur,*" she said, "*I'm
afraid of microbes!*"*

*The bishop merely turned pale and
shrugged his shoulders. As for the other witnesses, they found that quite
drole.*

25. – Worked passionately at an article on Jehan Rictus, *The Last Catholic Poet*. Article that could be an
act of charity at the same time as an act of justice.
Lord knows I have primarily the soul of that poor
poet in view.

Furious madness of automobilism. A race had
been organized from Paris to Madrid, and it was a
delirium for several days.[78] So from Paris to the extremity of French territory, with the route in Spain
protected by regiments. The life of the nation was interrupted for the amusement of millionaires. They had
fabricated machines going at unheard-of speeds, very
superior to that of the most rapid trains. The result,
easy to predict, was the crushing, the pure and simple
murder of a dozen people. Some of the perpetrators
themselves were wounded, in too few numbers, alas!

That modern thing appears more and more demoniacal. Imagine the horror of those two or three
hundred hideous cars launched like cannonballs and
chewing up, each in its turn, from one end of the hori-

[78]A race...: The Grand Prix of 1903.

zon to the other, the same bloody shreds! There are consolations. One of those cars caught fire and the driver was fortunately carbonized.

29. – Finished the article on Rictus. I do not think that any work of this genre has cost me more, nor do I believe to have ever written anything with a greater heartfelt enthusiasm.

8:40 in the morning, a train of employees. Those people, who all know each other, arrive invariably with a small sack or a small basket of provisions in hand in order to eat lunch at the office. They shake hands, and from the start of the year to the end of it they exchange the same seasonal pleasantries, the same commonplaces which they will be buried in, after which they will have pretended to die.

31. – A person, whom I have a really strong desire to slap, speaks to me about charitable works practiced by rich Christians. It has gotten to the point where I can no longer think of those cursed people without being deeply upset.

June

2. – Unpublished article:

The Revenge of the Vile

Ecrasons l'Infame[79] – VOLTAIRE.

What was needed was an epoch when nobody had anything anymore to do and no longer knew where to go at all, which unleashed the furious madness for speed. May whoever is able to explain that anomaly explain it.

And behold a man, ten thousand rich men, having no need whatsoever to earn their living, nor any desire above all to accomplish anything appropriate, vulnerable only to the goad of an imbecilic vanity of sports and who passionately risk their carcasses to arrive somewhere, anywhere whatsoever, two hours earlier than the express train. To suppose that one of them had an interest of some sort, a veritable interest to find himself as soon as possible in a specific place, assuredly that person would immediately get out of his automobile in order to jump on the first train. And this would be, for the span of his life, a bright idea, – well, pointless.

Ah! the swine! the swine! the swine! Die, each and every one of you, says the Gospel of the twentieth century. Several ultimately left their skins be-

---

[79]Ecrasons...: French for "Let's crush the vile."

hind, which is not very interesting, but altogether they crushed six or eight people. Collective murder, which none of those rich men will be prosecuted for. In a country of industrial and scientific so-called progress where it is understood that everyone must resign himself patriotically to being crushed to small pieces under the hoof of migratory bison, it would be grotesque to want anyone to be held responsible for anything.

"Truth is on the march," said the Cretin of the Pyrenees.[80] It is the same game. A child who writhes in agony or who does not even have the time to writhe, parents in despair, families in mourning, orphans, widows howling with grief and sorrow and their arms raised to heaven, what is that compared to what is at stake: ensuring that the "Continental tire" or the "Mercedes automobile" triumphs? (The crushing Mercedes!) For we are talking about commerce here, and business is business.

I know, right? from the moment that Mme. du Gast hasn't got a single morsel of her skin in the game, that flesh so dear to the prince de Sagan,

---

[80]Cretin of the Pyrenees: Émile Zola. See Je M'Accuse... for more on the Cretin of the Pyrenees.

and our friend Rodolphe Darzens didn't take the rap, it is quite certain that no one gives a damn. The pestle is made for [grinding] the poor, everyone knows that.

I dare say even that there is an evident firmness of the soul, an indisputable stomach *to be able to drive over human tripe, while traveling through the woods and the fields like a bolt of lightning, and never have a second thought. To think that a little ragamuffin worth nothing at all, the son of a peasant, an errand boy for a rural notary, who was run into* for life, *in the vicinity of Versailles or Châteaudun, by the first car, could have been pummeled, crushed, kneaded successively by the 254 other cars that were going one hundred or one hundred-fifty per hour, in the direction of Madrid. The flowers of the beautiful landlady, consumer of the poor, must have contracted a certain smell which counted, doubtless, for a great deal in the voluptuous dilatations of her person. For the rich do not amuse themselves, do not really enjoy themselves, except when they crush. That is the human and sixty-times secular experience. One needs to be stupid like a cyclist or an automobilist to doubt it.*

The future is, moreover, this: Every individual taken in flagrante delicto *of reading, comprehension, imagination, or thought will be judged dangerous and probably roasted like a ferocious animal. When cretinism gets to this point, – of talking, as seen in the* Journal, *about the "brazen pilots who have consecrated their lives to the triumph of mechanical locomotion" and "for whom the automobile is life," – how is it possible that the most unbridled anthropophagy should not become a law?*

"Oh! if you had seen poor Marcel lying inanimate at the side of the road!" How many others had he already assassinated the poor *Marcel? "The event I had participated in was a battle in which there are both the wounded and the dead," tells us the same Rodolphe. If one were younger, the light charcoal drawing of a Wagram of idiots or demented murderers would make a person jump up and shout to the confines of heaven. In the times when Christianity was not defunct and when there was still a sense of honor of some sort in France, the warriors of that ilk would have had their arms and legs lopped off promptly and their entrails thrown to the dogs. One of those goitrous malfeasors was carbonized.*

*There is always that. "One admired
the* Bits," *continues Darzens, struck
by a fit of unconsciousness. The so-
called "race" cars, hideous from the
moment of their creation, have they
not become funereal and, if I might
dare say, funeral, having assumed, obviously, the shape of biers and hears-
es?*

*It is evident that every ambitious auto-
mobilist is* a premeditated assassin,
*given that such a sport implies, know-
ingly and almost necessarily, the massacre of all animate creatures who
could be met on the road. That is formal, absolute, indisputable, and the
unprecedented sloppiness of contemporaries is alone capable of explaining the ignoble patience that encourages that murderer.*

*Two years ago, finding myself in a
country mortally afflicted by automobilism, I counseled the exasperated
farmers to greet the passing automo-
bilists with a shit pump. I went even so
far as to recommend an obstacle before and after, at the ends of isolated
roads, followed by the destruction of
the machines by blows of an ax, a
thorough smashing to smithereens
without special treatment for the exalted tourists, male or female. But every-*

one bawls, and nobody does a thing. It is universal cowardice and pusillanimity.

Never have the poor been so screwed, that much is certain, but never have the poor so greatly permitted it. That flatters them, it seems, to be crushed by machines that cost nearly one hundred thousand francs. It is said and it is printed that the automobile industry employs an incalculable number of workers, that it will employ tomorrow double or triple that number, which gives reason to hope that in the end it will employ all workers without exception. Two thirds of the population of France and its colonies will fabricate exclusively countless automobiles by the means of which they will daily and studiously crush the remaining third. It is possible that that is our fine destiny. It would be a levy in mass for the good war of the perfect stupefaction of the French. About ten years ago, the bicycle seemed to have attained that result by a bound. Already now nobody reads anything anymore. But the automobile is an instrument of progress to break, bury, and crush everything.

Of course, the cultivation of the fields is abandoned, and it could assuredly

be that we all die of hunger while go-
ing so quickly. I do not know whether
there is an inextricable difficulty there,
and it is not up to me to figure it out.
Nevertheless, that circumstance
changes nothing of the undeniable fact
of the idiotification of people who
were once the first of the earth. This is
serious in a different way than the
eventual crushing of individuals or
multitudes.

If an infect multimillionaire, enriched
by criminal speculations and filled up
on the substance of miserable wretch-
es, should happen to be flattened
stupidly or ignobly against a tree or
against a wall, impurifiable from then
on, while perpetrating, in contempt of
others' lives, a doltish exploit of
speed, two hundred journals, the next
day, will award him a martyrdom and
glorify in that decaying carcass a vic-
tim of duty *and* THOUGHT!!! *Not one*
person would mention participating in
the decease of human Reason.

Formerly, there was the marvelous se-
lection of Blood and Soul which is
called the aristocracy of virtues. To-
day, there is the selection of money
which naturally produces the aristoc-
racy of imbeciles and assassins, repre-
sented by the 255 Paris-Madrid auto-

mobiles.

3. – Enormous sadness. By God's permission, I suffer, for the thousandth time, that pain of believing that I am lost.

Read Henry Houssaye's *1815* which hardly consoles me. Nothing is sadder than that end of magnificences. Napoleon and France seemed to me less fallen in Thiers than in Houssaye. That obviously results from the superiority of documentation of that latter.

Fatigued by this reading, I fall back into the hands of the enemy.

4. – Read in several papers:

The Phonograms of H.H. the Pope Leon XIII. – *H.H. the Pope Leon III has deigned to choose the Phonographs X... in order that his voice might be registered forever for the good fortune of the faithful. The Sovereign Pontiff has uttered in two Phonographs the prayer of* Ave Maria *and the solemn* Benediction *given March 3, in Rome, on the occasion of his Jubilee... His Holiness' two phonograms are on sale...* Ave Maria, *10 francs, the* Benediction, *12 francs. See our catalogs.*

5. – Great! Here I am dreaming of the deacon now. In my sleep, I saw that pastor, that curate of countless works. The poor man had just founded the work of "Neighbors"! Clearly, that's stupid, but in the mirage of a dream it was so plausible, and it was such a gem of ridicule!

Read *1815*. Learnt the following, which Thiers, I believe, said nothing about: Napoleon, on return from Elba Island, could have unleashed the passions of '93, which were merely sleeping, and become in that way a very redoubtable Jacobin king.

7. – Solemn renewal of Véronique's first communion. She has put on last year's white robe again and I accompanied her to the church, seeing her from afar and finding in her a big resemblance to my wife. I knew that that resemblance existed, but I hadn't sensed it until today... Where is she, at this moment, my sorrowful wife and what assistance can she give to her poor old child?

The *Occident*, an art review, speaks about *l'Oblat*. Huysmans is called the "sole religious writer."

As it is today, the Trinity, the third mass with the third discourse by the deacon, always speaking to the children about their parents, some of which children probably have neither father nor mother.

I renounce going to vespers where there has to be a fourth discourse by the deacon. Jeanne returns home appalled. That furious ass vociferated for three-quarters of an hour, letting himself go, on and on, until he became a kind of energumen, defying his listeners, almost throwing the glove down and triumphing by their silence, finally declaring himself determined to speak until he lost his voice. That sermon, which surprised the canton, is explained charitably by the hypothesis of an excellent and prior lunch. The deacon is fat and he carries his meat well.

8. – *Letters of direction* by the Reverend Father Judas (Didon). Vanity of a gymnast and sentimentality bordering on lust.

9. – To the director of a review that I imagine prospers (and which ceased to exist after several months):

> *... I do not know your sentiments with respect to myself. Would you consent to publishing a critical study by me on Huysmans? That work being able to have twelve hundred lines is pushed to the limit, vehemently perhaps, in some places, but without injurious violence. I wanted to protest, in the name of absolute and integral Catholicism, against all kinds of religiosity, being a contemner, to the same degree, of the candy-stick religion of rue Saint-Sulpice and the Dutch beet sugar of J.-K. Huysmans.*

12. – SUBMISSION FOR PUBLICATION:

Letters by J. Barbey d'Aurevilly to Léon Bloy, with a portrait of and an autographed letter by J. Barbey d'Aurevilly. *Société du* Mercure de France.

It is known that Léon Bloy was, for more than twenty years, a regular visitor of Barbey d'Aurevilly.

These Letters by J. Barbey d'Aurevilly to Léon Bloy *offer, by consequence, the double interest that is attached to the author of the* Diaboliques *and the complicated author of* The Desperate Man, *the* Mendiant ingrat, *and the* Exégèse des Lieux Communs.

These letters go from 1872 to 1878. Some, extremely curious, refer back to the literary beginnings of Léon Bloy, who deplores that the heirs of his old friend's estate, by permitting him to publish this collection, have forbidden him all commentary and any preface. His memories and documents of literary history will go then, – more bitterly – into another book for which he will have no need of authorization and in which Barbey d'Aurevilly will be recounted by the only writer still alive who knew him well.

The Letters by J. Barbey d'Aurevilly to Léon Bloy *are preceded by a very fine portrait of the great writer on his deathbed.*

17. – Article on the famous painting by Félix Jenewein, *La Matinée du Vendredi Saint*, a beautiful color lithography which I received a copy of from Moravia. (Article published in the *Mercure de France*, September 1, 1903. Félix Jenewein died suddenly, last January 5, struck with joy for being elected to the Academy of Arts of Vienna. January 1905.)

The Morning of Good Friday

Dopoledne Velkého Pàtku – Jest odsouzen, bude ukrizovan.

Ante meridiam Feriæ VI in Parasceve – Damnatus est, crucifigetur.

Such is the inscription or rather subscription of this work that has strongly affected souls. It is not a thing of yesterday. It is a painting that was remarked on enough, in 1895, at the exposition of Vienna, for which its author became immediately famous in his Czech lands, the which are honored moreover to have let him die of hunger for a very long time, out of respect for the Gospel which does not want prophets to be honored in their fatherland.

Can anyone say, however, that he was a prophet, that man? Does it suffice to have a soul open to the wind blowing in every direction, like the redoubtably inhabited cave of a dangerous mountain? In that case, it is really a prophet in question here. "He is condemned, he will be crucified." Félix Jenewein heard that enormous sound which shook the world, as if a Titan, having seized it with both hands, had undertaken in a fit of rage to pull it off its hinges, and he wanted to make others hear it so that they might tremble in turn. For painters have the power to make things heard *through the eyes.*

Prophets are people who remember the future. *Their being placed right in the center, the future is before them and behind them, to their right and to their left. Time not existing in itself, any more than space, all that belongs to the senses is identical in the Absolute.*

One needs to read the testimony of the unequaled Anne-Catherine Emmerich who had, at the beginning of the last century, the privilege of being the ocular and auricular witness to the Dolorous Passion.

Not long after the recitation of the condemnation of Jesus, recalling the most terrible phrase that men have proffered:

"Every time," recounts that prophetess of the past, *"that I am meditating on the dolorous Passion of Our Lord and I hear that horrifying cry of the Jews, 'Let his blood fall on us and on our children!', the effect of that solemn malediction comes before my eyes and it makes me sensitive to marvelous and terrible images. I seem to see, above the people who are crying, a dark sky covered in bloody clouds from which exit things like sticks and glaives of fire. It is as if that malediction penetrated them to their bone marrow and reached the children in the belly of their mothers. All the people appear to me enveloped in tenebrous darkness: their cry leaves their mouth like an arrow of dark fire that comes back to them..."*

I do not know whether Félix Jenewein read the visionary of Dulmen who is, without question, the greatest one can read, but it is certain that, in one manner or another, something entered into him of the divine Terror of Good Friday.

His painting is not complicated. Mary

is standing at the center, in the fore-ground. She has received the blow without falling over, *no matter what the saint says, because she cannot fall, because the Mother of the living cannot fall. Who would sustain the blue or grey sky if she fell? That warrioress sustains the sky on the tip of the lance that pierced Jesus' side, like the Gauls claimed to do with their pikes. But above all she is, in truth, the Mother of the living and it is for that reason that the Gospel shows her standing at the foot of the cross, looking on a scene that would kill lions.*

She is standing then, her hands joined on that famous Belly that Christians name each day, and which bore the Salvation of the world. Her head is turned dolorously, but her half-closed eyes do not leave this earth where the Son of Man will die.

Horrible grief assaults that Tower of David like an armed multitude, that Ivory Tower that one cannot take and which suffers. What is needed so as to see the end of that agony is that there be no more men. She may have tri-umphed; She may have died, one cer-tain day, or merely fallen asleep, for one does not know; She may have been taken up into the sky where she

reigns supreme, just a tad below God;
She may be honored and almost wor-
shiped, for nearly two thousand years,
on golden altars, in diamond cathe-
drals which the angels themselves, incapable of suffering, could have built;
as long as there is a poor person, the
Immaculate Virgin will stand, her
chest full of daggers.

That, under the aureole, in sublime derision of the azure mantle that Christian iconography has always lent to
Mary, forgetting that she is primarily
the dolorous Fountain where they take
their source, all the rivers of fulfilled
Desire, lost Love, Tears of blood, Pity
that gives death, Expiation that one
cannot escape, Horror and Terror that
run through humankind like so many
Danubes.

Sentimentality wants by all means that
the Virgin Mother be an idol of honey
in the azure, in the middle of flowers.
There are three or four hundred thousand demons to hide the crenelations
and loopholes of that Citadel of Compassion. Some do not wish to know
that She is, before everything and after
everything, the resident, the inextirpable intern of Golgotha; that she has
her feet in the Blood of her Son, that
her eyes and her visage are in blood

and that her mantle, assuming it had been a translucid blue before the torments, is splattered with the blood of the Flagellation, with the blood of the Crown of Thorns, with the blood of the Lance, with all the spurting scarlet that She received in full when the high mass of Redemption was celebrated.

One absolutely refuses to understand that it is impossible for such a Mary not to always have in mind the atrocious behavior of the executioners of such a Child, their physiognomy of possessed men, their irremissible insults...

Go tell that flock of renegades who are called modern Catholics that every time a sweetness is procured for us by a catastrophe: the fire of a bazaar well-patronized by martyrs *in gala dresses, which beggars have no idea about and which the precious Shroud of Our Lord Jesus Christ would not redeem; the unexpected eruption of a good old volcano that Sodom and Gomorrah thought was sleeping and which snuffs out thirty thousand lives in one blow; the collision of trains or ships, cyclones or earthquakes, without prejudice to gratuitous massacres that have been, until now, the historic and ineluctable resultant of every sen-*

timental exacerbation; – try then to make them listen, those contemners of Justice, that it is the "clement Virgin" who is taking a stroll in her realm, waiting for the frightening Day of her plenary manifestation. Maledictio Matris eradicat fundamenta.[81]

Why would anyone want her to spare anyone, She who has immolated her own Child? For Mary's consentments are the instruments of the Passion of Jesus Christ, not in a symbolic or metaphoric way, but in a substantial fashion, and that is not different from how the most holy doctors of the church have understood it. "Mary mounts Calvary calmly," said Father Faber, "in order to assist in the murder of her dear son of Bethlehem."

Saint John who accompanies her has fallen onto his knees behind her, his hands clenched over his heart. And he remains frozen, without strength or light. Ephesus is far away, Patmos is farther, and the "Son of Thunder" is actually struck by lightning. Later, when the "Mirror of Justice" of the Litanies will have burnt his eyes out and after he has passed through Domitian's [vat of] boiling oil, there

---

[81]*Maledictio...* Latin for "The Mother's Malediction uproots the fundament."

*will be something to write that will
make the world clack its teeth until the
consummation of the centuries. But today, Good Friday, he looks completely
wiped out.*

*And the entire tableau is around those
two Beings like a hurricane. There is a
half dozen individuals and one gets the
impression of a multitude. The power
of the painter constructs this mirage.
It is the enraged multitude and so terribly prophetic of itself, as recounted
by Anne-Catherine, nineteen centuries
after the Gospel. The Hebrews, saved
formerly by the Red Sea and impatient
to return to it, vociferate for the flood-
gates of adorable Blood to be opened.*

*To the left, a parabolic, anachronistic,
synthetic, indefinable soldier, a sort of
adventurer of carnage taking after the
praetorian, the cataphract, and the
Calabrian brigands simultaneously,
seated on a boundary stone green with
fear, and his legs boorishly planted
one on top of the other, sniggers while
looking at the discolored, mystical
Rose, the Morning Star in its pallor.*

*At some distance, a fat priest suggests
one knows not what diabolical wickedness to a squalid Yid come from
Poland to attend the Crucifixion. To
the right a saturnalia of the year one*

thousand or the year forty: a naked man, horribly coiffed by a kind of monstrous coleopterous helmet garnished with antennae which makes him look like a devil, carried in the arms of two other masked scallywags, raises above the crowd, like a labarum, a derision of a crucifix, foul worn-out dish towel, tied up and suspended to a crosspiece on top of a broom handle, – figuram crucifixi in baculo quo verritur[82], *an explicator wrote to me – sacrilegious masquerade that infinitely pleases the populace.*

That admirable tableau which its author does not believe allegorical is extremely strange. I found in it, for example, what is unencounterable, I believe, elsewhere. The riffraff, drunk with joy and holding their sides laughing, as one says, have the uniform gesture of crossing their hands behind their back, palms in the air, looking thus like invisibly chained captives. Qui potest capere, capiat.[83]

19. – Rented a new domicile. Our girls will finally

---

[82]*Figuram... verritur:* Latin for "the symbol of a crucifix on a stick by which to sweep."

[83]*Qui... capiat:* Latin for "May he who can understand, understand."

have trees and a garden.

Short theological discussion with a priest on the subject of sanctifying Grace and the *absolute* non-worth, according to him, of good works accomplished outside a state of grace. My opponent is a rigorous theologian, a priest of the kingdom of Jesus. I am of the kingdom of the Holy Ghost. I plead philosophically for the perennity of the human act and theologically for the right of grace of the Legislator. We do not come to an understanding and I willingly cede, not being, moreover, equipped for the debate.

21. – Remarkable word by the mother Mary, that old pretty woman: "Monsieur Bloy, so modest a man!" I didn't know that I had earned that praise. Nobody, to this day, had noticed. Would I have, unbeknownst to myself, put a fire in that granary?

22. – Oh! the priest, the horrible priest who gives nothing to anyone, and who, having inherited a fortune in order to apply himself to good works, employs it solely for usurious dealings and lives in peace in appalling contempt of the diocese! I imagine, however, that the majority of his brothers must envy him in secret.

Saw our new residence again. Doubtless we will be happy there, if God gives us the wherewithal. But how much cleaning will it take? The filth of that house exceeds all rhetoric and the present occupant, a widow to make altar saints stand back, is a prodigy of rubbish and vermin.

24. – Nativity of Saint John the Baptist. This was demonstrated to me: Every time someone says the *Magnificat*, Saint John "exults" in his mother's belly.

I am assured that I scandalize Cochons-sur-Marne. Several spouses of Jesus are horrified by a man known to write nothing but nastiness and who takes communion every day.

25. – *1815*. Waterloo. Same painful impression. Ever the God of war's plans aborting because of the infirmity or perfidy of his lieutenants. Having to write on Napoleon, I would like to be able to show perfectly that destitution of contemporaries of the greatest of men, who should have been, for lack of superior comprehension, heroes of devotion and obedience, *heroes of admiration*, – which the poor soldiers were, but which the leaders were not. It seems to me that there would be something to write about there, of a beauty to pierce the heart of God, like a lance.

26. – A note from Henry Houssaye: "All my thanks. Those *Letters* are truly worth publishing. I was happy to see the terrible and gentle Barbey d'Aurevilly come alive again in them."

27. – "One must leave everything. *One must leave the*

day after tomorrow." – JEANNE.

1815. I would like it to be over, it is too painful. What a bizarre incertitude at the heart of man; stranger still, what a need for incertitude; or rather what an admirable presentiment that nothing is definitive in this world! Even though I know that cruel series of disasters, it is impossible for me not to hope, each instant, that they *will not happen.* I want to persuade myself that at Ligny, d'Erlon will obey his emperor, that Ney will obey him at Quatre-Bras, finding his earlier resolve again, that Grouchy finally will deign to listen, at Wavre, to his officers and his soldiers. No matter what I do, the terrible and so unjust in appearance misfortunes of that war always surprise me... If only everyone were mistaken, however! If only the battle of Waterloo continued still!...

28. – To Jehan Rictus:

> *My article on you will never be modified nor attenuated. I will write it* in conscience, *and I do not wish to change anything in it. Only, when I publish it in volume, I will be forced to make – in the notes at the bottom of the page – an otherwise very fraternal and very gentle reservation. However accommodating I might be and whatever my will might be to enter into the mind of your marvelous vagabond, I must not espouse nor appear to approve the manner – appalling for me –*

in which you speak about the Love for Madeleine, page 115; the love for Montmartre or for Montparnasse [are] very different from the infinitely pure and supernatural dilection for the Gospel. There are things that must not be touched.

29. – To an artist who gives me the honor of preferring me to all his contemporaries:

I am happy to hear that Barbey d'Aurevilly's Letters *have interested you. I was not permitted to write a preface or add commentaries, and I am annoyed by that.*

What ravished me is your appetite for the Salvation Through the Jews *which is incontestably the best of my books and which nobody, ever, speaks to me about. I confide to you, as to a very old and very sure friend, that sorrow which is – at the core of my life, completely at the core of my life, – a great bitterness.*

You wrote to me, in September 1900, a letter that did not displease. Oh! on the contrary! I have a horror of prophets or visionaries who do not turn water into blood and who do not resuscitate the dead. But you like my

Salvation Through the Jews, *you fulfill that act of justice of picking up out of the dust and darkness that poor, despised little book. So you are really my brother and really the friend of God. "He who loves greatness and who loves the abandoned, when he passes beside the abandoned, recognizes greatness, if greatness is there." That magnificent expression is by Ernest Hello, who was an abandoned.*

There is, for me, only one way of conceiving of sin against the Holy Ghost, irremissible sin. *It is the* lack of love, *a terrible crime, very exactly delineated by Saint Paul, 1 Cor. XIII. All that one can say or write about it, outside of that, is precisely bullshit. Modern Catholics who are beneath everything and who merit all forms of torture, practice that sin by disobeying the formal precept of* taking communion every day, *by rejecting the* "panem quotidianum supersubstantialem," *encouraged in that by homicidal priests. I hope to write what will be needed when the time comes. God will not let me die of hunger or despair...*

P.S. You say the Vulgate speaks to the future. You're completely wrong there. The Vulgate is the Holy Ghost, without past or future. Time *does not exist.*

30. – Sent to my Jesuit the article on Rictus published by the *Mercure* and before writing the last chapter of the *Dernières Colonnes de l'Eglise*. Foreshortened and parabolic explication: "*Christus evomens Phariseos, cœnat libenter apud istum principem publicanorum.*"[84] Added: "Not an easy task, this new book, and particularly nauseating. I assure you that it does no good to tarry with Coppée or Brunetière, principally when one is *jacens ad januam divitis, ulceribus plenus, egens micis et nullis canibus ulcera lingentibus.*"[85]

1815. Waterloo, page 314. A guide, Joseph Bourgeois, trembling with fear for his name. When asked what the emperor was like, he said: "His face was like the face of a clock wherein one would not dare read the hour."

Sermon by the deacon on I do not know what. He affirms that his audience is an assembly of saints, *dilectis Dei, vocatis sanctis.*[86] I was the saint closest to him when he made that beautiful discourse, and I believe that my presence must have bothered him.

---

[84]*Christus*...: Latin for "Christ vomiting Pharisees, dines willingly with that chief publican."

[85]*Jacens*...: Latin for "Lying before the entrance to a rich person's house, covered in sores, in need of crumbs, and no dog licking his sores."

[86]*Dilectis*...: Latin for "Beloved of God, called to be saints," (KJV). Romans 1:7

July

3. – The deacon, given over this evening to a kind of vehement senility, offers us something like the funeral oration of an individual whom he does not name, but *who was rich*. That said in a half voice with an expression of infinite piety and respect. That rich person then was consumed with desire to *be useful*, to the point that he died because of it. No explanation, no detail of that death that must not have been any less curious than edifying. That martyr had an ambition, we are told, to be a "member of the municipal Council and the county Council, in order to be in a better position to be useful," which gives us a glimpse into that fine lout.

4. – I cry to Mary like a desperate man.

5. – Sunday of the Precious Blood. I request that that blood be changed into *Money* for me, in conformance with the exegesis.

It is the festival of Swine. Ignoble joy of that crowd. When the bourgeois rejoice, it is the same thing as when they are afraid. They look like devils.

6. – When will it please God to tear out from my heart the thorns that are torturing me?

7. – Reread the *Bonne Souffrance* in view of the
Dernières Colonnes. Suavity of Coppée's stupidities.
"I am less unhappy than before," he says. What a fine
epigraph! I expect pleasure for those who read me
and for myself.

8. – We are excessively miserable, grief crushes me,
and it is not by the reading of that rotten Pharisee that
I might be consoled.

10. – Speaking to a priest about the coming death of
Leon XIII, I declare, once more, to have always seen
in that pontiff an obstacle to God. He refuses to follow me, saying that Leon XIII has been admirable for
workers, a merit quite unknown to all the workers in
the universe. When a priest is excellent, one finds that
in him.

11. – A citizen of Nîmes came to see me. We speak
about the anti-religious campaign in the provinces
and the dreadful role played by Charbonnel, in the
process of becoming a sort of potentate through the
lodges, and acting by means of his vile journal on the
ministry even, with nameless authority.

13. – Horrible heat. In order to refresh myself, read a
hundred pages of Bourget's *Étape*, always with an
eye toward the *Dernières Colonnes*, where that friend
of Hanotaux naturally has his place. The academician

of ladies is so mediocre that he escapes ridicule even. His stupidity is inconsistent and elusive.

14. – Doctor X is an attentive physician, but pluvious. He is one of those who say: "I am so pressed for time that I never have the time to read," but then goes on to talk for half an hour about the Franco-Russian alliance or the incompetence in hydrostatics of the gendarmerie sergeant, with each of his clients.

15. – There are certainly some good priests who deplore Leon XIII's inertia in the affairs of Armenia and the present persecution. They blame, while groaning, the condescension of that pontiff receiving the Taxils and Brunetières, but without understanding that his horrible politics is a crime of the same sort, even greater. Such is the misery of the contemporary Clergy, and there is no remedy... A good paraphrase of the *Unam Sanctam* bull by Boniface VIII, in collaboration with the Holy Ghost, what a luminous slap [in the face]!...

16. – Continued *Étape*. Ah! I was right to call Bourget the "Eunuch"! He is unprecedented in impotency. Castrated heart, frozen and crystalized intelligence. He is not even boring with any vigor. A sort of interest sustains his miserable book, which one might say is sprinkled with the scrapings of a serialized novel.

18. – What a sacerdotal mind, that which consists in taking in souls *after* works!

19. – Leon XIII is in agony and behold the Introït of this Sunday, introït that must dominate the entire week: *Omnes gentes, plaudite manibus: jubilate Deo in voce exultationis. Quoniam Dominus excelsus* TERRIBILIS...?[87]

20. – Sending of the *Lettres*: "To my friend Alexandre Roy, victor of Tyre and victor of Babylon. It is Barbey d'Aurevilly that one would need to ask for a dedication for this book *which I am not the author of* and which could be so remarkable if not for the stupidity of a woman who had unfortunately the power of opposing my plan for a preface and a commentary that I alone in the world could write."

21. – Leon XIII died yesterday at four o'clock in the afternoon. It is more than twenty years now that I have been waiting for his successor.

23. – Worked on the chapter on Bourget (*Dernières Colonnes*) with a bit of energy and a fair amount of disgust. That author is one of the contemporaries whom I have *repaid* the most. He is so low and so stupid that I do not know what motivates him.

---

[87]*Omnes gentes*...: Psalms 46:2-3.

24. – I live like a brute in the company of Bourget. Happily the chapter is finished this evening.

26. – To numb my sorrow in the most beautiful of all dreams, reading in *Napoleon* by Norvins whose sublime illustrations by Raffet so greatly exalted my sad childhood.

27. – Cut this out of a newspaper:

> *Rome, July 26. – The* Voce della Verita *publishes the text of the document on parchment deposited in the Pope's coffin. That document edited by the Jesuit Father de Angelis, is a biography of Leon XIII, accompanied by several allusions to the evil of the times. It concludes by saying that Leon XIII was a pope to whom any other perhaps could never be compared in terms of goodness of soul, greatness of intelligence, integrity of life, sanctity of behavior, and the ardor that he put into consecrating his entire existence and all his strength to the service of the Church and Christ.*

Eh! well, I vehemently put forward the name of my patron saint Léon the Great, and a rather large number of others, among whom the martyr pope,

Saint Martin the First, who preferred a horrible death and the outrages of an entire world to the complicity of sophism and heresy that was proposed to him.

29. – I have the opportunity to meet a pious and intelligent priest. But I feel alone in his presence. He belongs to the sacerdotal generation formed by Leon XIII. I am a Catholic of the *Syllabus* and of Boniface VIII.[88] At some distance from strict Dogma, impossible to find common ground.

31. – To Albin Michel, publisher:

> *Jehan Rictus tells me that you are exceptionally equipped for a launching. You would be the man I have been looking then for many years now. Not having found him thus far, I have become a kind of "old master," very well known in the literary world and very unknown by the larger public.*
>
> *Today the Conclave begins. I have formulated a plan for a short book that can be read in one hour, in which the presumable role of the future Pope would be presented in substance. That in the literary form that one knows me for, and which pleases or exasperates so many people. Fifty or sixty pages would suffice. Is that something you*

---

[88]Boniface VIII: Pope from AD 1294-1303.

would be interested in? I would set
down to work on it as soon as you for-
mally accept.

August

1st. – The enormous torment that I saw the poor Hello suffer, more than twenty years ago, that of [one's prayers] *not being granted* and appearing to pray in vain, has become my torment. It seems to me that I no longer obtain any result and that the thing which is, each day, more necessary, is precisely what is refused to me most firmly. Dreadful discouragement, very bitter tears that remind me of the old days, certain ineffable days in the past.

2. – Noticed the surprising liturgical prayer of Saint Alphonse de Liguori at mass: *Sacerdos magnus qui in vita sua suffulsit domum et in diebus suis corroborav-it templum*,[89] *quasi Ignis effulgens et thus [sic]* ARDENS IN IGNE.[90] Words that seem completely supernatural when one thinks that the Conclave is presently reunited for the election of the Pope IGNIS ARDENS!!! Such things pass before my eyes like flashes of lightning, letting me know that God is here and that I am, ever also, the same desolate wreck in a torrent.

---

[89] *Sacerdotus...templum*: Ecclesiasticus 50:1-2. Latin for "the high priest,... who in his life repaired the house again, and in his days fortified the temple."

[90] *Quasi... igne*: Ben Sira 50:9.

To Jehan Rictus:

I do not expect great things from your publisher. I am aware of too much ignorance in these folk, their prompt stupidity, and above all the ambient scoundrel consulted by them... You know what there is to say about me literarily. As for my beliefs, my doctrines, do not be afraid to distinguish me violently from other Catholics, not fundamentally *of course, but in every other manner. In a word, affirm, raise your voice even that I am a Catholic, it is true, but* not a boring *Catholic, because I am an* ABSOLUTE *Catholic. That would be the originality of my small book. A petition of theocracy according to the* Syllabus *and Boniface VIII, the great Pope at the end of the XIIIth century, – in this time of imbeciles and cowards, it would not be banal. You will say: Bloy will do what he has done so many times before, he will say the most revolting things for the modern mind, the most incompatible with the automobile and the wireless telegraph. He will invoke, in order to say them, arcana that is the least imbued with traditional philosophy and theology, but all that in a form that a traveling salesman and a street peddler might understand or think they do. Etc...*

*As for dough, you will see what can be
gotten from that monsieur. But I do
not want you to be fed up with me, my
friend. That would render me complicit in the iniquity of the most hateful
louts. We are, the both of us, pastors.
Our role is to shear and not to be
shorn. It is true that our flock has become so many swine that it is no
longer a question of shearing, but only
slaughtering. If you bleed one of your
beasts then hold my portion for me.*

3. – For the beautiful feast of the Discovery of the
relics of Saint Stephen, Protomartyr, mass by the abbot Galette, babbler, stammerer, potbellied, miserly,
Blind-Mans-Buff priest and hearse driver. It is all I
can do to ward off disgust and horror. If I had the
misfortune of finding myself in a place where there
was no one but that priest, I would be forced to renounce every practice.

Response from Albin Michel. Formal refusal,
irrevocable. When a man writes: "I regret to inform
you," one can be sure that there is nothing to do about
it and that the information is as deceitful as the regret.

4. – That Galette has an idiot brother. Would that he
might care for him. It is the most precious thing he
possesses. We call them the innocent where I come
from. When he dies in the middle of his money and

amidst his sacrileges, that poor creature will speak for him perhaps.

Learnt, this evening, of the election of the patriarch of Venice who has taken the name of Pius X. This news saddens me, far from rejoicing me, and also I sink into depression. I had so desired an extraordinary event! It is always the same thing. An Italian and an old man!

5. – I enter church only to exit it immediately, the sacrilegious Galette saying mass. All day, I hold in my heart the image of that little turd.

8. – To Raoul Narsy:

> *I read in the* Occident *which is sent to me regularly, I do not know by whom or why, several lines by you, expressing a degree of affinity. But, in those lines that are at this moment before my eyes, you say: "A J.-J. Rousseau," comparing me cruelly to that son of Onan, to that vile masturbator of others and himself; you call me a "pessimist"!!! me, the famous optimist without equal or companion, incorrigible and perpetually conned! Our epoch not being exactly an epoch of thinkers, very few have understood that Marchenoir is a* philosophical *"desperate man" and nowise a* theo-

logical one. In other words, he expects nothing from men, but he expects EVERYTHING *from God.*

You also call me "discouraged," forgetting that I continue to fight back, and more than ever, at fifty-seven years of age, abandoned by everyone, riddled with horrible wounds and tortured by poverty.

Finally, you say that "I proclaim my defeat," when it is exactly the opposite that could explain my life. Supposing that I consider myself vanquished – which is not the case – I would never admit it, unless ironically. Is it then so difficult to understand me?

(I cited that letter whose interest is mediocre, uniquely because the addressee appears to be a Catholic of benevolence. If those sorts judge me thusly, what must I expect from others?)

9. – When one is incapable of great crimes, one is incapable of holiness. That truth by M. de La Palisse exceeds the abilities of a professor of religious philosophy come a great distance to instruct us.

10. – To Georges Rémond who seems to have completely abandoned us. I congratulate him on his translation of a "Life of Nicholas Poussin," from Italian

into French, curious adaptation that the *Occident* just published. I tell him that having so rarely obtained justice, I would think to merit that treatment if I refused it to others.

11. – Beginning of the execution of Paris, condemned for a long time now to perish by fire. Vast conflagration of the Metropolitan, at the metro station called *Couronnes!* The newspapers announce the discovery of 85 dead. That for the debut of the pontificate of *Ignis ardens*.

12. – What a mortal wound Reason seems to have received! Always the same thing! Everyone is persuaded that a bad tree can give good fruit.

21. – Enormous scandal. A rich man, who led a bad life, just died. First-class funeral with a deployment of unprecedented sumptuousness. Everyone runs to church to see it. Bitterness to think that with a portion of the money spent vainly on that carcass we could have been delivered!

What I am told about the ceremony makes me regret having stayed at home. It appears that that resembled a solemnity of devils. At each of the four corners of the sumptuous catafalque, there was, for people's astonishment or terror, an enormous lamp giving off a *green* flame. That gave something of a surreal definition to the deceased, in the middle of a torrent of lights. An orchestra savant come from Paris played authoritatively all that he liked, and over all that, mixed with incense and the suint of beasts, floated a strange and penetrating odor of *mildew*.

The only thing missing was the terrible peripeteia recounted in the story of Saint Bruno and painted by Lesueur, where the dead man sits up and says to the crowd: "I'm a damned man!" What would have been the countenance of our deacon who refused, several months ago, the Christian sepulture to an indigent because of concubinage and who tolerates today, joyfully doubtless, these alarming obsequies of a cohabitant estimated at fifteen thousands of francs?...

22. – I think of Saint Bernard whose feast day it was the day before yesterday, and I say to the Holy Virgin that the celebrated *Memorare* by her great friend becomes for me, each day, more difficult. *Non esse auditum a sæculo quemquam,*[91] said that priest. Alas! And what about me. It is for so long a time that I supplicate you to deliver me! Then I think of all the other liturgical or non-liturgical prayers, and I tell myself that each of the words pronounced by us in praying *is forever*, and that we will find their multitude at the hour of death and even after the hour of death.

24. – This evening, the sensation of taking our last

---

[91]*Non esse*...: From the *Memorare*, a Catholic prayer to the Virgin Mary soliciting her assistance.

supper.

30. – Saint Fiacre (See entry on the same date in 1901). Discourse by the deacon to gardeners. Jesus *ingenious* (!) to the point of imagining this *comparison:* "*Pater meus agricola est.*" My father is a gardener! His garden, it is our soul, "*hortus conclusus.*" I renounce to express what that homily's imbecility inspires in me.

September

2. – To a poor man who is about to die:

> *... I cannot encourage my wife to write to you. You have so completely disappointed her! She has this strange and lugubrious impression of having held out her hand to a man who was drowning, having believed she was about to save him, only to see herself rebuffed by that man who preferred death. You are surprised to have been thought a* Protestant. *It is quite simple. You reject confession and you say that you do not believe* all *the dogmas taught by the Church. If that is not Protestantism, I give up on knowing the meaning of words...*

6. – With respect to Iconoclasts, spoke of the enormous and totally mysterious importance of images. Idea to develop: God made man in his image and he made him *of the earth*. In Deuteronomy, chapter IV, he expressly forbids his people imitating him in that.

8. – Our new domicile is being prepared. A team of laborers work for three days to disinfect the walls and the parquets. Those men, although habituated, are surprised by so unusual an odor. But the house is nothing compared to the inhabitant, mephitic widow of a poor devil, an old officer who just died. That person, truly appalling, resembles a teeming and pestilential city in Asia, where all the filth and all the vermin would be on display. It is true that one washes, degreases, disinfects, scrubs, cures by smoke the habitation; all the same I grow serious thinking that it is going to be ours. Then there is that torturous thorn, that cruel point that is the feeling of my perfect impotence, or our utter destitution. If our present poverty continues, not only would we be unable to profit by that lodging, we would not even be able to live anymore.

9. – My new landlady, bourgeoise in a classic, ugly way, informs me that the stinking officer's wife whom we are going to replace is a serious drinker, a regional drunk, a zealot of the most ancient Poland. Naturally.

11. – Sudden departure of a young man whom we

gave hospitality to for *two months*. He leaves us, almost without saying a word, crushing us with his disdain. Having, by dint of energy, reached twenty years of age, that athlete had dreamt of making me benefit generously by his experience, by giving me lessons in literature and piety. Poorly recompensed by his effort, he took off, filled with a huge satiety of men.

(I didn't want to say any more about that poor child whose stupidity and pride made us suffer for sixty days. He believes himself called to the sacerdocy.)

12. – All the newspapers are filled with Renan and the inauguration day of his statue in Tréguier. The very low domestic of the Lodges, the dirty renegade persecutor, Émile Combes, father of the scandal of the "Carthusian million,"[92] tomorrow will go and give a discourse in honor of the famous jackass, the *denigrator of democracy*. Six thousand soldiers have been mobilized in order to surround the orator, menaced by slaps or, at minimum, by torrents of shit.

14. – I was hoping that the inauguration of the statue of Judas would have been the occasion of some bloody conflict. At least the Bretons should have hermetically locked the doors to their homes and shops, and sold neither a crumb of bread nor a glass of wine.

---

[92]Scandal of the "Carthusian million": in French, "*l'affair 'du million des Chartreux,'*" refers to a scandal that Combes' son Edgard was accused of being involved in, regarding blackmail of the Carthusian religious order in France.

Absolute interdiction, complete mourning. But we are in the twentieth century. Everything had to be, and has been, mediocre. All the displeasure that the bandit and his companions experienced came from above. It rained uninterruptedly. Mud underfoot and in people's hearts.

Jeanne was insulted this morning by a bourgeoise woman whom she owes nothing to, but who hates, instinctively, people of our sort. What a diabolical joy [there would be] in this infamous town if they saw us perish! *Spes unica!*

17. – Someone tried *to see* the miserable Galette's *eyes*. Impossible.

Atrocious poverty, fortunately and miraculously unknown.

18. – I know a priest, otherwise excellent, of the diocese of Tarbes who believes, inexplicably – like so many other modern priests – *that a bad tree can produce good fruit.*

I have seen in his hands a Protestant translation of the Bible which he judges superior, *closer* to the Text than the Vulgate. When one loves the Church, it is enough to make a person cry. That abbot has too much wit. When *Colonnes* appears, I will address a copy to him with these words: "From a devotee of the Vulgate who asks that one crucify him in Latin."

23-29. – The disorder of moving is in my soul. Since our marriage, this is the twelfth time, of which twice in Denmark.

30. – Saint Jerome. In the presence of the modern exegetic school, I feel the most tender love for Saint Jerome and his Vulgate. I see him alone, just as I am alone. I am perhaps *his only friend*.

October

2. – SS. Guardian Angels. I speak to my guardian angel, to that invisible companion who was, for half a century, witness to all my torments and who must have great compassion.

The clerk of the court of the Justice of the Peace informs me of a claim for 25 francs filed by a bitch to whom I do not owe them.

3. – I am always thinking about my book on money, for so long now. What a chapter I could write on landladies, pocketing what one gives them with a frightful disinterestedness in the anguish of their renters – anguish able to turn, nine times out of ten, into agony! I see that Madame Corbillard, old knacker with yellow teeth, who rented to us and who wants to be paid in advance, like all those damned people; I

always see her with the same gesture one uses to force-feed geese, methodically slipping into a long, silver-mesh purse, the poor pieces of money that were like blood drawn from my veins, which represented, – for so many days! – the life of my poor children, precious and execrable money which she hadn't even any need for, and which I saw disappear while having difficulty holding back a sob. And that enormous sacrifice must be renewed in three months.

5. – We subsist on the last of our poor exhausted credit.

6. – I learn that the deacon has profited by a serious malady that befell the sacristan, by depriving him of his employment, under pretext that the poor man, the father of a family, sometimes drank a little glass, without affecting his service which he excelled at. Novel viciousness that would complete that Pharisee if he had any need of being completed.

8. – On the path of the church. ME. – The more we go towards God, the more we will be united, that is to say brought together. Human beings are not parallel but convergent, and God is their hearth. Each soul is a ray of Divinity, which it is a part of, as of a sun, which must one day resorb it.

JEANNE. – *Et sanabitur anima mea*,[93] is said at

_____

[93]*Et sanabitur anima mea:* Latin for "And my soul will be healed."

communion. We are the ill, but Mary is our hospice: *Salus infirmorum*. The healing, in that hospice, is sanctity.

Such thoughts allow us to support the horrible life of this world.

Our portion appears to have run out. Agony of sadness. I attempt to work, but it is nothing but a crying for everyone. Ridiculous and enormous complication.

10. – The ways of the rich are enough to make Him who watches over the swine of the Parable vomit.

11. – In Vienna, Austria, Mirbeau when interviewed declares that Napoleon was simply an idiot.

In Clermond-Ferrand, Combes, inaugurating (again) a statue of Vercingetorix, throws in the face of that Gaul that there was never so amiable a government as his (that of Combes', naturally).

13. – Paris. The *Assiette au Beurre* asks me for an article on the Sultan. Infamy and ignominy of that bookstore where one sees only abject physiognomies.

Writ summoning me to the justice of the peace, Friday, in order to hear myself "sentenced" to pay 25 francs to that bitch plus expenses. Cost 4 fr. 45.

My physical horror for that sort of paperwork is, I think, an inborn trait. Their very sight unbalances me, despairs me.

14. – Dedication of *Colonnes* to René Martineau, a "Tourangeau found by God in order to spice up a bit this desalinated province whose swine began no longer to want the prodigal son."

15. – Another letter to a priest: *Dormientibus somnia-tor.*[94]

Extraordinary. The Redemptorists of boulevard Ménilmontant, who are to be expelled, had themselves photographed *palms in hand!!!*

Angustia creberrima.[95] Heart in a vice.

17. – Mass for eight hours. The deacon imagined to have the rosary told out loud, at the same time as the celebrant said the mass, such that it is equally impossible to follow either. Result desired by the devil and procured by ten thousand priests each day.

To the Judge of the peace:

It is certain that my literary enemies who are very numerous, would have

---

[94]*Dormientibus somniator:* Latin for "a dreamer to those who sleep."

[95]*Angustia creberrima:* Latin for "very tight anguish."

infinitely rejoiced yesterday, in your audience, for my very perfect humiliation.

Exhausted by five hours *of waiting, standing in the atmosphere that you know, dejected to death, by fatigue, disappointment, and disgust, when my turn finally arrived, it is totally indisputable that I had lost all ability to respond and that I was no longer in a state to defend myself. To see myself at the bar* in such company, *under the eye of an ignoble public, I felt like I was soaking in a pool of filth and you saw me speechless almost, which, anywhere else, would have astonished many people. I saw myself so totally disarmed! What an appearance that made, a man of my sort having to dispute with such a slut, were I not idiotified and paralyzed from the get-go. As for presenting witnesses, for a thing that happened* without witnesses, *and under the unique cover of good faith, how is it possible? In a like case, an honest man is fatally and indubitably conned.*

There would be one resource, however. The intuition of the good judge, at least the reasonable and certainly equitable induction drawn by him from the known morality *of people. But it appears that that did not happen. I felt it the very moment I appeared, and I immediately lost all hope.*

I have then the honor of informing you that, while renouncing my right, I consent to pay, me, a very poor writer, to Mme. de J., the sum of money that I do not owe her and which would be very beneficial to my dear little girls who are deprived by that stinking woman.

I will effect this payment, as well as that of the iniquitous expenses of stamped paper, with a profound feeling of indignation and horror.

19. – Employed in our vegetable garden, which has a furious need to be worked, is a very poor man, formerly a gardener, now infirm and living on not much more than alms at the sill of the church. Rude work for that miserable wretch, because the garden, rather large and given over to the most shameful abandon, resembles something of a dumping ground. But he puts the time in to it and that will be, I think, a rather honorable manner of sharing what God gives us with one of his friends.

21. – Forced to comply, I pay a visit to the court clerk of the Justice of the peace who presents to me a bill for 34 francs, payment due immediately, with no possibility of paying half now, half later. If I cannot pay,

it will start all over again. Such is justice. I pay.

And that rascal of a judge with a face of smoked herring who did not deign not to respond to my letter which I had the distinguished honor of writing to him! I return home, with clenched heart, thinking about that sow that gets drunk on the pink blood of the little children of Bethlehem.

It is clear that Jesus wants, in his capacity as Pontiff, to test me as engineers test a bridge, that is to say by putting the heaviest weights on me.

23. – Article for the *Assiette au Beurre* (published October 31, 1903):

Thirty Years of Assassinations

The present sultan Abdul Hamid II, younger brother of the sultan Mourad and nephew of the sultan Abdul Aziz, is the second son of the sultan Abdul Medjid. Grandson of Mahmoud the Reformer, *he is the 34th Padishah of the Osman Family and the 28th since the taking of Constantinople.*

So therefore since May 29, 1453, day of the taking of Constantinople by Mohamet II, there have been in the same time period: 28 sultans; 50 popes; 16 so-called Christian kings, not to mention a dozen emperors or presidents of the so-called French Republic; 15 Catholic kings or queens of Spain; nearly as many very faithful majesties in Portugal, among whom an Em-manuel the Fortunate, *who appeared, at one point in time, on the verge of renovating Alexandria; a small group of German emperors; no less a num-ber of English, Polish, or Scandina-vian monarchs; and I do not know how many subaltern potentates. Au-gust rabble, allegedly Christian.*

Supposing that that magnificent Pros-titute of the East and West, which goes by the name of Constantinople for nearly sixteen hundred years now, had been surprised like a maiden by the appalling Ottoman brute, Christians and their monarchs would have had time, after four and a half centuries, to disinfect the Occident.

Of course, there were magnificent ef-forts. Nicopolis, Lepanto, and Vienna are among the sublime frescoes of Christian heroism. But what difference does it make? A unanimous will would have been needed, the permanent ob-stinate, indiscouragable coalition of every power, and it is Europe's inex-pressible shame that Mohammed's vermin should always be found on the sex organs of the civilized world.

I say the sex organs. *"Venter meus in-
tremuit ad tactum ejus,"[96] as that canticle sighs. When someone touches
Constantinople, the world trembles
from head to foot.*

*Here is what I wrote on March 14,
1897, – about the time of the Cretan
horrors – to Henry de Groux whom I
thought was intelligent and who was
in effect, but who so sumptuously for-
sook me four years later:*

*"... Don't get so worked up over the
Greeks. There is not a less interesting
people in the world, and all the fuss
one makes about them is nothing but a
vile joke. I absolutely refuse to sympa-
thize with those schismatics, inhabitants of a land devoted for three thousand years to all the demons and
whose ancestors in the middle ages
made all the Crusades fail. Their history is nothing but a trail of rottenness
and blood.*

*"The present attitude of Europe is per-
fectly vile, of course, but don't you see
that all this Greek noise is designed
mostly to make people forget about
Armenia whose dreadful massacre has
not inspired any of our chivalrous students talking today to have themselves*

[96]*Venter...*: Latin for "my womb trembled at his touch," Song of
Songs, 5:4.

killed for Greece, which would be extremely stupid if anyone took them at their word?

"However, you know what Armenia is, don't you? It is the most mysterious country in the world, the place chosen for the Reconciliation. *It is there that the Deluge had an end, and where human Multiplication began.*

"For a dozen centuries at least, there has never been anything but one Eastern affair, a triple-faced and tripartite affair: Extermination or at least expulsion of the Muslims, extermination of the Greeks, and conquest of the Holy Sepulcher. All the rest is idiotic or deceitful.

"But to think that that Leon XIII who practiced politics while two or three hundred thousand Armenian Christians were being cut to pieces: Ah! one must have a robust faith..."

After the Armenians and the Cretans, it is finally and completely naturally the Bulgars' turn. There is no older score to settle, History being a sempiternal reiteration. Always Bulgaria for two thousand years. For Byzantium, – Greek, Latin, or Turkish, Christian or infidel, – it is a secular anguish. At the beginning of the XIth

*century, at the beginning of the Cru-
sades, there was a frightening man
among appalling men. He was a
Byzantine emperor, a Basileus the col-
or of blood, an extraordinary captain,
in the way that Hannibal was. He also
had sworn to exterminate a people,
but, more fortunate than Hannibal, he
succeeded. Bulgaria being at that time
a dangerous empire for Constantinople, he decided that there would be no
more Bulgaria nor even Bulgars. For
forty years, he didn't take off his
boots, he didn't dismount his horse,
and when he went to lie down to die,
that nation no longer existed. He is
called Basil II, the Bulgar Slayer. I do
not know of a more terrible epoch in
history.[97]*

*Listen to this. It happened that one
day, dragging behind him fifteen thousand prisoners who were hampering
his march, he divided those wretches
into companies of one hundred men,
had their eyes gouged out, except for
one out of the hundred who had only
one eye gouged out so that he might
serve as a guide for his comrades. He
sent them in that condition back to
their king, who was struck with horror
and collapsed, and did not regain his*

[97]The Bulgar Slayer: Bloy treats of the Basileus and the period in
his *Constantinople and Byzantium* (Sunny Lou Publishing, 2022)

senses except with so violent a beating of the heart that he died two days later. You have to read about this history in Gustave Schlumberger.

Now try to compare Abdul Hamid to that! Having seen that man of war from the XIth century, try to imagine that abominable maniac, always trembling for his ignoble skin and immolating entire peoples with his own crap.

You will see the camels of a coarse and crude driver, as Voltaire wrote, speaking about Mohammed. I never cite the patriarch of imbeciles, but that inversion appears to me to have something striking about it when I consider the filthy merchant of peanuts so licked by the Hanotaux and the Delcassés.

One of his historians, Pierre Quillard, makes the observation that the sultan, whatever his name is, is always and necessarily an individual without any intellectual heredity, in his capacity as the son of a slave, the law even interdicting the sovereign from making any alliance with a woman of middling condition, with the daughter of a functionary, for example!

One easily imagines the results of that hateful monarchic constitution. Abdul

Hamid is indisputably what one can imagine as the most successfully execrable and monstrous [of sultans]. The imagination becomes discouraged and succumbs before that atrocious idiot whose only thought is for the conservation and protection of his carcass and who seems to know no other joy than massacres or tortures. One knows about the appalling murders of Armenians, but there had been the massacres of Arabs in Yemen, the massacres of Druses in Lebanon, the massacres in Asia of the Kurds, Lazi, Circassians, or the Albanians in Europe, whenever they weren't acting as executioners themselves. He had massacred, near Mosul, perfectly inoffensive Yezidis. He had massacred the Hellenes in Crete and in Epirus. He had massacred in Macedonia the Bulgars, Serbs, and Vlachs. He had massacred thousands of Turks by drownings in the Bosphorus, strangulations in prison, suppressions in a land of exile. Jailer and probably assassin of his own brother, the Sultan Mourad, he had sent to himself at Yildiz, like an Object d'art, the cut-off head of Midhat Pasha, to whom he owed his elevation to power.

All that did not suffice for him however, for that happens at a distance. He had need of seeing the blood, hearing the sobs and hurlings of despair, the delicious spectacle of convulsions and agonies. He has then privileged tortur-ers who work before his eyes, in his palace. Enlightened amateur, he gives them advice and is honored with hav-ing invented several tortures himself.

One gets what one deserves, even when one is a Turk. Would to God that wicked man could exterminate his en-tire empire! But the inertia of Europe is complicit with that assassin and, permitting him to cut the throats of his European peoples even, it is a specta-cle of ignominy, enough to desiccate the tongue of a prophet!

When Abdul Hamid dies, which will happen soon, one will see the Hano-taux and all servile diplomatic scum be afflicted. They will go to Byzantium in their culottes and, so that the funer-al procession might be totally magnifi-cent, they will make them act perhaps like the horses in Suleiman's cortege, which were seen shedding tears be-cause they were made to breathe in through their nostrils I do not know what lacrymogenic powder.

24. – The *Dernières Colonnes de l'Église* is available

for purchase.

25. – To another benefactor:

Monsieur,

I have received the 40 francs that you have confided to an extraordinary man who does me the honor of loving me to the point of begging for me... I do not know all his steps... He has visited you, so be it. It appears even that it is terribly difficult to be received in your house, when one is not an academician. Through me he learnt that I am not an unknown person to you, he saw you as rich, finding such instructions at your door, and he wanted to hope nonetheless.

It is true that I am in danger – once again – but I would not have dared that. Knowing me to be very poor, literary folk have decided that I was a beggar, and I made of that honorable insult a panache for the proudest of my books. In reality, I have never known how to beg. My voice is not suited for anything but imprecation or hosanna. When one has read ten of my pages one is hooked.

You have given 40 francs. In your place, being unable or unwilling to do what was needed, I would have given nothing at all. Why humiliate an artist who suffers, not without nobility? If I had wanted, like so many others whom you know very well, I would not be poor. One knows that in the world of letters, but nobody says it. The book that you sent me will save me perhaps. Some people believe in a humble success. Would to God! The enormous injustice that I endure and that two innocents suffer would seem to be forgettable *if I obtained only a little of what is due to me. Life is so short and so vain!*

Send me your third volume when it appears. The name alone of Napoleon bursts out with love as if it were the Name of God, and I will speak of your work differently than others, it is probable. Only, do not inflict humiliations on me. I have already suffered too much, if you only knew!

26. – Apropos of a cleaning woman as nasty as all the others: There are no more servants in a society that no longer recognizes God for its master.

27. – Learnt of Rollinat's death *in a madhouse*. His wife, even stranger than he was, died *enraged*, it is

said. What a terrible end for an artist who impressed me so deeply at the beginning of my literary life! Never have madness and death been invoked in that way. His art was a sort of chronic blasphemy. His poetry summoned his music and together the two made the devil appear not long thereafter. I remember a month spent with him, in dark Berry, on the edges of the Creuse, in 1882. The "eminent" Haraucourt, who rudely left us later, was our companion and must not have forgotten that trip, notwithstanding his memory being as mediocre as his talent or his heart. I have tried to describe, in *The Woman Who Was Poor*, that sinister place.

30. – A liturgical dedication of *Colonnes*: "To the abbot Victor Charbonnel. *Ecce sacerdotulus qui in diebus suis displicuit Deo, et inventus est nequam, et in tempore iracundiæ, factus est anathema.*"[98] (No reply.)

31. – At church our deacon approaches, full of smiles, to thank me for the copy that I had expedited to him with this dedication: "From the black sheep to the good pastor." – "I protest against the 'black sheep,'" he says to me, but he does not protest against the "good pastor."

---

[98]*Ecce*...: Latin for "Behold the little priest who displeased God in his day and is found to be good for nothing, and, in irascible times, is made anathema."

November

1. – All Saints Day. I pray to the Holy Virgin and the Saints to deliver me from the sight of others who sully me and drive me to despair.

     Copious note from the baker. All that is far from eternal Life.

3. – Continual expectation and anguish. We owe, at the present hour, more than 800 francs, and some of our creditors become threatening. I stick to my little book which will die perhaps with me. I try to persuade myself that the end of my old torment is near and that my *Colonnes* could be the occasion of it. One no longer knows how to get by.

4. – The pastor's near visit is announced. That fat pastor, impressed by my book of a lamb, has decided finally to set foot amongst us – after three years.

5. – A grocer whose name is ridiculous sends me an inexact statement, insolently inexact. In vain, I point it out to him, I prove to him even, that he has cheated me by 20 francs. His accounting is infallible. I feel, as with the shitty official of last month, that I am vanquished in advance and that I will need, in order to find peace – the justice of the peace! which leaves me, once again, cleaned out. Nothing I can do. Books of account are taken as evidence in courts of justice!...

I vomit into an abyss.

6. – I clearly affirm that the modern Catholic world is a reproved, damed, absolutely and irremediably rejected world, a vile world that the Lord Jesus is *fed up with*, in a most complete fashion, a mirror of ignominy in which he can no longer see himself without feeling *fear*, as in Gethsemane.

A Sacamer, ironmonger and coal merchant, whom I owe 110 francs to, had been begged not to inflict a commercial settlement date on me. That young and brilliant husband of the eldest daughter of the Dépendeurs had a letter brought to me, written in an abject style, saying that he was going to "fire on me." Jeanne, having tried to persuade him to wait for me and do nothing about it [for now], found in him a most excellent lout who insolently refuses. I decide to accept the bill. Ignorant as I am of the procedural garbage, all attempts at resistance to these scoundrels would be pointless and would cost me horribly dear.

8. – A sublime Czech by the name of Josef Florian, who propagates me as much as he can in Moravia, and who writes me letters much more precious than diamonds, expresses this simple idea that I would have need of a "translator from heaven."

10. – Visit finally by the deacon accompanied by a missionary who looks as though he had just come

back from living with savages in Oceania. That merciful and fat deacon did not think he could, in all conscience, deprive me any longer of this favor. But he has come with visible fear, and it is for that reason that he is accompanied. Grotesque meeting. I have never seen a man more uncomfortable, more powerless to extricate himself from an awkward situation. He could not find a word to say, not the semblance of a word about my book which was however the pretext of his visit. "I made it a point to read it in its entirety before coming," he said to me, for he belongs to the multitude that thinks it knows how to read. Nothing more, if not some extremely vague commonplaces about I do not know what.

Serious like a mule that one might load with very heavy relics, I was able to be decent, to avoid every regrettable word. But the extraordinary unintelligibleness of that visitor, infinitely out of his element at our house, made me feel pity. He departed at the end of half an hour.

11. – Another effect of the *Colonnes*. My Jesuit wrote to me saying that his conscience makes it a duty for him to *separate from me*, the manner in which I speak about Leon XIII appearing unacceptable to him.

I had thought about taking out an ad in the *Semaines religieuses*. Idea of little worth, that publicity being the most limited of all, and the directors of the *Semaines religieuses* being almost always inexpugnable imbeciles.

12. – *Lourdes*, volume by a young (?) occultist, Grillot de Givry (?) who wrote *Xrist*, cites from Greek and Hebrew, and says he is "a forgotten columnette." Life is short. The epigraph, nevertheless, makes me pay attention. *Congregationes aquarum appelavit Maria.*[99] Certain phrases here and there seem to me to have a superior mark. Undertook the reading of that book which appears to be uniquely for the glory of Mary.

> From Jeanne:

> *If God gives us but little, it is because it is impossible for him to give us any more, for reasons that are hidden to us. That makes me think of our poor gardener, the beggar on the church sill whom we cannot pay at this moment, who suffers because of us, but who would be unjust if he accused us. And I am seized by an immense pity for God, a mysterious and supernatural pity.*

13. – Continued with yesterday's reading. Disenchantment. The occultist ends up possessing all the pride particular to those people and the incredible pedanticism with which they drape their nothingness. He calls himself "the initiate of Hermes, the mysteri-

---

[99]*Congregationes*...: Latin for "Congregations of water addressed Mary."

arch of antique beliefs." I obviously have nothing to do with such a man.

15. – An old cleaning woman, whom we had believed to be a treasure sent by God, gets drunk. Everything that happens is preferable to what could happen.

17. – The grocer with a ridiculous name, mentioned earlier, definitively and comminatorily refuses to modify his addition. Once again, that imbecile undertakes to prove to me – by his books – that his accounting is exact. I have already responded to him: "I will read your books when you read mine." But he does not like the counsel.

It is said and even written, I think, that merchants' books of account are "taken as evidence." Why? It is something that no one will ever know. I have already expressed that idea. What prevents a grocer to inscribe whatever he pleases in his book, then to put out invoices with fantastic claims and, if one complains, responds: "You have lost one or more intercalary invoices. Here is my book that *proves* that I made deliveries to you which you deny having received"?

It is quite certain that a merchant's books of account would always condemn me, being much more trustworthy than the Bible. A doubt expressed on their exactitude would attract the ire of all judges.

Continued all the same the reading of *Lour-*

des, that strange book received on the 12th. I have great difficulty understanding who the author can be, whose talent is undeniable, and who greatly interests me when he puts a mussel on his occultism.

18. – To the grocer with the ridiculous name:

> *Monsieur,*
>
> *I send to you herewith a postal order for the sum of 128 fr. 30, for which you will be kind enough to send to me, in return, a statement of quittance of all monies owed. My time is precious and I do not want to lose it in useless demands or contestations. Your books are nothing to me, and you know perfectly well that I am in the right to complain. I prefer to pay what I owe rather than dispute with a grocer over an ignoble question of money. Only, I advise you to pay more attention to your accounting. Not everyone will be as accommodating as me...*

Three hours later, a visit by the grocer's wife, bringing quittance and chastisement. "Monsieur," she says to me, "grocers are every bit as worthy as writers!"

I received this terrible blow with appropriate humility. I even went so far as to recognize, by bowing to the ground before that Nemesis, that grocers are worth much more, which seemed to "throw her

for a loop," as my old comrade Alphonse used to say
with such authority.

19. – Prospectus which I admit to being the author of,
sent by the *Mercure* to a large number of ecclesiastics:

Les Dernières Colonnes de l'Église

COPPÉE, THE REVEREND FATHER JUDAS,
BRUNETIÈRE, HUYSMANS, BOURGET, ETC.
THE LAST CATHOLIC POET

By Léon Bloy

*People know that Huysmans' conver-
sion is one of the works of* LÉON BLOY,
*the only one that had a bit of success.
The celebrated Catholic pamphleteer
having been the visible instrument of
that extraordinary change, nothing is
more curious than to see today the disciple judging the master.*

At the same time, LÉON BLOY *judges
several other writers received only recently into the Church and whose zeal
as converts appears to him a bit cum-
bersome.*

*When one knows the power and the
originality of the author of* La Cheval-
ière de la Mort *(Marie-Antoinette) and*

The Son of Louis XVI, the announcement of a similar work suffices to excite curiosity to the highest degree in these times of religious crisis.

20. – To Jeanne speaking to me about the correspondence that she finds sometimes between the movements of her soul and the liturgy: "The Liturgy is so supernatural that it is quite simple to say that it really exists in us, that it is *imprinted* in us like a result of the sacrament of Baptism and the sacrament of Confirmation." Incredibly fecund idea.

21. – Spoke about an abbot Loisy who appears to have taken the lead among those who make war on the Vulgate and Saint Jerome. It is the modern inclination, and the best are on that slope. Negation pure and simple of the sacred Text. Never has the faith run up against a greater danger. On the subject of the fruit from the forbidden tree that that school judges mythical, I say that that fruit, *that apple is no more a myth than the Eucharistic Species*, and that with the Holy Ghost affirming that fruit one must believe on it as on a visible and sensible reality, at the center of a tourbillon of mysteries.

The Christian who communes under the consecrated species eats Life – a mystery. Adam and Eve ate Death under the species of the forbidden fruit. Another mystery certainly identical.

22. – To Grillot de Givry:

Monsieur,

I know nothing about you, your name even was unknown to me, and I received your book with extreme defiance. Already little satisfied with my contemporaries, Catholic contemporaries above all whose idiocy and cowardice can surprise the most inveterate imbeciles: I was put off, what is more, by the occultist formula that was nearly impossible for me to digest. The epigraph, however, convinced me to read you. As a disciple of Grignion de Montfort and one of his last supporters of the Catholic Absolute, I stopped seeing then what, in your book, might appear to me onerous or difficult, and you have certainly added to my personal vision of Glory. A Christian today giving to Mary what is her due, it is the most surprising of all miracles.

I hope, sir, that you will not be indifferent to this vote of confidence by an old writer renounced by all those whom he had perhaps the mission to instruct, abandoned by all the hateful faithful *whose duty would have been to assure him his bread and who works for twenty years now for the Reign of God and for justice, all the while agonizing in poverty.*

(No reply. To declare that one is poor is the secret for turning someone to stone. Medusa had to be poor. I knew, through Péladan, that contempt for the poor is an arcana of Occultism.)

24. – Invitation for 30th. That will be the great Fall. One could bring the world along.

25. – Amusing note by Eugène Grasset on Huysmans, apropos of *Colonnes*: "I find his books indigestible since he renounced spices."

The privation of wine and sorrow exhaust me. A person brings me a franc, another person two francs. It is as if Jesus on the cross let fall three drops of his blood.

28. – "The Angels are voluntary mirrors." MARY OF AGREDA.

29. – I have friends whom my persistent misery embarrasses and whose delicacy consists in appearing persuaded that all will work itself out at the precise moment when the death rattle comes. When the anguish is enormous, one would almost wish – a totally strange impression – for a disaster so that one can say to them: "See how cruel your surety was!"

To a passionate friend who comes around every eighteen months:

> *I want to believe that you will come finally, one day or another, and I consent even to receive your young painter friend. Only... (I say* only*) on one condition. You write to me telling me that that adolescent has read, "by chance," the* Exegesis of Commonplaces, *and that he has read only that* one *work of mine. Now, in order to be received in my house, he needs to have read at least* FOUR *of my books, among which* The Desperate Man *and the* Femme pauvre. *I owe it to myself to demand that from unknown people who desire to see me, not wishing, – at my age and not even having become an academician, – to be visited like a dangerous animal. I require, moreover, that my books not be read* by chance. *Those points accorded, you can execute the maneuver. I will be "welcoming" if I am still alive, which is not altogether certain.*

December

1st. – The previously-mentioned Sacamer claims to have presented the bill to me yesterday, which is false. That "couillon de ratepennade,"[100] as Rabelais says, had planned, with an extremely shitty bailiff, that nasty little trick of adding expenses, while *forgetting* to present me with their dirty piece of paper. Fortunately, I remembered in time, and I paid my judicial obligation, not without having inundated Sacamer with the expression of my sentiments, which exasperates him, to judge by the yelling heard after I closed his door. I was hoping in vain that, running out after me, he would come and collect several slaps on the sidewalk. I would not have shown myself to be stingy, I could have even added several kicks in the pants, but he would have needed to ask me for them.

2. – Reading the *Avertissements* by Bossuet, on a horribly cold day, while drinking ice water, – I recommend that to anyone wishing to practice chastity.

God always wants to be impenetrable, and he is more than ever when he seems to say to his aggrieved friends: Look at me.

4. – Abundant snow on our poverty. "Sorrow is a grace that we have not merited," Jeanne tells me.

7. – To André Martineau, a very young child who, hearing tell of our poverty, called on his parents to send us the several francs that he possesses:

---

[100]*Couillon...*: French for "bat testicle," or "testicle of a damn rat with wings."

My dear little friend,

You are Léon Bloy's benefactor. It is something that you cannot yet very well understand. But if, keeping this letter, you re-read it in twenty years, when the poor Léon Bloy will be underground, you will weep with pity on thinking of the earthly life of that poor wretch of a writer. At the same time, you will weep for joy on remembering that the power was given to you to console him for several hours...

A person who wants to do me some good passes the word around that I am a drunk.

8. – Apropos of a bookstore's invoice, the payment of which is demanded insolently, Jeanne points out to me that the end of the year is a time resembling that of a *hallali*. All the dogs, gobs ajar, rush forward.

10. – Eighth anniversary of the death of our little Pierre. We have no more dolorous a memory. I implore the protection of that innocent become our *Benoni* in heaven.

Conference in Paris, rue du Bourg-Tibourg, with the very poor, who love me. It is a humble circle of Christian workers and goes by the name of *Hope*. Modern little catacomb under a landlord. No one is less of a lecturer than I am. I get by as best I can with lectures. Those in the audience, determined to admire anything it pleases me to make them listen to, is contented. But I cannot admire myself, no matter what I do. Here is the peroration of prattling announced under this title:

The People of God in the Twentieth Century

... and the People of God? you ask me. Haven't I demonstrated that to you? Formerly, more than three thousand years ago, the People of God were the Hebrew people. They did not lack miracles: Jehovah led them by the hand through the middle of the waves and into the desert, for the astonishment and extermination of other peoples. Since Jesus Christ, the people of God is each one of us, it is me, it is you, the carpenter, you, the locksmith, you, the office employee, the cesspool emptier, or the poet. It is anyone who is poor, anyone who suffers, anyone who is profoundly humiliated. It is an immense flock in solitude, an infinite multitude of sad hearts in search of Paradise. There are those who barely earn their bread, who never have a free hour for the cultivation of their souls, and who finish by renouncing it.

Besides, who could instruct them,

guide them, encourage them? The clergy, insufficient in terms of number, is almost always of a frightful mediocrity. As for those Léon Bloy types, when they can be found, they are strangled, suffocated so much so that it is impossible to know them, and there is no means to hear them. Then what? Nothing remains but bosses or landlords. Frankly speaking, it is not enough.

However, souls, they exist! You have been bought, paid a large price for, said Saint Paul. I believe it! nothing less than the Blood of God was needed! Those things there are things that we cannot understand.

But what we do understand, very well, is that nothing in the world or in hell would be capable of paying for our souls. "I am the son of a man and a woman, so far as I'm told. That surprises me. I thought I was more than that!" Those words were written by a totally modern poet who was as wretched as possible. Pascal is burning with glory for much lesser words.

The saints have affirmed that if by divine permission a soul could be seen for it is, one would die this very instant, as if thrown into a furnace or into a volcano. Yes, the soul of whom-

soever it might be, the soul of a bailiff, the soul of a concierge, would consume us.

Ah! Lord, behold a sad people of God! a strange and inconceivable people of God! A perpetual and universal procession, a torrent of flames more incandescent than the stars and which do not even know themselves! Sirius, Aldebaran, Altair, or that terrifying star of the Constellation of Hercules at which our sun precipitates itself with an accelerated speed of several thousand leagues per second; – such stars, I say, absolutely covered by darkness, unsuspectable but certain, as they have cost all the Blood of Jesus Christ: it is what the People of God are composed of. Furnaces as large as worlds, but invisible, and not knowing themselves to be furnaces...

It is a monster to think about, it is to die of admiration to tell oneself, for example, that here is a poor copyist, eighteen to twenty years old, a very poor rascal of an employee who scratches on administration paper while copying stupidities or nastiness, who will continue thus until the day he dies finally, without any hope and growing stupider with each passing day, and whose soul, however, cost the

life of the Son of God!... Tell yourself,
after that, that that miserable wretch
is still an aristocrat, a kind of nobility
or bull's Eye, in comparison to other
slaves. Keep in mind that there are
hundreds of millions of others who do
not even know that God exists, and
whom one batters to death from morn-
ing to evening. Is it to them that Jesus
Christ said: "Quit everything, sell ev-
erything, renounce everything and fol-
low me?" Clearly, as nobody is ex-
cluded from the evangelical predica-
tion. Only that multitude can respond:
"We have nothing to quit, nothing to
sell and, possessing nothing, not even
our bodies nor our souls, we do not
know what to renounce. We do not
refuse to follow you, but we are dis-
tressed, hundreds of millions of dis-
tressed souls living in darkness. If we
grope to the right, is that your Heart,
o Jesus! is that the Wound in your
side? If we grope to the left, is that the
Devil that comes to take us by the
hand?... Consider this, if you please, o
Lord, that there has never been a God
who had a more lamentable people."

My dear friends, we say that or we do
not say that, but it is certain that our
entrails shout it, if not for ourselves, at
least for our completely disinherited
brothers.

*The service of God is hard. Only hyp-
ocrites will tell you the contrary. It has
cost me, myself, twenty years of tortures, perfect ignominy, and the death
of two of my children killed before my
very eyes by the fiercest poverty. However, I do not want to complain. Suffering is an infinitely precious grace
that nobody is worthy to judge. So
much the worse for me if I am too
much a coward to ask for a supple-
ment.*

*I have come to tell you that we are all
together extremely interesting miserable wretches, as we are the People of
God, not being landlords. But this language can only suit souls, and I naturally supposed yours. Your souls! Ah!
I always think of those invisible furnaces! Interrogate the first bourgeois
to come along. He will tell you that the
serious thing to do in life is to fill up
on tripe. By that account, I have never
been serious, and I declare that I do
not know how to speak to people of
flesh and blood. You have just experienced an example of that.*

13. – Atrocious existence, terrible bitterness. What a
disposition in which to receive the Liturgy on this
Third Sunday of Advent: *Guadete; iterum dico:
Guadete*. The Deacon, whose stupidity grows ram-

pant, seems driven to chase away the faithful from his church. He no longer allows anyone to choose his place. By his order, the seats are stringed together so that it is impossible to take one away and sit by one-self, if only to escape the stink of a group. One will need from now on to be parked according to his fanta-sy and pay through the nose. He had the nerve to speak about that from the pulpit. It is a shame for ec-clesiastical authority to confide an important parish to a priest who is so completely devoid of intelligence and goodness.

14. – I leave Bossuet at the Vth *Avertissement* to that scoundrel Jurieu. That controversy where terrestrial impunity and the divine right of kings is affirmed makes me nauseous. At a distance of more than two centuries, that pedagogue coming from the other side of the gulf of the Revolution and, when all peoples writhe in agony on the sills of the Holy Ghost, is much more than strange.

I am, moreover, as ill disposed as possible to welcome that old-fashioned stuff. The idea alone that, in fifteen days, I will need to hand over to my landla-dy, who has no need for it, a found (?) sum at the price of what humiliations! and which represents our subsistence for a month, – that infernal idea little pre-pares me for respect for the powerful sons of bitches of this world.

15. – We begin again no longer to be able to feed our

children. The postage of a necessary letter, 30 centimes, a bleeding straight from the carotid, a flow of blood!

16. – I think a lot about our little ones who died, about the "house that sings," Jeanne's beautiful and sorrowful tale; I ask for assistance from those innocents, and I weep.

17. – If God continues to conceal his Hand, this memorandum will soon become the journal from the edge of the Raft of the *Medusa*.

19. – Very painful impression caused by the fall of one of the great trees in our vicinity. Devastation that afflicts us and disgusts us already in our new domicile. Yesterday morning our hearts tightened when we saw lying down on the ground an entire row of those magnificent poplars that had attracted us here, and the sound of those trees [swaying in the wind] gave us the illusion of being near a forest. We could have wept.

But today, seeing and *hearing* one of them fall, I felt an extreme sadness, an immense satiety for this world. The savages have an obscure fear of natural forces, the *elementa mundi*,[101] as the ancients said, which can turn them away from destroying a beautiful thing. But the bourgeois, a superior brute, is incapable of that fear. The beauty of God's Face, to them, is not

---

[101]*Elementa mundi*: Latin for "elemental spirits."

worth the effigy of Louis-Philippe or Napoleon III on a one-hundred-sous coin. The mother of the faller of our poor trees, an illustrious shopkeeper, gave the real response several days ago: "If it wasn't us, it would have been someone else!" she said with a great nobility of expression. If Judas was selling his Master, fifteen deniers, all the more to profit by. Why let a business opportunity slip away?

This evening, the terrible postman threw into our box a long letter by a Greek cretin, by an idiot from Athens who wants to make historical reprimands to me and to give me advice on returning to reason by leaving a religion of imposture. It is my article on Abdul Hamid that has unleashed that Hellenic patriot, that descendant of Marathon warriors.

20. – Beautiful dream, last night. I was in Paris, I entered, I do not know how, the Sainte-Chapelle. A dreamlike Sainte-Chapelle which soon became the House of Mary. Not the humble House in Nazareth, but the splendid House, the glorious House. I cannot express the sensation of warmth and supernatural sanctity that I felt. It is the impenetrable mystery of dreams. Impossible also to explain this fact that I was charged with feeding a very gentle furnace which warms the entire house. From time to time a golden grill lifts and I push into the middle of the flames large branches, similar to those of our poor cut-down trees. Those branches bend easily and *willingly* in order to enter the furnace... I woke up gently, sweetly, prepared to receive the joy or the sorrow that it pleased God to send my way.

21. – A bit of work and reading, but with what a thorn bush around my heart!

22. – Read this, that the Académie Goncourt has set aside a prize of five thousand francs for the best book... There are at most three in that group, Huysmans, Descaves, and Mirbeau, who know that that prize will never be awarded to me and that I die of poverty very justly. Finally, would that God might fill them with blessings, – the God Emmanuel who will be born in two days, and would that he might have pity on the old ass and old bull that I have reunited in my person!

23. – Horrible cold in church by the will of our pastor who prefers an ignoble lucre to his duty. He makes collections for the heating and he never heats. Danger for the rare faithful, and a putting to flight of the infidels, not to mention the scandal. Those things there are met with on one's deathbed.

24. – At the *Commerce* cafe. Quick note. An unknown individual has just entered. Almost immediately afterwards, another individual enters exactly similar to the first. Then a third, then a fourth, then ten, twenty, fifty, five hundred, one cannot count them. The cafe is full, bursting with people who are absolutely the same, who are *one*. And behold the be-

ginning of the end of cafes, the beginning of the end of the world!

Frightening image come from Denmark in a Christmas album: *Jule Roser*. It is a Lutheran adoration of the Infant Jesus by the Scandinavian Pharisees whom the painter wanted to make touching and much more venerable than Catholic saints. Some are kneeling, hands joined, indescribably abject. But that is nothing. There is Mary, a monstrous Mary, imagined by I do not know what filthy damned people. The artist, extremely habile, has poured out all his art to represent a *vulgar* Mother of Jesus, hideous in vulgarity. The ignoble ugliness of that face is calculated to fill Protestant hearts with joy. On its knees, a child whose visage is not seen and who appears hydrocephalus.

[Something] to hold on to, in order to dishonor Protestantism. I wrote this below it: *Lutheran Noel* – ADORATION OF BAD SHEPHERDS.

25. – Noel. Even today, the deacon does not provide heat. At high mass, I was frozen to the bone, and I had to endure for three quarters of an hour the babbling of the greedy old man. He said, several days ago, to his unfortunate sacristan, a father of six children, and basely paid: "I do not like needy employees."

Avarice being a passion that grows with age, it is frightening to think of the last days of that priest.

26. – A good man who thinks he has read me, offers me his counsels. He shows me the good way which consists in being gentle and resembling other Catholics whom it is manifest that God is delighted with.

27. – A young gentleman with the terribly Genevan name of Morerod and calling himself a painter, is introduced to us as an "admirer" by an old, half-savage friend. Welcome as good as circumstances permit. Unable neither to regale him, nor to gratify him in any way, I speak with gentleness and give him two of my books (I have never seen him again).

31. – In the *Mercure*, long supplication by Péladan to the Pope "for the reformation of canons in the matter of divorce." Indissolubility annoys him. Sophism common to all heretics: *Charity* called to the aid of passion. Joséphin was more amusing when he was Sar and when he took the Princess Paule for a stroll through all the bordellos in Paris.

1904

Sorrow is a grace that we have not merited...

January

1ˢᵗ. – I learn with satisfaction about the fire at the Iroquois Theater, in Chicago. That consoling incineration of landlords makes me think, once more, about the conflagration of Paris, predicted so many times.

2. – Formerly, there was the delirium of grandeurs, today it is the delirium of pettiness.

"Why would we leave Cochons-sur-Marne?" Jeanne says to me. "Here, at least, we are known, people despise us. Elsewhere, it would be difficult perhaps to find that again."

4. – Visit to our landlady who refuses, as rent payment, a very good security offered by the *Mercure*, gracious advance on *Mon Journal* which will be published in the spring. She says that the acceptation of a security would expose her to losing her *privilege of a landlady*, by putting her on the same footing as such and such other creditor. In other words, she would no longer have the recourse to sell our furniture at a low price, – which must be for creatures of her type, a divine joy, above all when there is an artist and small

children to make suffer. Content and proud of that expression which would dishonor an honest galley
slave, she consents to give me one month's extension.

A more consoling word by another old woman
whom Jeanne utilizes for sewing and who came this
morning, passably drunk. I do not know why she told
me "she has nothing to reproach herself for." As I fe-
licitated her while envying her, because of the bad
state of my conscience which does not give me the
right to attribute to myself that permanent testimony,
I attracted this strong reply: "Monsieur, it is doubtless
because you are instructed!"

5. – No news from God.

7. – "Communion is not permanent." Response by our
dear deacon to a question that one can probably
guess. "Charity also is not permanent," someone voluntarily retorted. The extraordinary unconsciousness
of such an expression reanimates in me the old desire
to write a novel of observation which would be entitled *Cochons-sur-Marne, canton seat*. I would depict
the deacon with the character traits of a saint operat-
ing some miracles and accomplishing just the opposite of the ridiculous or revolting acts that one knows
here.

8. – The onerous necessity of making money by [pen
and] paper forces me to recur to the talents of an ex-

bailiff revoked for I do not know what turpitudes and who gives a discount in order to dry the tears. That excellent man is always mistaken when rendering money. With clients like myself, it never fails.

We were speaking of something, it had to do with I do not know what *acts* that we said had to be accomplished. Suddenly Madeleine puts before our eyes her little missal opened to a page of acts of faith, hope, and charity, saying to us: Behold!

10. – To the deacon:

> *You may have noticed, over the last three years, that we are Christians, my wife and I, and you understood that we go to church in the hope of finding peace. Since then, how could you approve of pious people who, without any provocation, without the shadow of a pretext, insult us in your church? This is what happened today for the second time.*
>
> *My wife, attending high mass with our youngest daughter, was horribly insulted by a lady R. whom I've noticed one time only and whose extreme vulgarity made us take her for a domestic. My wife was in perfect alignment and could not have in any fashion been in the way of that bourgeoise woman who had, moreover, many*

empty chairs in front of her. One must believe that the lovable creature was drunk or possessed, for she did not stop complaining scandalously and even worked herself up into a fury by proffering cries and injuries, without there having been any means to hope that she might calm down, at the price of any concession whatsoever.

You know that a well-bred woman is without defense in cases like this. A very soft plea to remind her that she was in the presence of the Holy Sacrament only served to exasperate the shrew. It is also extraordinary that you hadn't noticed a thing.

Such then is the situation. The scandal can happen again. Supposing that you are the master in your own church, I am persuaded that you would want, and that you are able, to oppose a continuation of that disorder.

This evening we decided not to send that letter, sure that the deacon would find fault with us.

11. – There are nothing but bailiffs and discounters. Having received, from the women religious to whom we owe 40 francs, an insolent and comminatory demand [for payment], the housekeeper, whom we sent, returns with a receipt for 44 francs, 4 francs in surplus

for absolutely illusory supplies, and a hypocritical letter in which our "dear children" are spoken of. Ah! they were right to expel those bitches, and how well God knows what he allows!

Death of the painter-sculptor Gérôme. Newspaper copy for a week. Sudden death. One of the last acts by that contestable artist, who was treated by the World with so much gentleness, was to say, apropos of me who never asked him for anything, that he had decided, *in the future*, no longer to give anything to anyone.

12. – Someone speaks to me again about Mother Mercédès whom certain people believe to be very advanced in the supernatural life. It appears that that saint Thérèse of contraband and contramark considers herself called, since the time in her mother's belly, to the most dazzling aureole, declaring that penitence is not her way, that she has need of the joy and glory of the Resurrection and that the Sufferings of Jesus Christ interest her little.

"Could you not vigil one hour with me then?" says the Savior in agony. "I do not sleep, my dear Master, as you can see. I enjoy myself before your Face covered in blood, and the little souls, whom you gave me to instruct, kiss my feet with a very great respect. It is thus that I am united in following you. You suffer opprobrium and tortures so that I might be in delight, and I have nothing better to do than to desire it. As for the poor who are your dolorous members, is it not just that they pay for your Elect, and what has

your Elect got to do with the lamentations or supplications of those savages ignorant of your splendor?"

13. – I ask God to grant me the grace of at least a few
centimes, not to demand everything from his poor
debtor, to give me finally a bit of joy, of security.

14. – Nothing is more necessary to me than wine. In
consequence, my merchant refuses, with a panache
and stars, to continue extending credit to me. I never
tire admiring the power that all these flunkies have to
walk successively on two feet or four paws, according
as they sniff riches or poverty.

15. – Letter from my Jesuit, long and bizarre but extremely conformant with the traditions of his Institute.
He is afflicted to "no longer be able to follow me,"
because of certain audacities in *Salvation Through
the Jews*, for example, and because of my lack of esteem for modern Catholics whom I understand poorly. Finally, and it is in this that I believe I discover the
hand of his superiors, he insinuates that if I consented
to transform myself to the point of conceiving affection for those people, *I would be delivered*. Well,
well! Fancy that!

       A certain abbot Purgatoire, a student of abbot
Loisy, does not understand that it is important to the
faith that Moses be believed the author of the *Pentateuch*. What does he believe then? It is however true

that there are superior men who reach the end of a very long life without having ever understood anything.

Response to my Jesuit:

... I don't ask that anyone follow me "to the end" nor even for one hour. I limit myself to asking for a little justice... You speak to me about Catholics whom "I have never known how to turn to account" and for whom I could still "do an enormous good." That good, you know that I have ardently desired it, and that I have never been able to accomplish it. Today, what could I do? I have the inexpiable defect of passing for a writer of genius. So I die in poverty. You understand me. It has gotten to the point that if, by a miracle, certain Catholics became aware of me suddenly, finally, it would most likely be too late. The baker to whom I owe a great deal can, tomorrow, refuse me his bread. I know that in your communities each religious is individually poor, but he has only the care of his soul, and the charge of no human life weighs on him. Tell me, do you believe that there are many among them who can, I don't say understand, but glimpse only the enormous catastrophe expressed by these simple words: The refusal of the baker?...

16. – In his letter, my Jesuit told me incidentally that Ernest Hello appeared quite insignificant when one read Saint Thomas. Priggish and insane comparison. May as well compare a sumptuous, set table and a grain of wheat, while forgetting that the grain of wheat can become the Body of Jesus Christ. And that [religious] is my Judge!

17. – Issue of the *Assiette au Beure*, illustrated by Géo Dupuis, aka our Dupuis de Montrouge, my converted Calvinist. All that is needed now is the anticlerical caricature and that fascicule of the *Assiette* is precisely dirty.

19. – I reproach myself for never having said a word about the ancient abbatial church of Saint Furcy. An exhaustive archeological and historical labor would need to be performed on that horribly profaned ruin. Transformed into an outright loathsome *furno*,[102] that baptistry of Brie resembles a brothel house for vagabonds. That place, where the Sacrifice was offered for centuries, is now a stable, and the old stones that were friends of the saints, who protected generations of poor people against the cold or heat, have become the walls of dancehalls or urinals... As seldom as I can, I pass by that humiliated and venerable facade that dies of nobility amidst the rubbish, and which is certainly the one beautiful thing in the area

---

[102]Furno: furnished lodging or building of furnished lodgings.

that nobody, ever, looks at.

20. – Letter from a group of young invalids, calling themselves "Catholic students of Gand" and proposing a stupid questionnaire to me for publication in an *almanac*. I could refer them to Cambronne.

23. – New and extremely miserable letter from my Jesuit. More lessons and counsels. I do not recognize the good qualities of Catholics and, while groaning, one recognizes that it is too late to set me straight.

> Response:

> *It is cruel to propose enigmas to a man who is dying, primarily after having given him a glimmer of hope. If it is not possible to obtain better, I ask at least for silence. What more humble salary for a worker who has borne the weight of the day and paid for some including yourself certainly?*

24. – To the sender of a hundred francs:

> *I do not wish to inflict on you the banality of a thank you. One knows that I live on alms and I have no shame, having before me a row of about fifteen volumes which would have assured me a comfortable living and even much more than that, if I had*

*written them to please men. However
distant you are from me in your sentiments and your thoughts, I do not believe you could despise that.*

Read the first installments of a serialized novel: *The World of the Living*, published by *Quinzaine*,
the work of a young writer, Jacques Debout, with
whom I have had the occasion to correspond (see
February 6, 1903). It is a frank and generous wine,
but a tad green and has need of the bottle. There are
very beautiful parts. The author could very well write
a masterpiece one day, but he still needs to control the
adjective better, to rein in the adverb and the partici-
ple, to get rid entirely of the quitch from pious im-
agery, perhaps also from certain commonplaces, not
in expression, but in thought. The mark of a writer is
the glinting word, one meets it here rather often.

(*The World of the Living* was just published in
book format, by the publisher Beauchesne. February
1905.)

25. – To stay warm, worked on *Mon Journal*. Tale of
our captivity in Denmark. What an agonizing memory
and how similar to all my other memories!

29. – Complete distress. I was alone with Madeleine.
I went into the shadows near the stove to weep.
Madeleine understanding that I was suffering, came
and put herself on my knees and caressed me tender-
ly. May God bless her eternally!

30. – Ever preoccupied with the project of a novel that I would modestly entitle: *Cochons-sur-Marne*, a lovely and fresh idea presents itself to me. There is room to presume – given the duration of the Prussian occupation in 1870 and 1871, and considering the common sense that the bourgeois class justly pats itself on the back for, – that the majority of present citizens in this canton seat were fabricated with German semen. What an illuminating character trait!

   Read in Remy de Gourmont's *Epilogues*: "Saint Paul is, for me, nothing more than a mediocre and *frivolous* writer. – The word of God is intolerable, *like that of the Scribe*, except in music." Dreadful poverty of intelligence and more dreadful state of the soul! And to say that that is acquired! When I knew that miserable wretch, in 1893, he would have been horrified to write that. It is true that back then...

31. – This Septuagesima Sunday is the dawn of Redemption and begins with a dolorous moaning. The Gospel is that of the workers of the eleventh hour. It would seem that it is this Sunday itself which is signified by those workers in the sense that it must be *paid for*, honored as much as other Sundays until Easter, being thus both the first and the last simultaneously, given that it is by *it* that one begins. Idea more or less clear that I will draw what I can from, a bit more later.

February

2. – Candlemas. To a poor wretch who is going to die without the sacraments:

> ... *Today it is Candlemas, that is, the feast of that old man the saint who made the promise not to die before having seen the Christ and who received finally in tears, in his arms, the infant who was the Light of the world. Dear friend, if you wanted, you too could receive him and your consolation would be infinite. Have pity on yourself, have pity on us, have pity on Jesus Christ who is at your door and who implores you.*

3. – Surprised to hear a mass that is not a *requiem* but which has, however, the epistle and Gospel for the departed, I interrogate the priests who don't know anything and do not understand any more than I do. Verification made, I learn that Saint Odilon, abbot of Cluny, in the XIth century, whose feast day is marked for today, in the *Ordo* of this diocese, instituted the feast of the *Commemoration of the Departed* (November 2), which makes him a totally extraordinary personage and I am surprised, once again, by ecclesiastical ignorance.

In my lay ignorance, I could not help following the mass of Saint Blaise[103] while praying to that *Apotropean*, that auxiliary, that patron of my choice, to pay my baker, my landlady, and all the rest, God willing.

To Frédéric Masson, freshly elected academician:

I am perhaps not unknown to you. Some twenty years ago I practiced the profession, little recommended, of an errant writer, a lone literary scout. I earned what so many others sought in vain: a legend. I have my legend, like Napoleon and some wicked men. It is what has emboldened me to write to you.

I would like to finish my life with a book on Napoleon. I have this great man in my blood to the point that it is difficult for me to speak about him without losing or recovering something of my equilibrium. Now, I cannot procure indispensable works such as yours except by the practice of begging, indigence being the natural consequence of my choice.

Do you want, then, dear sir, to have sent to me those of your books that treat of Napoleon and his family? I know perfectly well what I am asking

---

[103]Saint Blaise: one of the fourteen Auxiliary Saints, whose intercession is considered efficacious.

*of you. I am not unaware that this type
of request is particularly disagreeable
to an author who cannot always give
his books away with extreme facility.
Yes, sir, I have the experience of that
annoyance. However, I dare inflict it
on you because I am very poor, in
truth, and also because I have something to say about Napoleon, even after you. A kind of crowning of a literary existence that has been rather sorrowful.*

*(No response. There is loutishness in aca-
demia.)*

4. – The poor sacristan tells me his troubles. That
poor man is hatefully oppressed by the deacon who,
not content with overworking a father of five children, whom he remunerates shamefully, even gives
him difficulties for the payment of his miserable
wages.

A terrible sadness descends on me. The old
lady Corbillard, our avaricious-yellow landlady sends
her male domestic with a letter. The rascally wench
demands that I pay her immediately, or she will issue
an eviction notice. Unable to contain myself, even in
the presence of that man, I expressed myself so violently that I lost my equilibrium for the rest of the
day. "I will respond tomorrow to your ugly ape."

5. – To Corbillard:

Your letter is an enigma of the most disagreeable sort. I do not succeed in understanding why, from the get-go and with no known motive, *you treat me like a vagabond and a criminal. This behavior is so unexpected that it appears to me explicable only by the effect of a calumny received with particular complaisance.*

When you refused the excellent value of the offer that I made to you, it was understood that you would wait for me until February. Good faith on the one hand, and benevolence on the other, being supposed, as happens between honest people, I was preparing to settle with you in fact during the course of this month which has just begun. How was I to anticipate a declaration of war? It is incredible.

If you cannot stand our presence on your property, we will leave all the more willingly given the cleaning of this infect place was done as poorly as can be. Already we are infested by the thousands of fleas that remained, I imagine, in the gaps in the parquet. We have seen bugs even. What will it be like in summer? I think, madame, that you should not, in good con-science, *rent your house to other people before having renovated it from top to bottom. At the price of 700 francs, one has a right to a habitable lodging. It is a question of rudimentary* equitableness.

There is another thing. I had to pay a gardener at 2 francs a day for 40 days for the clearing and preparation of the vegetable garden which was not, as you know, but a mass of garbage. If I cannot profit from that expense, it would seem just of you to take it into account.

Finally, I present to you herewith several bills for various repairs that, by your own admittance, should not be at my expense.

(One will see, a little later on, the noble response by that old woman to whom I had been stupid enough to send a copy of *Colonnes*, as if I had sent a magic lantern to a mole. She is probably a childhood friend of Coppée's.)

We are refused credit here and there. One would think that there is someone who demolishes us everywhere [behind our backs].

6. – We were already without wine, meat, and coal. Now we are without any more water. The landlady responds to a housekeeper, the messenger of our complaints, with a lie and an insolence. New letter:

Madame,

I am afflicted to see a person of your age lacking in good faith. You know perfectly well that the kitchen pump was in bad shape, given you have, three or four times, sent a worker who declared to us that it was worthless and that you were simply trying to economize at the expense of your renters. I am still waiting for a response to the letter that I had brought to you yesterday. I understand that you have the repugnance of seeing intellectuals and well-bred people in your house, but a bit of correctness and justice would still be in order.

Depressed by our privations and forcing myself to work all the same, I feel around my heart that atrocious claw that I know and that would soon be the death of me, when a new viciousness by the knacker came to add to my already excessive distress. That enraged bitch wants to be paid before Monday evening, if not she will add late *fees*. Dying with ill-humor, strangled by indignation, I pay a visit to an individual whom I know, the bailiff Br. in whom I had had the incredible surprise of finding a reader of my books and a friend. He is interested in my situation, promises to see the object, and does not despair of obtaining a delay.

7. – Sexagesima Sunday. After a deep sleep by ex-

hausted people, we drag ourselves to church. *Exsurge, quare obdormis, Domine?*[104] Is it not for us that the Liturgy speaks? What a memory! It was on this same day in 1895, when we were so terribly wretched, that Véronique, who was unwell, said to her mother while kissing the crucifix: "Little Jesus sleeps on his cross, we must wake him up!" Those days of death, are they going to return? (See last year, February 15.)

My friend the bailiff kept his word and succeeded. I will not be strangled immediately. She will wait for me until the end of the month, but she wants me to leave in April. As for the indemnification to us for the bad condition of the house, nothing doing. We must find the means to escape this cursed place.

8. – Impossible to sleep in this villa with fleas. It is quite clear that we could not live here during the summer. Something even more baneful and more dangerous than the vermin could very well have been left here by our predecessors.

The newspapers speak of imminent war between the Japanese and the Russians. Danger perhaps for the entire world. Commencement, God willing, of greater things.

A friend, as poor as we are, came to suffer with us at our house for one hour. Every line in his face, Jeanne said to me, thinking of that ravaged physiognomy, is a promise of Beatitude.

---

[104] *Exsurge...*: Latin for "Rise up, Lord, why are you sleeping?"

9. – Terrible day! The lack of wine and fortifying ali-
mentation, the threat of a lack of coal, the *human* certitude of being unable to feed our children tomorrow,
the impossibility of continuing to live here and the
impossibility of escaping, the apparent abandonment
of everyone and the evident hostility of so many people; finally, and above all, that infinitely dolorous expectation of a liberator who never comes; all that together puts us two steps away from despair. While we
stiffen our wills, our house is shaken by a tempest and
the sky is sad like death without God. For whom then
do we suffer thus? And I was able to work, to write
books with these tortures! That will be taken into account at the Last Judgment.

10. – Commencement of the Russo-Japanese war.
Mysterious laws want that by virtue of universal solidarity there be a connection between that colossal
event and our humble and dolorous destiny. What is
that connection?

Journalists of the antechamber or the stable
have published that Mme. Lebaudy, the known multimillionairess, acknowledging Christianly the iniquity
of her riches, has decided to give *restitution*, by helping the poor. I know that kind of charity! Pharisaism
to make the hills boil! Several good ecclesiastics have
written to her for me. I wager anything one wants that
they will not succeed even in getting a letter to her.

(I won, naturally. But had she received it, how

would they expect that woman, who busies herself with national politics to please God, that she should concern herself with me? She has enough work to do buttering up the ponces of the *Bonne Presse*.)

13. – It must be terrible to be rich. Even when one wants to do good, as that Lebaudy is claimed to want to do, one is forced to make oneself invisible, like devils.

Regular eviction notice by my knacker, with this clause: "If you remain until April 15, that will be fifteen days that you would need to pay me above and beyond the three months in course." Yes, my dear, I will pay you, your *furno*!

14. – To a moribund:

> *Are you still with us? Can you read me, can you write to me or dictate a letter? Have you given to your deso-late soul the consolation it had need of? We have suffered for you to the point of agony. I say for you, because since the news of your danger we have offered everything, given everything so that Jesus Christ might accept you. And we have been so profoundly, so terribly miserable, these last few days, how much we hope for you! At that price, it seems to us that something truly precious must have been truly*

paid.

Now, my friend, I have one last thing to ask of you. You will give it to me, if God consents. You know that there is not, properly speaking, a death. "Vita mutatur, non tollitur,"[105] *so says the Liturgy. When your life then will have* changed *and you will finally be in the Light, I adjure you, by the living God and with his holy Permission, to manifest yourself to me. I have an immense desire to know what my Creator and my Savior want from me, and if I am or am not on his path. I know that that can be requested humbly, and that there are many examples of similar communications.*

After your departure, your friends will pray for you. Our prayers will be a continuation of our terrestrial correspondence. They will benefit you doubtless and, I hope, attract to me in particular the exceptional grace that I ask for tearfully. Adieu!

(August 27, 1904. Last night I saw in a dream an old man near death. As all things happen in dreams, in the simplest manner in the world, that old man became, in order to die, a very small infant who faded away before our very eyes, while penetrating us with sweetness and divine love. I have forgotten ev-

---

[105] *Vita mutatur, non tollitur:* Latin for "Life changes, it is not taken away."

erything, except that it was a feeling of Paradise. Several hours later, news of the death of the old librarian Alexandre Roy, addressee of the letter that precedes.)

18. – Horrible weather of melted snow. I think of our landlady who would be so joyous to put our children out on the street...

19. – I am told that *Colonnes* has wrecked havoc here. A rich and old shopkeeper, a woman, who has her opinions about literature and who practices, I'm told, the imperfect subjunctive, does not accept my *Révérend Père Judas*, becoming indignant, along with many other enlightened devotees, that frequent communion should be permitted to so little charitable a man. That marquess of the cash register dazzles the poor deacon who sees in her a Maintenon[106] and who consults her probably with the sacerdotal respect appropriate to piles of ecus!

I am struck by the idea for a novel or short story in which a pious bourgeoise woman would have an exalted devotion for Judas, because he was a priest and even bishop, unable to distinguish him from Saint Jude the Apostle.

21. – Torrential babbling on the part of the deacon who, not content with reading the bishop's pastoral,

---

[106]Maintenon: presumably a reference to Madame de Maintenon (AD 1635-1719), the second and "secret" wife of King Louis XIV.

not a thing of which I have the opportunity to grasp, speaks, before and afterwards, interminably. I was able to catch something at the beginning. With respect to I do not know what, he thundered and fulminated against those who, possessing any power whatsoever, abuse it to oppress their subordinates. That Pharisee is scary. When he finally descends from the cathedra, after bawling so much, I was able to admire, one more time, God's justice in the abjection of that face of a stupid priest, vain and pitiless, dressed in the canonical robe and carrying against the hollow of his stomach, very ostensibly, the cross which he puts on the back of others with so much satisfaction. It is time to leave. This is too much.

22. – I saw in a dream a multitude of people come from afar expressly to help us and who filled our home. They were the dead.

Pavuli petierunt panem et non erat qui frangeret eis.[107]

23. – Why do priests receive so much clairvoyance to refuse and so little light to give? Another question. If a fat or slender curate decides that the sacrament of baptism be administered on such and such a day, must the vicar, *par obéissance*, refuse Regeneration to a dying child? JEANNE: Obedience becomes the tomb of love, when love is not the cradle of obedience.

---

[107] *Parvuli*...: Latin for "The young the young children ask bread, and no man breaketh it unto them." Lamentations 4:4 (KJV).

24. – Complaints after complaints. Terrible life! And the instinct of ferocity on the part of the bourgeois who make them [the complaints] rush all at once, like dogs after the quarry,[108] after a poor wretch who succumbs. Worked however, as I really needed to. The worst misfortune is to have a need for men: one is immediately crucified *to the left* of Jesus Christ.

25. Saint Matthew. I writhe, weeping, at the feet of the Apostle of the Holy Spirit and Eternal Life. As others do not respond to me, you at least, give me a response!

26. – On top of everything else, the physical pain of a forced, but very complete, fast, which is necessary to make during Lent and meritorious by acceptation. We are all stunned by it. Fortunately the children do not suffer yet. Why does God treat the poor who love him – so strictly?

28. – In my distress, I addressed myself to the Reilles, scant gifted parliamentary riffraff, but supreme Catholics who have slaves underground, like Belgian Catholics. I am bound to obtain at least a helping hand, on the recommendation of two or three de-

---

[108]Dogs after the quarry: The image of the dogs, or hounds, of rich people hunting down the poor like quarry is further developed, in a very terrifying manner, in Bloy's "Introduction: Hallali" in *Blood of the Poor* (Sunny Lou Publishing, 2021).

ceased and supposing myself supported by the attorney Joseph Menard, an acquaintance of the family who was formerly my friend. It is a priest who took the first step. Impossible to see those funny fellows. Joseph Menard, the only person visible in the antechamber, sent the messenger away, with the insolence of a domestic, a person whom he should have respected at least the character of.

That attorney Joseph Menard, ambitious without genius, destined as much for approval as for kicks in the pants, *possesses* an old painting that belongs to me. I had, one day of anarchy, confided it to one of his brothers. This latter, more interesting but less virtuous, having died some time afterwards, Joseph found it more expedient to hold on to the object than to return it to me, estimating the occasion, moreover, very providential for recuperating half a dozen pieces of one hundred sous. For it is in this way that I am *The Ungrateful Beggar*. There is nothing more costly than that sinecure.

I have often thought, above all when I saw my little ones in agony, of that poor painting subtitled *by an enemy of the* JEWS, the which painting has perhaps a great worth and would be such a resource for me! I add that that anti-Semite profited by the occasion to annex several papers of Léon Bloy, me, confided to the same deceased and vainly asked for for twenty years now.

The attorney Menard, refuge, shelter, roof and garrison of widows and orphans, is one of the last confidants of divine mercy. I will pay him back, that fellow, he can count on it!

What madness to have hoped, for a single moment, for whatever it might be from those cursed people who represent the most vile members of the Catholic world, the Catholic world of the Fathers of the Assumption, *the which have a rule forbidding them from giving alms!* (See the *Mendiant Ingrat*, p. 395)

March

1ˢᵗ. – We stopped suffering yesterday. According to Jeanne's expression, it seems that, for three days now, – since the visit by a poor coal man come to request, him also, money, and who, not obtaining it, left us the two sacks of coal all the same, – one might believe one senses a *hinge* turning finally, the hinge of the good door which did not want to open until now. God will do what God wants, we have no fear of him or men.

2. – An old multimillionairess who wants to do nothing, alleging her *charges*, counsels the Society of men of letters! the bureau of charity!! finally... M. Loubet!!!

3. – It is a joy that I have never known, that of not having dogs at my heels, that of no longer hearing the yapping gobs and devouring jaws behind me, that of stopping finally in safety, at any hour of the day, to

drink from God's fountain.

Having been able to settle up with my knacker, one of the clerks of my friend the bailiff who took care of that disgusting operation, brings me quittance and a message. The leech claims that I am liable to her for the doors and windows. I respond to that clerk that he should ask her if I don't also have the duty of sleeping with her.

4. – Another landlady, less hermetically closed to intellectual life, as she takes lessons in literature from Gaston Deschamps, Mme. Frusquin, née Visible, already honored by my suffrage, is scandalized by a sermon where the poor are spoken of respectfully. Someone whose patience is short, objecting that wealth is condemned in the Gospel: "Then," she says, "the Gospel is *exaggerating*."

In *l'Autorité*, reply by Marc Sangnier[109] to Paul de Cassagnac[110] saying: "Your intentions are good, but your work is bad, given you are a Republican." In spite of that reply, I was aggrieved to think like Cassagnac. I do not believe that there is vainer work than *Le Sillon*.

Only, Sangnier, despite his wrong ideas, all the same goes out to the poor. I am with him then, and I want to let him know it.

---

[109]Marc Sagnier (AD 1873-1950), a French Catholic politician who founded *Le Sillon*, a Catholic social movement.

[110]Paul de Cassagnac (AD 1843-1904) a French politician and journalist who founded the journal *l'Authorité*.

Sending of *la Femme pauvre*: "Marc Sangnier, what have you got to do with that old cadaver de
Cassagnac, when the living writer of these pages
comes to you?"

7. – I am told that a deacon of a diocese in Manchuria
had given, on New Year's Day, 5 francs to the sacristan and 5 francs to the porter. Surprising largesse.
But the poor devils didn't take long to find out that
the two pieces were false. Complaint to the deacon
whose response was this: "They were passed on to
me, I had to pass them on in turn."

8. – Overheard this at the *Commerce* cafe: "Have you
read *Quo Vadis?*" "Yes, but I cannot read much of it
at one time, it's too *absorbing*, too deep. That demands too sustained an attention."

11. – Return of a cleaning woman who had been
turned away. We want to hope that that drunk will
bring a little mercy to our home. We had replaced her
by virtue itself which we had to send away, the day
before yesterday.

Copied for the printer the important letter to
the mathematician that one can read in *Mon Journal*,
p. 260. It is one of my best passages. The addressee
who disappeared so suddenly from my life, in 1899,
and who has become for me a phantom, will have
been merely the occasion of speaking to others.

13. – A beautiful and gentle sun on *Lætare* Sunday and for us the continual expectation, the expectation of God, the expectation of the Saints, the expectation of help, of a loving place to live, of a beginning of deliverance.

We learn that the old gardener-beggar, whom we had given work to out of charity and who cost us about 80 francs, speaks many bad things about us behind our back and that the curate, happy to hear those calumnies, propagates them. That beggar, is he not his brother, and are they not, the both of them, like Corbillard and all the riffraff here?

15. – Paris. My first trip on the *metro*. Gigantic work, I admit, and not devoid even of a certain *subterranean beauty*; but what an infernal noise, certain danger, probable death – and what a death! – all the times that one descends into those catacombs. Impression of the end of fountains of water, the end of trembling woods, dawns, and twilights in the prairies of Paradise. Impression of the end of the human soul!

16. – I am informed that the painter Georges Rouault, a student of Gustave Moreau, is fascinated by me. Having found at his master's home the *Femme pauvre*, previously sent, with these words: "To Gustave Moreau, to avenge M. Folantin," that book touched his heart, wounded it incurably. I tremble to think of that poor wretch's punishment.

A young man who was our guest last summer, for two months, responds to my sending of *Colonnes*. The poor fellow is uniquely full of himself and does not perceive it. Will he ever perceive it? He asks pardon to begin with, or rather he writes formulaic expressions that seem good for expressing that, and immediately after he begins to *be witty*.

17. – Another story about the deacon of Manchuria. In January, three ill-fated undertakers came to ask him for their New Year's gifts. Response: "I have decided that in the future I will no longer give New Year's gifts except in the month of July."

20. – "Those people owe money everywhere!" Such is, sung over us, the scalping song of the honest people of this canton.

23. – Enormously painful search for a lodging in Paris where we want to live from now on. Found finally an apartment surrounded by trees that would content us, without an extraordinary concierge who coos while puffing out his chest, with the dignity of an old guinea fowl who believes himself still on display.

Sad return. I'm cold and I see black. I think of Jesus Christ forced to pay his rent. The Verb of God would have a landlord![111]

---

[111]The Verb of God would have a landlord: see chapter 13, *Blood of the Poor*, where Bloy develops this idea further.

24. – Georges Rouault has embarked, not for Cythera, but for my deserted and gloomy island, [with] his friend and comrade, Georges Desvallières, another student of Gustave Moreau, and behold them both searching for subsidies, raising deniers for my release. I owe it to Auguste Marguillier, the dear secretary of the *Gazette des Beaux-Arts*, for those two hearts; he has always been favorable to me in spite of the drawbacks of my *ingratitude*. I tell him how glorious it is for me, in my old age, that those good men take the trouble thus to come to my aid and break the rocks on the minor roads and byways.

27. – Palm Sunday. Impression at mass this morning. A small child was crying. Then I had something like a vision of a lake of sadness and darkness, above which floated an enormous silence. And that silence was broken suddenly by the solitary cry of that small child, the only being who could make himself heard among the eternal and desperate men lying about that place. For it was a very particular vision of hell.

Discourse by the deacon. Butterflies snatched in flight: "I am very content with being the curate... I find life to be very good... The *cement of prayer* is worth more than Portland cement. Etc."

28. – Full of good will, I wanted to listen attentively to an instruction. The preacher who is not however the deacon, begins to speak about "the business of

salvation," a vestral and shopkeeper expression which he seems taken with. I fall asleep. If he was speaking about SANCTITY, I would have woken up like a horse to the sound of a trumpet.

29. – Last letter to my Jesuit:

> *My dear Paul,*
>
> *I was hardly thinking to write you, limiting myself to thinking sadly of you, since the day when you declared to me your desire to "separate" from me. Will you permit me to confess, without bitterness or recrimination, that* I did not understand, *habituated as I am to consult, in all cases, your infallible patron and firmly deter-mined not to be wiser than him. Now, your letter implied such an erasure, so total a confiscation or abolition of chapter XII of the first book of Corinthians (*divisiones gratiarum, divisiones ministrationem, divisiones operationum – ad utilitatem*), that I felt that you were completely lost to me. You believe now, in contempt of Saint Paul, that all Christians must be thrown* into the same mold. *I was not mistaken then about the Jesuits, alas! And we can no longer understand each other... Adieu then, my dear Paul. If I die before you, as is proba-*

*ble, remember sometimes the poor
writer who was not a Jesuit, but who
gave you Jesus Christ all the same.*

April

1st. – Two things contradictory in appearance and,
however, certain, observed at Corbillard's place. That
harpy is vexed to lose renters and, on the other hand,
she would have so wanted to make us suffer! Mali-
ciousness and avarice gnaw at each other while howling from the depths of her old entrails. She can no
longer be a landlady.

2. – I think that there are injustices that God has need
of in order to balance I do not know what, like merchants tossing weights onto the pan with the merchandise in order to verify their heaviness.

3. – Response by my Jesuit who is not resigned to
losing me, but who makes things worse by telling me,
more or less, that I am a heretic, in no uncertain
terms, that "certain of my assertions are destructive of
dogma." It is page 129 of the *Salvation Through the
Jews* that he cannot swallow. "Is it a metaphorical as-
similation or an absolute affirmation?" Such is his cir-

cle of Popillius.[112] How to explain to him that it is neither here nor there? How to get it through his brain filled with formulas that the difficulty stops and the circle is broken as soon as one brings near to that redoubtable page 129 the liturgical prayer of Holy Saturday: *Lucifer, inquam, qui nescit occasum?*[113] Very rare Christians who still employ their reason will notice that it has nothing to do, here or there, with metaphor, any more than rigorous affirmation in the sense of revealed doctrine, but simply noting the *mystery, the* PRESENCE *of the mystery,* to the scandal of imbeciles or pedantic theologians who claim that everything is clarified.

4. – Easter Sunday. When the glories of Easter come, the soul is seized by a particular sadness that can be translated in this way: "I am with Jesus in his Resurrection, not having been with him in his Death. I did not suffer with him, my fast was a derision. It is therefore without any right that I rejoice with the Saints, and it would be tantamount to dying of shame without the incomprehensible divine Pity."

6. – I know a truly pious priest whom I love, and who annoys me to no end. There is in him a need for contradiction, above all in matters of exegesis and even

---

[112]Circle of Popillius: a reference to the circle that Gaius Popillius Laenas supposedly drew around Antiochus, ordering him not to step out of the circle until he had given him an answer. The story is told by Titus Livius.

[113]Lucifer...: Latin for "Lucifer, I say, who knows no setting."

liturgy, which paralyzes me. He spoke to me today about the Pope, altering the names of saints known or supposedly apocryphal or nonexistent, although venerated by all the Church for centuries. The idea that the Canon of the Mass could be revised does not trouble him. Me, I find a principle of despair in it.

8. – *Mon Journal* is finally completed, and that will pay for my move. Enormous work knocked off in a few weeks, despite everything, and which I have just written the last lines of. Will God allow me finally to live from my work like other laborers? a grace that I have been asking for tearfully, for so long a time!

12. – Change of address, escape, deliverance. No other incident except the presentation, by the domestic of the odious Corbillard, of a note for 32 fr. 20 for doors and windows and the rent from the 1st to the 12th of April. That sum, under the circumstances, is as just as a pint of my blood. Of course, she will never factor in the much greater sum that the garden cost me, received in the state of a dump and transformed, any more than certain repairs devolving on the landlady whose reimbursement has been totally *forgotten* by that honest woman. Clawed by vermin which the renovation brought out in that house, *I pay what I do not owe* in order to escape more quickly, but I want to hold on to this note, a muniment of ignominy and bourgeois iniquity.

The miserable woman, whose death is probably not very far off, will go before God then, with the bread of my poor children in her old gob!

 – Montmartre, February 1905.

Index

Other Books by the Publisher

Fanchette's Pretty Little Foot by Restif de La Bretonne

Je M'Accuse... by Léon Bloy

My Hospitals & My Prisons by Paul Verlaine

Salvation Through the Jews by Léon Bloy

Words of a Demolitions Contractor by Léon Bloy

Cellulely by Paul Verlaine

Ecclesiastical Laurels by Jacques Rochette de la Morlière

Flowers of Bitumen by Émile Goudeau

Songs for Her & Odes in Her Honor by Paul Verlaine

On Huysmans' Tomb by Léon Bloy

Ten Years a Bohemian by Émile Goudeau

The Soul of Napoleon by Léon Bloy

Blood of the Poor by Léon Bloy

Joan of Arc and Germany by Léon Bloy

Fêtes Galantes & Songs Without Words by Paul Verlaine

Joys by Francis Vielé-Griffin

The Son of Louis XVI by Léon Bloy

Septentrion by Jean Raspail

The Resurrection of Villiers de l'Isle-Adam by Léon Bloy

Poems Saturnian by Paul Verlaine

The Biography of Léon Bloy: Memories of a Friend by René Martineau

Fredegund, France: A Book of Poetry by Richard Robinson

The Good Song by Paul Verlaine

Swans by Francis Vielé-Griffin

Constantinople and Byzantium by Léon Bloy

Enamels and Cameos by Théophile Gautier